When People Want Punishment

Against the backdrop of rising populism around the world and democratic backsliding in countries with robust, multiparty elections, this book asks why ordinary people favor authoritarian leaders. Much of the existing scholarship on illiberal regimes and authoritarian durability focuses on institutional explanations, but Tsai argues that, to better understand these issues, we need to examine public opinion and citizens' concerns about retributive justice. Government authorities uphold retributive justice – and are viewed by citizens as fair and committed to public good – when they affirm society's basic values by punishing wrongdoers who act against these values. Tsai argues that the production of retributive justice and moral order is a central function of the state and an important component of state building. Drawing on rich empirical evidence from in-depth fieldwork, original surveys, and innovative experiments, the book provides a new framework for understanding authoritarian resilience and democratic fragility.

Lily L. Tsai is the Ford Professor of Political Science at the Massachusetts Institute of Technology (MIT) and the Director of the MIT Governance Lab (MIT GOV/LAB). Her research focuses on accountability, governance, and political behavior in developing contexts, particularly in Asia and Africa.

CAMBRIDGE STUDIES IN COMPARATIVE POLITICS

OTHER BOOKS IN THE SERIES

Continued after the index

When People Want Punishment

Retributive Justice and the Puzzle of Authoritarian Popularity

LILY L. TSAI

Massachusetts Institute of Technology

CAMBRIDGE
UNIVERSITY PRESS

University Printing House, Cambridge CB2 8BS, United Kingdom

One Liberty Plaza, 20th Floor, New York, NY 10006, USA

477 Williamstown Road, Port Melbourne, VIC 3207, Australia

314–321, 3rd Floor, Plot 3, Splendor Forum, Jasola District Centre, New Delhi – 110025, India

103 Penang Road, #05–06/07, Visioncrest Commercial, Singapore 238467

Cambridge University Press is part of the University of Cambridge.

It furthers the University's mission by disseminating knowledge in the pursuit of education, learning, and research at the highest international levels of excellence.

www.cambridge.org
Information on this title: www.cambridge.org/9781108841474
DOI: 10.1017/9781108882545

First published 2021

A catalogue record for this publication is available from the British Library.

Library of Congress Cataloging-in-Publication Data
NAMES: Tsai, Lily L., 1975– author.
TITLE: When people want punishment : retributive justice and the puzzle of authoritarian popularity / Lily L. Tsai, Massachusetts Institute of Technology.
DESCRIPTION: New York : Cambridge University Press, 2021. | Series: CCPO Cambridge Studies in Comparative Politics | Includes bibliographical references.
IDENTIFIERS: LCCN 2021009247 (print) | LCCN 2021009248 (ebook) | ISBN 9781108841474 (Hardback) | ISBN 9781108794862 (Paperback) | ISBN 9781108882545 (eBook)
SUBJECTS: LCSH: Authoritarianism. | Dictators. | Criminal justice, Administration of. | BISAC: POLITICAL SCIENCE / General | POLITICAL SCIENCE / General
CLASSIFICATION: LCC JC480 .T75 2021 (print) | LCC JC480 (ebook) | DDC 321.9–dc23
LC record available at https://lccn.loc.gov/2021009247
LC ebook record available at https://lccn.loc.gov/2021009248

ISBN 978-1-108-84147-4 Hardback
ISBN 978-1-108-79486-2 Paperback

To Max and Carys for who I am,
and to Edward for the life I have

Contents

Figures

viii

Tables

Acknowledgments

It is a great pleasure to express my gratitude for the many conversations and collaborations that have shaped this book.

First and foremost, this project relied heavily on opportunities to collect data and conduct fieldwork under challenging conditions. Much of the research that undergirds this project would not have been possible without the help of Minh Trinh, Liu Shiyao, Wen Yingying, Scott Rozelle, Zhang Linxiu, Lü Xiaobo, Zhang Ping – and especially Wang Jianying, Tian Wuxiong, Lu Xing, and Wu Guojin, who were nothing short of heroic in the field. I am deeply grateful to all in China who generously shared their time and their thoughts. It is their experiences that form the foundation of this book.

I have also been gifted with brilliant students over the years and working with them led to avenues that enriched the book greatly. Research collaborations with a special set of former students, now colleagues – Guillermo Toral, Leah Rosenzweig, Tesalia Rizzo, Ben Morse, and Nina McMurry – illuminated aspects of this project that I would not have otherwise seen or developed. I also thank Paige Bollen, Yiqing Xu, Yue Hou, Alec Worsnop, Yuan Xiao, Blair Read, Ye Maoliang, and Yang Liangsong for their valuable research assistance at various stages.

I continue to be indebted to Liz Perry for her steadfast support, Tony Saich and the Ash Center at Harvard for giving me a place to start the research, and Margaret Levi for her always incisive feedback. I also thank Fredrik Sjoberg, Hannes Hemker, Tiago Peixoto, and Jonathan Mellon for collaborating on valuable cross-national research that helped to put the project in comparative context.

Valuable feedback and opportunities to present parts of the book generously came from Mary Gallagher, Miriam Golden, Saad Gulzar, Melanie Manion, Jean Oi, Tang Wenfang, and Paul Collier. Thanks also to Teppei Yamamoto, Dan Posner, Roger Petersen, Danny Hidalgo, Suzanne Berger, and Adam Berinsky for their feedback at various stages of the project, and a special thanks to Dick Samuels for providing careful comments on the entire manuscript and instigating the writing of an entirely new Chapter 6. I am also grateful to Chappell Lawson and David Singer for our writing groups and asking hard questions about what I really wanted to say with this project. Conversations with Rob Blair, Vishal Gujadhur, Aidan Miliff, and Jeffrey Javed helped to crystallize parts of the argument at key moments in the process.

At the Massachusetts Institute of Technology (MIT), I have been particularly indebted to Rick Locke, Andrea Campbell, Charles Stewart, and Melissa Nobles, who provided time, resources, and at one point when it was badly needed, a literal "room of my own."

Colleagues and partners at MIT Governance Lab (MIT GOV/LAB) also generously shared ideas and experiences that enabled me to put the questions of accountability, corruption, and citizen–government relations in global perspective. Speaking on a panel with Rakesh Rajani many years ago proved to be a fateful stroke of fortune from which many good ideas and, more importantly, much fellowship have sprung. I am also grateful to the following people for opening my eyes in myriad ways: Ester Alkonga, Ben Armstrong, Annie Baltar, Walter Flores, Florencia Guerzovich, Khuram Hussain, Michael Jarvis, Noelle Lee-Okoth, Varja Lipovšek, Alfonsina Peñaloza, Manang Pura, Bing Van Tooren, and especially Alisa Zomer, who worked tirelessly to create the time and headspace for me to finish this book.

Financial and institutional support for this research was provided by the Department of Political Science and the Department of Urban Studies and Planning at MIT; the Ash Center for Democratic Innovation and Governance at the Harvard Kennedy School; and the World Bank.

At Cambridge University Press, I thank Sara Doskow, Cameron Daddis, Robert Dreesen, and two anonymous reviewers for their support of this project. I also thank My Seppo, Danny Tobin, and Michelle Cerna for helping to prepare the manuscript – and especially BreAnne Fleer and Anna Weissman for their outstanding work in getting it over the finish line. All errors and omissions remain, of course, my own.

Family and friends have sustained me throughout the process in countless ways. Meejin Yoon and Eric Höweler gave us the gifts of vistas and children's laughter in our summer visits. Gatherings with them and with Ana Miljački, Lee Moreau, Rosie Jones, Paul O'Gorman, John Shovlin, and Kristel Smentek helped to refill my bucket when it was empty.

I am deeply grateful to the Young Family – especially Rosemary Young for giving her love and energy so freely and generously during our field trips to Kenya – and to Stephen Tsai, Franny Coe, and the Coe Family.

To my parents, Huei Chu Tsai and Cheng Kween Lee: I find that I never stop learning from the two of you because you yourselves never stop trying to do better and be better. It is endlessly inspiring and humbling. When the kids were born, you told me that they would bring great responsibility and endless joy. This has indeed been true of being a parent. But I want you to know that the same has turned out to be true of being your child: It is a joy, and an honor, to be your daughter.

To my husband, Edward Young: After eighteen countries, two children, cholera while nursing, and now a global pandemic – I'm grateful, yes, for your patience, commitment, and seemingly bottomless capacity for cracking jokes. We are never bored, which in and of itself is a gift. But how you do this all while bushwhacking your own trail through work, immigration, and fatherhood – and encouraging others to do the same – this makes me feel awe.

Finally, to Carys and to Max, my "little sleep's heads": As I write these last words of the book, I am thinking back to its first days of fieldwork when I was also becoming your mother. Max, I felt your first kicks in a van driving across the Jilin countryside; now, here you are, always hanging back to make sure others are okay, even when you could easily be the first to finish. Carys, I can still see you setting out on your first crawl in Kirinyaga, no trial and error, just zero to perfectly competent in three seconds.

One of the great privileges of writing a book is being able to speak across the years and distances that may separate us. For me, there is no greater joy or privilege than telling you that I am so proud to be your mother. No book will ever match it. Many waters cannot quench it.

The Puzzle of Authoritarian Popularity

Why do authoritarian leaders appeal to so many? When we talk about the kind of government we want, whether in casual conversation or in public opinion surveys, many of us say we want the power to choose our leaders and to have a voice in how these leaders make policies and decisions. Many ordinary citizens, in established democracies and around the world, subscribe to the ideal of a government "of the people, by the people, and for the people."

So why are there leaders in authoritarian regimes who are popular and trusted by their citizens? Perhaps even more puzzling, why do people in democratic regimes vote with increasing frequency for leaders who openly promise to subvert the liberal institutions we say we care about? When do citizens believe that illiberal leaders in both authoritarian and democratic regimes are responsive to their concerns, so much so that they make the effort to contact authorities with these issues, and comply willingly and actively when authorities ask for their cooperation? Why do people sometimes view authoritarian leaders as fair, just, and morally upstanding?

To answer these questions, we need to recognize that societies and the individuals within them have a deep-seated need for social and moral order. We want our leaders to make sure that we live in a stable and secure society. If the world seems chaotic or our place in it is threatened, the right to free speech or the freedom to assemble may seem like remote ideals rather than things of immediate value. These abstract principles can pale in comparison to more concrete, everyday concerns of fighting to keep what we have and figuring out how to protect our children.

Authoritarian regimes and authoritarian leaders in democratic regimes that take actions to allay these fears can thus become quite appealing, particularly when anxieties are high. For better or worse, people look to leaders to identify – and punish – plausible culprits for the instability and insecurity we feel.

This book argues that authoritarian leaders become genuinely popular because ordinary people care deeply about what philosophers and psychologists call *retributive justice*. Government authorities uphold retributive justice when they affirm society's basic values by punishing wrongdoers who act against these values. People everywhere want to know that bad guys will get punished. In places where people are not sure this will happen, they may prefer government leaders who convincingly demonstrate that they will fix this problem, regardless of how undemocratic or incompetent these leaders are in other ways.

AUTHORITARIAN POPULARITY AND DEMOCRATIC DISSATISFACTION

Little attention has been given to the public opinion and the bases of popular support of authoritarian regimes. In recent years, we have mostly studied authoritarian regimes as a function of elite choices, resources, and constraints. We explain the persistence of authoritarian regimes as a result of elite politicians and decision makers who collude in power-sharing agreements;[1] who are independent from the influence of democracies in the West; who have built strong ruling party organizations;[2] and who strategically use elections and other seemingly democratic institutions to co-opt and repress potential opposition.[3]

What we have not done is look systematically at when and why authoritarian regimes are genuinely popular. Why have we focused on

---

[1] Milan W. Svolik, *The Politics of Authoritarian Rule*, Cambridge University Press, 2012.

[2] Steven Levitsky and Lucan A. Way, *Competitive Authoritarianism: Hybrid Regimes after the Cold War*, Cambridge University Press, 2010.

[3] Jason Brownlee, *Authoritarianism in an Age of Democratization*, Cambridge, UK: Cambridge University Press, 2007; Jennifer Gandhi, "Dictatorial Institutions and Their Impact on Economic Growth," *European Journal of Sociology* 49, no. 1 (April 15, 2008): 3–30; Jennifer Gandhi and Ellen Lust-Okar, "Elections under Authoritarianism," *Annual Review of Political Science* 12, no. 1 (2009): 403–22; Barbara Geddes, "Stages of Development in Authoritarian Regimes," in *World Order after Leninism*, edited by V. Tismaneanu, Marc Howard Morje, and Rudra Sil, 149–70, University of Washington Press, 2006; Beatriz Magaloni, *Voting for Autocracy: Hegemonic Party Survival and Its Demise in Mexico*, Cambridge University Press, 2006; Edmund Malesky and Paul Schuler, "The Single-Party Dictator's Dilemma: Information in Elections without Opposition," *Legislative Studies Quarterly* 36, no. 4 (2011): 491–530; Alberto Simpser, *Why Governments and Parties Manipulate Elections*, Cambridge University Press, 2013.

elites and institutions rather than on the opinions and actions of ordinary people? At least part of the explanation is that many of us, as political scientists in the United States, thought that democracy would become the only game in town and that the twenty-first century would see the global consolidation of democracy. So far we have been wrong. More than thirty years after the fall of communism and European colonialism, people all over the world have become deeply disappointed in their democratically elected leaders and, worse, in their democratic institutions. Despite the global spread of national elections, we have seen the persistence – and sometimes strengthening – of authoritarian leaders and regimes.

Our dismay at what we call "authoritarian resilience" means that the puzzle we have wanted to explain has been the persistence of illiberal institutions that existed in the authoritarian regimes we thought would democratize. And perhaps our empirical investigations have sometimes also been shaped by assumptions that regimes without individual rights and civil liberties cannot actually be genuinely popular with their citizens. When citizens in authoritarian regimes voice approval and trust in authorities on public opinion surveys, we wonder whether their responses are due to desirability bias and fear of political repression or retaliation.[4]

This assumption, however, is becoming hard to defend. Citizens all over the world increasingly turned toward less liberal and more authoritarian leaders in the first part of the twenty-first century – even as they continued to say that democracy is the best form of government.[5] Magufuli in Tanzania, Duterte in the Philippines, Orban in Hungary, Buhari in Nigeria – despite some degree of election irregularities, all of these leaders were popularly elected by citizens who responded to their promises of combating corruption, crime, and terrorism, no matter what the cost. Illiberal leaders are often genuinely popular with ordinary

---

[4] Daniel Corstange, "Sensitive Questions, Truthful Answers? Modeling the List Experiment with LISTIT," *Political Analysis* 17, no. 1 (January 4, 2009): 45–63; Daniel W. Gingerich, "Understanding Off-the-Books Politics: Conducting Inference on the Determinants of Sensitive Behavior with Randomized Response Surveys," *Political Analysis* 18, no. 3 (January 4, 2010): 349–80; Kirill Kalinin, "The Social Desirability Bias in Autocrat's Electoral Ratings: Evidence from the 2012 Russian Presidential Elections," *Journal of Elections, Public Opinion and Parties* 26, no. 2 (April 2, 2016): 191–211; Rory Truex and Daniel Tavana, "Implicit Attitudes Toward an Authoritarian Regime," *The Journal of Politics*, 81, no 3 (2019): 1014–1027. www.journals.uchicago.edu/doi/full/10.1086/703209.

[5] Stefan Dahlberg, Jonas Linde, and Sören Holmberg, "Democratic Discontent in Old and New Democracies: Assessing the Importance of Democratic Input and Governmental Output," *Political Studies* 63, no. 1 (August 28, 2015): 18–37.

people. During Duterte's use of extrajudicial violence in his war against crime, public support for Duterte did not substantially waver.[6] After winning the 2015 election with just over 50 percent of the vote, Magufuli's approval rating, one year into his presidency, was around 90 percent despite increasingly repressive policies toward the media, civil society, and freedom of speech.[7]

In many democracies, levels of public trust and political participation are declining over time.[8] Citizens are increasingly cynical about democratic institutions and disillusioned about the way that democratic processes function.[9] And when people are dissatisfied with their democratic government, they are less likely to engage in political action. Doorenspleet, for example, finds that perceptions of government performance are the strongest determinant of democratic discontent in African democracies. Among citizens who prefer democratic regimes over nondemocratic ones, those who are dissatisfied with the performance of their democratic government show lower levels of political participation and are less politically interested.[10]

Against this backdrop, authoritarian China has become one of the most popular and trusted regimes in the world, raising the question for many observers of whether there is a viable, nondemocratic "China model" for governance. Observers often wonder at how the Chinese state has been able to increase its capacity to collect taxes, build institutions, and secure high levels of voluntary cooperation from its citizens.[11] Regime support

---

[6] Gill Boehringer, "Asia-Pacific: Duterte's Drug War: Violating Rights for a Quick Fix," *Alternative Law Journal* 42, no. 3 (September 16, 2017): 233–36.

[7] Carolyn Del Vecchio, "The Political Participation, Engagement, and Perceptions of President Magufuli among Students at the College of African Wildlife Management," 2016. *Independent Study Project (ISP) Collection.* 2351. https://digitalcollections.sit.edu /isp_collection/2351

[8] See, for example, Dalton's analyses of data from the World Values Survey, Eurobarometer, International Social Surveys, and Comparative Study of Electoral Systems. Russell J. Dalton, *Citizen Politics: Public Opinion and Political Parties in Advanced Industrial Democracies*, Cq Press, 2013.

[9] Russell J. Dalton, *Citizen Politics: Public Opinion and Political Parties in Advanced Industrial Democracies*, Cq Press, 2013, 1; see also Devra C. Moehler, *Distrusting Democrats: Outcomes of Participatory Constitution Making*, University of Michigan Press, 2008.

[10] Renske Doorenspleet, "Critical Citizens, Democratic Support and Satisfaction in African Democracies," *International Political Science Review* 33, no. 3 (June 25, 2012): 279–300.

[11] Anna Ahlers, *Rural Policy Implementation in Contemporary China: New Socialist Countryside*, Routledge, 2014, cited in Bo Rothstein and Aiysha Varraich, *Making Sense of Corruption*, Cambridge University Press, 2017, 104; Alfred Tat-Kei Ho and Meili Niu, "Rising with the Tide without Flipping the Boat – Analyzing the Successes and Challenges of Fiscal Capacity Building in China," *Public Administration and*

for China has been robustly high in both domestic[12] and international Chinese public opinion surveys such as the World Values Surveys, the Asian Barometer Surveys, the Pew Surveys, the Chinese General Social Surveys, and the Chinese Urban Surveys. These patterns hold, regardless of how the survey questions are worded – whether respondents are asked about "support for the central government," "trust in the Communist Party," "trust in the central government leaders," "confidence in the key political institutions," "approval of China's political system," or "satisfaction with central government performance."[13] According to the 2000 World Values Survey, China had the highest levels of institutional trust, even compared to established and new democracies, and in the 2013 World Values Survey, 85 percent of respondents in China had a great deal or quite a lot of confidence in their government, the second highest among the 59 countries surveyed. According to the 2018 Edelman Trust Barometer, China had the highest levels of trust in government, among both informed citizens and the general public, out of the twenty-eight countries surveyed.[14] Tang finds that 77 percent of Chinese survey respondents believed that their government was responsive to their demands compared to only 36 percent in democratic Taiwan, where respondents share the same cultural factors that might lead to similar ways of responding to survey questions.[15]

Are these levels of support real? Or are they due to survey respondents who are worried about saying something critical of a repressive government? Research on this question suggests that much of this support is genuine. Using list experiments, Tang estimates that only about 8–10 percent of respondents hide their unhappiness with the central government.[16] Other scholars have argued that citizens in China have

Development 33, no. 1 (February 2013): 29–49; Mattias Ottervik, "Conceptualizing and Measuring State Capacity: Testing the Validity of Tax Compliance as a Measure of State Capacity," The Quality of Government Institute (QoG) Working Paper Series, 2013, 20. https://core.ac.uk/download/pdf/43558814.pdf

[12] Bruce Dickson, *The Dictator's Dilemma: The Chinese Communist Party's Strategy for Survival*, Oxford University Press, 2016.

[13] Wenfang Tang, "The 'Surprise' of Authoritarian Resilience in China," *American Affairs* 2, no. 1 (2018): 101–117.

[14] Tonia E. Ries, David M. Bersoff, Sarah Adkins, Cody Armstrong, and Jamis Bruening, "2018 Edelman Trust Barometer: Global Report," 2018. www.edelman.com/sites/g/files/aatuss191/files/2018-10/2018_Edelman_Trust_Barometer_Global_Report_FEB.pdf

[15] Wenfang Tang, *Populist Authoritarianism: Chinese Political Culture and Regime Sustainability*, Oxford University Press, 2016.

[16] Wenfang Tang and Yang Zhang, "Political Trust: An Experimental Study," in *Populist Authoritarianism: Chinese Political Culture and Regime Stability*, edited by

little reason to fear government punishment of criticism as long as it remains individualized. King, Pan, and Roberts find that Chinese internet users can be highly critical of the government and politically active as long as they do not attempt to organize collective action.[17] Even after accounting for political desirability bias, levels of trust and support for the Chinese regime remain higher than those for many democratic regimes. This level of support is also reflected in citizen engagement. More than a third of respondents in a nationally representative survey conducted in 2008 said that they had complained to authorities about government provision of public services.[18] If fear and distrust were strong, it would be hard to understand why so many people are willing to criticize government performance.

A RETRIBUTIVE JUSTICE MODEL OF CITIZEN ENGAGEMENT

So why do leaders such as Xi Jinping and Duterte garner such support? The answer, I argue, has to do with a concern that political scientists have thus far overlooked: Citizens care deeply about *retributive justice*, or the use of punishment to uphold what is fair and right. We want government leaders to show a commitment to punishing wrongdoers in society and especially within the government itself. When authoritarian leaders signal through anti-corruption campaigns, anti-crime initiatives, top-down bureaucratic control, and punishment of malfeasance that they are implementing retributive justice, citizens may express high levels of support, engagement, and cooperation, even when economic performance, democratic processes, and redistribution are lackluster or absent.

Wenfang Tang, 134–51, Oxford University Press, 2016; see also Lily L. Tsai, "Constructive Noncompliance," *Comparative Politics* 47, no. 3 (April 1, 2015): 253–79.

[17] Gary King, Jennifer Pan, and Margaret E. Roberts, "How Censorship in China Allows Government Criticism but Silences Collective Expression," *American Political Science Review* 107, no. 2 (May 1, 2013): 326–43.

[18] By comparison, the Afrobarometer survey in Kenya asks people whether they contacted a government official about anything (not just government provision of public services but also personal problems and requests for patronage): "During the past year, how often have you contacted any of the following persons about some important problem or to give them your views: An official of a government agency?" In 2015, only 22 percent of people in rural Kenya said they had taken action. More people in China's authoritarian regime contact government officials about problems with public services than in Kenya's competitive multiparty democracy. Lily L. Tsai and Yiqing Xu, "Outspoken Insiders: Political Connections and Citizen Participation in Authoritarian China," *Political Behavior* 40, no. 3 (September 11, 2018): 629–57.

We care about punishment, not only because it deters future wrong-doing or has instrumental value, but also because it's "only fair" for those who break the rules to suffer the consequences. We want them to get what they deserve.[19] Punishing wrongdoers confirms the importance of the social order and restores our confidence that society is indeed being governed by fundamental values and rules. It reestablishes predictability and reassures those of us who do follow the rules that we are not "suckers."

We also want the authorities to answer the question of who the bad guys are, especially when we are hurting, economically or socially. We want our leaders to find the culprits, to identify the *hostis publicus*, the "enemy of the people," as it was called in ancient Rome. They can be external – foreign invaders, say, or terrorists. Often, and more conveniently, they are identified as internal – criminals, drug traffickers, illegal immigrants, corrupt officials. We look to our leaders for assurances that government authorities are ready and willing to identify these wrongdoers and root them out. These actions tell us something about the moral commitments and benevolent intentions of those in office. When we see our authorities punishing criminals and wrongdoers, it can strengthen our beliefs that they at least care about right and wrong – even if we are not sure that crime and wrongdoing are actually decreasing.

And when the bad guys are part of the system – when the main problem seems to be corruption among government officials – we are particularly attentive to how our leaders respond. Are they willing to punish their own? Do they really care about upholding social and moral order? Or do they only really care about their hold on power? Anti-corruption punishment, as I explain in Chapter 2, can be a particularly compelling signal of the government's commitment to retributive justice – and thus a particularly powerful strategy for leaders seeking to mobilize popular support.

RETRIBUTIVE JUSTICE AS A "BLACK SHEEP" CONCEPT

Though Chapter 2 will also expand on this issue, it is worth taking a moment here to reflect on why political scientists have largely

---

[19] Morton Deutsch, Peter T. Coleman, and Eric C. Marcus, *The Handbook of Conflict Resolution: Theory and Practice*, John Wiley & Sons, 2011; John Rawls, *A Theory of Justice*, Cambridge University Press, 1971; John Rawls, *A Theory of Justice, Revised Edition*, Cambridge University Press, 1999.

overlooked the importance of retributive justice in governance and state–society relations. Why does retributive justice make us feel uncomfortable? One reason is that we associate it with our instinct for revenge. We often want those who hurt us to suffer, even when we do not have a moral or social justification.

Personal revenge and retributive justice are two different phenomena. Revenge or retaliation is instinctive and can occur without moral justification, while retributive justice is the deliberate use of punishment to reinforce social order and society's moral values. But we worry that retributive justice can be used rhetorically as an excuse for violence and degenerate into unrestrained vigilantism. Retributivism has thus been controversial as a basis for legal punishment because it can legitimate our "darker human impulses for revenge and retaliation."[20] The execution of revenge often follows the same guideline of "just deserts" on which retributive justice is based, making it easy to conflate the two, in theory and in practice. The biblical decree of "an eye for an eye" reflects a retributive justice imperative but also justifies more primitive urges.[21]

Compounding our unease with retributive justice are cases of authorities supporting the use of force to satisfy these primitive needs for retaliation. In the establishment of the South African Truth and Reconciliation Commission, for example, Braithwaite advocated against the retributivism associated with Nuremberg-style trials, favoring instead a paradigm of "restorative justice." Retributivism, he noted, stems from "the corrosive remnants of outdated survival instincts," and authorities should not legitimate these instincts.[22] In his history of punishment in the Western world, Friedland identifies retaliation as a consistent justification for punishment, even by government authorities. When someone is harmed,

[20] Mario Gollwitzer, Milena Meder, and Manfred Schmitt, "What Gives Victims Satisfaction When They Seek Revenge?" *European Journal of Social Psychology* 41, no. 3 (April 2011): 364–74; see also Geoffrey P. Goodwin and Dena M. Gromet, "Punishment," *Wiley Interdisciplinary Reviews: Cognitive Science* 5, no. 5 (September 2014): 562.

[21] Kevin M. Carlsmith and John M. Darley, "Psychological Aspects of Retributive Justice," *Advances in Experimental Social Psychology*, 40 (2008): 193–236.

[22] John Braithwaite, "Principles of Restorative Justice," in *Restorative Justice and Criminal Justice: Competing or Reconcilable Paradigms?*, edited by Andrew von Hirsch, Julian V. Roberts, and Anthony Bottoms, 5, Hart, 2003; John Braithwaite, "Restorative Justice: Assessing Optimistic and Pessimistic Accounts," *Crime and Justice* 25 (January 1999): 6, 7; see also Lucy Allais, "Restorative Justice, Retributive Justice, and the South African Truth and Reconciliation Commission," *Philosophy & Public Affairs* 39, no. 4 (September 2011): 331–363, footnote 73.

societies have broadly agreed that someone ought to pay for it, irrespective of whether the punishment has deterrence value or upholds social and moral order. To illustrate this point, he draws our attention to how societies even execute animals who maim or kill humans, identifying cases from twelfth-century France as well as today's United States: "Even after all these centuries, we too want in some visceral way to see people (or animals) *pay* for their crimes."[23]

Another reason we may shy away from studying or acknowledging retributive justice concerns is out of fear that government authorities use retributive justice as an excuse to eliminate political opponents and consolidate their power within the state. Recent anti-corruption campaigns, including ones in Nigeria, Senegal, Brazil, and Mexico, have been criticized for only targeting politicians in other parties and factions.[24] And even when anti-corruption campaigns genuinely seek to prosecute wrongdoers, effective implementation of retributive justice in developing countries has often led to use of the death penalty that violates liberal conceptions of rights. Andersson and Heywood point out that the international anti-corruption campaigns that gave rise to Transparency International and its Corruption Perceptions Index have had the unintended consequence of encouraging developing countries to use the death penalty "in ways that render their democratic record very problematic."[25] While they acknowledge that initiatives that rely on severe punishment such as those in Hong Kong and Singapore are often the most effective among the cases they study, they note: "If anti-corruption is elevated to the status of being the most important issue facing governments, does that contribute to legitimizing an approach to which the end justifies the means, for instance using very harsh means to

---

[23] Paul Friedland, *Seeing Justice Done: The Age of Spectacular Capital Punishment in France*, Oxford University Press, 2012.

[24] Economist Intelligence Unit, "Senegal," *The Economist*, 2017; John P. Frinjuah, "A 'Cry for Change' and President Buhari's Fight against Corruption," *Afro Barometer*, February 2018; Paul F. Lagunes and Susan Rose-Ackerman, "Why Brazil Is Winning Its Fight against Corruption," *The Conversation*, February 2, 2017.

[25] Andersson and Heywood note that international anti-corruption campaigns can have the unintended negative consequence of encouraging developing countries to use the death penalty in ways that render their "democratic record" very problematic – despite the fact that these countries are seen to have some of the more effective anti-corruption initiatives. Staffan Andersson and Paul M. Heywood, "The Politics of Perception: Use and Abuse of Transparency International's Approach to Measuring Corruption," *Political Studies* 57, no. 4 (December 2009): 746–67.

fight against corruption sometimes can be questioned in relation to legal security, the risk of arbitrary punishments, and human rights."[26]

Not surprisingly, legislators in consolidated democracies express concern that the broad discretion given to anti-corruption agencies can threaten constitutional freedoms and guarantees.[27] Klitgaard comments, "The power to punish can be devastating if it is abused or corrupted; consequently, governments tend to guard against punishments for civil servants." At the same time, concern for the protection of individual rights is often in tension with the effective implementation of retributive justice. While caution about the violation of individual rights may prevent abuses, "it also leaves most public managers with little authority to penalize the corrupt."[28]

One challenge is that in countries with relatively low state capacity and limited ability to monitor the behavior of state agents, government authorities who genuinely want to uphold retributive justice may have little choice but to rely on extreme sanctions, including the death penalty. The imposition of harsh punishments can be a rational strategy for controlling state agents, one that has been noted as far back as Plato, who argued, "The servants of the nations are to render their service without any taking of presents. . . . The disobedient shall, if convicted, die without ceremony."[29] Such "infinitely large penalties" can be the optimal solution for certain principal–agent problems.[30] Even when extreme sanctions

---

[26] Staffan Andersson and Paul M. Heywood, "The Politics of Perception: Use and Abuse of Transparency International's Approach to Measuring Corruption," *Political Studies* 57, no. 4 (December 2009): 746–67.

[27] De Sousa notes: "Unlike conventional law enforcers, ACAs [anti-corruption agencies] tend to benefit from a range of special (investigative) powers. The fact that this type of institutional response to corruption is traditionally associated with broad competences and special powers is controversial and is not always popular in democratic regimes. On the one hand, the decision makers and legislators fear the allocation of special powers to ACAs, on the grounds that their excessive use or abuse represent a threat to constitutional freedoms and guarantees; while on the other hand, the conventional law enforcers fear an inevitable loss of competences to the specialized agency. This explains why there are few of them in western democracies." Staffan Andersson and Paul M. Heywood, "Anti-Corruption as a Risk to Democracy: On the Unintended Consequences of International Anti-Corruption Campaigns" in *Governments, NGOs and Anti-Corruption: The New Integrity Warriors*, edited by Luís De Sousa, Barry Hindess, and Peter Larmour, 42, Routledge, 2012.

[28] Robert Klitgaard, *Controlling Corruption*, University of California Press, 1988, 79.

[29] Plato, "The Laws," in *The Collected Dialogues of Plato*, edited by Edith Hamilton and Huntington Cairns, Princeton University Press, 1961, 1225–1514, cited in Robert Klitgaard, *Controlling Corruption*, University of California Press, 1988, 78.

[30] Robert Klitgaard, *Controlling Corruption*, University of California Press, 1988, 78.

such as dramatic executions do not lead to more actual compliance from agents, such actions can help political leaders appear to be committed to retributive justice.

Rather than causing us to shy away from thinking about retributive justice, these dangers and concerns mean that it is important to do exactly the opposite. In order to understand how to prevent authorities from abusing their access to coercion and stirring up public concerns about retributive justice for political ends, we have to look empirically at how retributive justice concerns influence the behavior of citizens.

PRIOR SCHOLARSHIP

To be clear, this book's focus on retributive justice complements rather than competes with existing theories of public opinion and mass support. Its main objective is to highlight that retributive justice is one important criterion that citizens use to evaluate government authorities that we have generally overlooked. But there are, of course, other important criteria as well. Existing theories fall into two general categories: evaluations of performance and evaluations of distributive and procedural justice.

Performance Evaluations

A government's ability to promote the material well-being of its people has long been seen as a key source of citizen satisfaction and support for government leaders in both democratic and nondemocratic regimes.[31] A large body of research shows that economic performance affects regime support and durability in the long run, as well as vote choice in the short run.[32] Evidence from the case of China is generally consistent with these

[31] Margaret Levi, *Of Rule and Revenue*, vol. 13, University of California Press, 1989; Seymour Martin Lipset, *Political Man*, Vintage Books, 1960; Adam Przeworski, *Democracy and the Market: Political and Economic Reforms in Eastern Europe and Latin America*, Cambridge University Press, 1991; Susan Carol Stokes, *Public Support for Market Reforms in New Democracies*, Cambridge University Press, 2001.

[32] For a review of this literature, see Michael S. Lewis-Beck and Mary Stegmaier, *Economic Models of Voting*, Oxford University Press, 2007; see also Harold D. Clarke, Nitish Dutt, and Allan Kornberg, "The Political Economy of Attitudes toward Polity and Society in Western European Democracies," *The Journal of Politics* 55, no. 4 (November 1993): 998–1021; Steven E. Finkel, Edward N. Muller, and Mitchell A. Seligson, "Economic Crisis, Incumbent Performance and Regime Support: A Comparison of Longitudinal Data from West Germany and Costa Rica," *British Journal of Political Science* 19, no. 3 (July 27, 1989): 329; M. Stephen Weatherford, "How Does Government Performance Influence Political Support?" *Political Behavior* 9, no. 1 (1987): 5–28.

arguments. Public opinion polls over the past twenty years have showed a high level of support for the regime.[33] Many have argued that the Chinese Communist Party (CCP) deliberately adopted a "pragmatic" strategy of accomplishing concrete goals such as economic growth, public goods provision, social stability, and strengthening national power at the start of the reform period to replace a governing strategy based on ideology and mass mobilization.[34] Dickson finds that Chinese citizens generally see government public goods provision as improving and that attitudes toward provision are correlated with citizen satisfaction.[35] Manion notes that ordinary villagers see local congress delegates as advocates for local public goods to their constituencies.[36] The idea that the government's first priority should be the economic well-being of the people has historical roots in the Analects of Confucius, which states that the first task of government is the elimination of poverty.[37] Recent survey research and data from the 2002 and 2007–08 Asian Barometer also suggest that citizen ratings of the national economy and government performance are positively correlated with trust in political institutions and support for the current form of government.[38]

[33] In China, there is much discussion because we find a high level of regime support for China in public opinion polls. Jie Chen, Yang Zhong, and Jan William Hillard, "The Level and Sources of Popular Support for China's Current Political Regime," *Communist and Post-Communist Studies* 30, no. 1 (March 1997): 45–64; Tianjian Shi, "Cultural Values and Political Trust: A Comparison of the People's Republic of China and Taiwan," *Comparative Politics* 33, no. 4 (July 2001): 401; Wenfang Tang, *Public Opinion and Political Change in China*, Stanford University Press, 2005. Yet, China has failed to implement national elections. Jane Duckett and Hua Wang, "Extending Political Participation in China: New Opportunities for Citizens in the Policy Process," *Journal of Asian Public Policy* 6, no. 3 (November 21, 2013): 263–76.

[34] Hongxing Yang and Dingxin Zhao, "Performance Legitimacy, State Autonomy and China's Economic Miracle," *Journal of Contemporary China* 24, no. 91 (January 2, 2015): 64–82; Yuchao Zhu, "'Performance Legitimacy' and China's Political Adaptation Strategy," *Journal of Chinese Political Science* 16, no. 2 (June 9, 2011): 123–40.

[35] Bruce Dickson, *The Dictator's Dilemma: The Chinese Communist Party's Strategy for Survival*, Oxford University Press, 2016.

[36] Melanie Manion, *Information for Autocrats: Representation in Chinese Local People's Congresses*, Cambridge University Press, 2016.

[37] Daniel Bell, *China's New Confucianism: Politics and Everyday Life in a Changing Society*, Princeton, NJ: Princeton University Press, 2008; Wai-man Lam, *Political Legitimacy in Hong Kong: A Hybrid Notion*, Cambridge University Press, 2016.

[38] Jie Chen, Yang Zhong, and Jan William Hillard, "The Level and Sources of Popular Support for China's Current Political Regime," *Communist and Post-Communist Studies* 30, no. 1 (March 1997): 45–64; Neil M I Munro, Jane Duckett, Kate Hunt, and Matt Sutton, "Does China's Regime Enjoy 'Performance Legitimacy'? An Empirical Analysis Based on Three Surveys from the Past Decade," 2013; APSA 2013 Annual Meeting Paper,

Some believe economic performance to be particularly important for nondemocratic regimes like China because these governments cannot rely on democratic bases of legitimacy. Existing work, for example, has also found regime support to be correlated with citizen evaluations of the economy in post-socialist Russia.[39] Conversely, poor economic performance has been found to render authorities in authoritarian and hybrid regimes vulnerable to political challenges and defections,[40] resentment, and rebellion.[41]

At the same time, it is important to note that regimes usually survive economic downturns. Research on development interventions providing citizens with information about poor governmental performance also suggests that poor performance is not always salient to ordinary people.[42] Economic performance is one source of mass support but not the only one.

Justice Evaluations

As with this book, other studies of public support focus on whether people believe their government authorities uphold justice.[43] But most of this

American Political Science Association, https://ssrn.com/abstract=2302982; Tianjian Shi, "Cultural Values and Political Trust: A Comparison of the People's Republic of China and Taiwan," *Comparative Politics* 33, no. 4 (July 2001): 401; Zhengxu Wang, "Explaining Regime Strength in China," *China: An International Journal* 4, no. 2 (2006): 217–37; Dingxin Zhao, "The Mandate of Heaven and Performance Legitimation in Historical and Contemporary China," *American Behavioral Scientist* 53, no. 3 (2009): 416–33.

[39] Richard Rose, William Mishler, and Neil Munro, *Popular Support for an Undemocratic Regime: The Changing Views of Russians*, Cambridge University Press, 2011.

[40] Ora John Reuter and Jennifer Gandhi, "Economic Performance and Elite Defection from Hegemonic Parties," *British Journal of Political Science* 41, no. 1 (2011): 83–110.

[41] Ted Robert Gurr, *Why Men Rebel*, Princeton, NJ: Princeton University Press, 1970.

[42] John Gaventa and Rosemary McGee, "The Impact of Transparency and Accountability Initiatives," *Development Policy Review* 31 (July 2013): s3–28; Stephen Kosack and Archon Fung, "Does Transparency Improve Governance?" *Annual Review of Political Science* 17, no. 1 (May 11, 2014): 65–87; Varja Lipovsek and Lily L. Tsai, "What Do We Know about Transparency and Non-Electoral Accountability? Synthesizing the Evidence from the Last Ten Years," *Transparency and Accountability Initiative*, January 2018. https://mitgovlab.org/results/information-and-non-electoral-accountability-evidence-in-context/; World Bank Group, *Making Politics Work for Development: Harnessing Transparency and Citizen Engagement*, The World Bank, 2016.

[43] For example, see Robert Folger, Tom R. Tyler, Robert J. Boeckmann, Heather J. Smith, and Yuen J. Huo, "Social Justice in a Diverse Society," *Administrative Science Quarterly* 44, no. 4 (1999): 839; Tom R. Tyler, "Social Justice: Outcome and Procedure," *International Journal of Psychology* 35, no. 2 (2000): 117–25; Tom R. Tyler, Kenneth A. Rasinski, and Kathleen M. McGraw, "The Influence of Perceived Injustice on the

work has focused on either distributive justice, the fair allocation of resources by authorities, or on procedural justice, the use of fair procedures for decision making.

Scholars of nondemocratic regimes have noted that distributive justice and welfare provision are an important source of public support for government authorities. In the Soviet Union, the existence of a "socialist social contract" defined an implicit exchange whereby citizens acquiesced to autocratic rule and in return government officials provided them with social services, housing, and other benefits.[44] Similarly, in the Middle East, natural resource revenues enabled authorities to purchase societal support (or at least passive acceptance) with free health care, education, and other benefits.[45] Concerns about distributive justice have also been found to play an important role in explaining political attitudes.[46]

Survey research in China has also shown that distributive justice concerns are important to citizens. Whyte shows that while people generally support market competition, they also favor policies, such as minimum income and employment guarantees, that reduce persistent poverty and provide additional help to the disadvantaged so that they can compete on a level playing ground.[47] His findings also suggest that those with higher-status positions in the previous socialist system, such as urbanites, the well-educated, members of the Han ethnic majority, and those with links

Endorsement of Political Leaders," *Journal of Applied Social Psychology* 15, no. 8 (1985): 700–25.

[44] Linda J. Cook, *The Soviet Social Contract and Why It Failed: Welfare Policy and Workers' Politics from Brezhnev to Yeltsin*, vol. 86, Harvard University Press, 1993.

[45] Michael L. Ross, "Does Oil Hinder Democracy?" *World Politics* 53, no. 3 (2001): 325–61.

[46] Charlotte Cavaillé and Kris-Stella Trump, "The Two Facets of Social Policy Preferences," *The Journal of Politics* 77, no. 1 (January 2015): 146–60; Donald M. Taylor and Fathali M. Moghaddam, *Theories of Intergroup Relations: International Social Psychological Perspectives*, Greenwood Publishing Group, 1994; Heather J. Smith and Tom R. Tyler, "Justice and Power: When Will Justice Concerns Encourage the Advantaged to Support Policies Which Redistribute Economic Resources and the Disadvantaged to Willingly Obey the Law?" *European Journal of Social Psychology* 26, no. 2 (March 1996): 171–200; Morton Deutsch, "Equity, Equality, and Need: What Determines Which Value Will Be Used as the Basis of Distributive Justice?" *Journal of Social Issues* 31, no. 3 (July 1975): 137–49; Morton Deutsch, "Conflict Resolution: Theory and Practice," *Political Psychology* 4, no. 3 (September 1983): 431; Rupert Barnes Nacoste, "Sources of Stigma: Analyzing the Psychology of Affirmative Action," *Law & Policy* 12, no. 2 (April 1990): 175–95.

[47] Martin Whyte, *Myth of the Social Volcano: Perceptions of Inequality and Distributive Injustice in Contemporary China*, Stanford University Press, 2010.

to state-owned enterprises, tend to have stronger preferences for redistribution and more critical attitudes toward current inequalities.[48]

Procedural justice concerns have also been found to have an important effect on citizen attitudes and behaviors.[49] Procedural justice evaluations play an important role in whether citizens in the United States accept the decisions of authorities and to obey the law.[50] People are more likely to contribute to public goods and participate in institutions that they believe to be impartial and procedurally just.[51] Scholars of developing contexts have also argued that effective, impartial government institutions help to generate political support and legitimacy.[52] In the case of China, scholars

[48] Deborah Davis and Stevan Harrell, *Chinese Families in the Post-Mao Era*, vol. 17, University of California Press, 1993; Martin Whyte, *Myth of the Social Volcano: Perceptions of Inequality and Distributive Injustice in Contemporary China*, Stanford University Press, 2010.

[49] E. Allan Lind and Tom R. Tyler, *The Social Psychology of Procedural Justice* (1988), Springer; Heather J. Smith and Tom R. Tyler, "Justice and Power: When Will Justice Concerns Encourage the Advantaged to Support Policies Which Redistribute Economic Resources and the Disadvantaged to Willingly Obey the Law?" *European Journal of Social Psychology* 26, no. 2 (March 1996): 171–200; Rupert Barnes Nacoste, "Sources of Stigma: Analyzing the Psychology of Affirmative Action," *Law & Policy* 12, no. 2 (April 1990): 175–95; Robert Folger, Tom R. Tyler, Robert J. Boeckmann, Heather J. Smith, and Yuen J. Huo, "Social Justice in a Diverse Society," *Administrative Science Quarterly* 44, no. 4 (1999): 839; Tom R. Tyler and Kathleen M. McGraw, "Ideology and the Interpretation of Personal Experience: Procedural Justice and Political Quiescence," *Journal of Social Issues* 42, no. 2 (1986): 115–28.

[50] Tom R. Tyler and E. Allan Lind, "A Relational Model of Authority in Groups," *Advances in Experimental Social Psychology*, 25(1992): 115–91; Tom R. Tyler and Peter Degoey, "Collective Restraint in Social Dilemmas: Procedural Justice and Social Identification Effects on Support for Authorities," *Journal of Personality and Social Psychology* 69, no. 3 (1995): 482–97; Tom Tyler, Peter Degoey, and Heather Smith, "Understanding Why the Justice of Group Procedures Matters: A Test of the Psychological Dynamics of the Group-Value Model," *Journal of Personality and Social Psychology* 70, no. 5 (1996): 913–30.

[51] Tom R. Tyler and Steven L. Blader, *Cooperation in Groups: Procedural Justice, Social Identity, and Behavioral Engagement*, (2000), Psychology Press. The authors find that employees are more likely to engage in "discretionary cooperative behavior" – voluntary participation and contributions to public goods in the organization – when they see the organization as committed to procedural justice.

[52] See these citations from Stefan Dahlberg, Jonas Linde, and Sören Holmberg, "Democratic Discontent in Old and New Democracies: Assessing the Importance of Democratic Input and Governmental Output," *Political Studies* 63, no. 1 (August 28, 2015): 18–37; Sören Holmberg and Bo Rothstein, *Good Government: The Relevance of Political Science*, Edward Elgar Publishing, 2012; Pedro C. Magalhães, "Government Effectiveness and Support for Democracy," *European Journal of Political Research* 53, no. 1 (February 2014): 77–97; Bo Rothstein, "Creating Political Legitimacy," *American Behavioral Scientist* 53, no. 3 (November 12, 2009): 311–30; Bo Rothstein, *The Quality of Government: Corruption, Social Trust, and Inequality in International Perspective*,

have argued that even limited implementation of local democratic elections increases citizen evaluations of government responsiveness[53] and procedural justice. Public opinion surveys in 2010 and 2014 by Dickson indicate that urban citizens in China believe that the country is becoming increasingly democratic, at least in terms of government "by and for the people."[54] Direct exposure to competitive local elections can lead to higher levels of participation in politics and higher trust in local leaders.[55]

Performance evaluations and concerns about distributive and procedural justice are an important part of the story. But they are insufficient. They cannot account for why individuals and groups – rural residents, lower- and middle-income families – who often fail to receive the lion's share of benefits sometimes still support their authoritarian leaders with great enthusiasm. In the Philippines, even the rural poor seems to support Duterte. In Tanzania, unemployment is far higher among the young and educated,[56] yet Magufuli's approval ratings among these groups has ranged between 70 and 80 percent.[57] Procedural justice concerns can account for citizen dissatisfaction in places where democratic institutions are weak and problems such as vote buying, election violence, and repression of civil liberties are rife. But they cannot account for why authoritarian leaders are sometimes *popular*. A model of retributive justice helps to account for the popularity of authoritarian leaders and authoritarian regimes where democracy,

---

University of Chicago Press, 2011; Alexander F. Wagner, Friedrich Schneider, and Martin Halla, "The Quality of Institutions and Satisfaction with Democracy in Western Europe – A Panel Analysis," *European Journal of Political Economy* 25, no. 1 (March 2009): 30–41.

[53] Survey data collected by Manion in several provinces suggest that rural citizens believe that local people's congresses act as representative institutions. Melanie Manion, *Information for Autocrats: Representation in Chinese Local People's Congresses*, Cambridge University Press, 2016.

[54] Bruce Dickson, *The Dictator's Dilemma: The Chinese Communist Party's Strategy for Survival*, Oxford University Press, 2016.

[55] Pierre F. Landry, Deborah Davis, and Shiru Wang, "Elections in Rural China: Competition without Parties," *Comparative Political Studies* 43, no. 6 (2010): 763–90; Lianjiang Li, "The Empowering Effect of Village Elections in China," *Asian Survey* 43, no. 4 (2003): 648–62; Melanie Manion, "Democracy, Community, Trust: The Impact of Elections in Rural China," *Comparative Political Studies* 39, no. 3 (2006): 301–24.

[56] Isis Gaddis, Waly Wane, and Jacques Morisset, "Youth in Tanzania: A Growing Uneducated Labor Force," *Africa Can End Poverty*, 2013. https://blogs.worldbank.org /africacan/youth-in-tanzania-a-growing-uneducated-labor-force

[57] Carolyn Del Vecchio, "The Political Participation, Engagement, and Perceptions of President Magufuli among Students at the College of African Wildlife Management," 2016. *Independent Study Project (ISP) Collection*. 2351. https://digitalcollections.sit.edu /isp_collection/2351

redistribution, and economic growth either vary dramatically across individuals and communities or are uniformly weak.

RESEARCH DESIGN

The primary aim of this book is to document the importance of retributive justice descriptively, as something citizens care about, a criterion they use to evaluate government. If retributive justice is an important criterion for citizens, we should see certain causal relationships (e.g., providing citizens with information about anti-corruption punishment should lead them to have higher evaluations of the moral character of government authorities), and the book indeed evaluates these observable implications.

But the book's main claim is not causal but descriptive. It seeks to demonstrate that citizens care deeply about the provision of retributive justice. As Barrington Moore noted, "Stability and predictability in human relationships have some advantages even for the disadvantaged."[58] This book argues that retributive justice is one of the most important and perhaps the most fundamental public good that a government provides to its citizens.

The Case of China

This book uses China as a test case for demonstrating the importance of retributive justice concerns for a number of reasons. The most obvious one is that many view China as a paragon of authoritarian popularity. At the very least, it seems to be a stable authoritarian regime that does not rule solely through fear and coercion.[59] If we fail to see that retributive justice considerations play a role in citizen evaluations of leaders in this case, we might be doubtful that such concerns explain authoritarian popularity anywhere.

Second, there is an extensive body of empirical research that has demonstrated the importance of performance, distributive justice, and even procedural justice considerations in authoritarian China.[60] If we believe these findings, there should be relatively little variation left to

[58] Barrington Moore Jr., *Injustice: The Social Bases of Obedience and Revolt: The Social Bases of Obedience and Revolt*, Routledge, 2016.
[59] The sixth wave of the World Values Survey indicates that 85 percent of the respondents in China have a great deal or quite a lot of confidence in their government, the second highest among all fifty-nine survey countries.
[60] On performance, see Jie Chen, "*Popular Political Support in Urban China*," (2004), Woodrow Wilson Center Press; Jie Chen, Yang Zhong, and Jan William Hillard, "The

explain. So if retributive justice does indeed play a role in explaining citizen evaluations of government and willingness to interact with government authorities, then retributive justice may play an even more important role in cases where leaders do not satisfy these concerns about performance, procedural justice, and distributive justice.

China's size and diversity also mean that empirically we see extensive variation across localities in citizen evaluations of government authorities and in the delivery of economic performance, procedural justice, and distributive justice by authorities. This variation allows us to assess the importance of retributive justice concerns across a variety of different types of localities.

Finally, the question of whether retributive justice is an important source of public support has become particularly relevant to China itself over the past few years. After what many consider an extraordinary trajectory of reform and development, China is now seeing its lowest growth rates in thirty years, and grassroots democratic reforms have stagnated. With Xi Jinping's rise to power in 2012, anti-corruption campaigns have become the main focus of the Chinese government with increasingly frequent and intense punishment being meted out. Although a rigorous evaluations of Xi's policies are outside the scope of this study, as the data are largely drawn from before the intensification of his anti-corruption initiatives, the book's model of retributive justice can shed light on how these initiatives may be a way of "recession-proofing"

Level and Sources of Popular Support for China's Current Political Regime," *Communist and Post-Communist Studies* 30, no. 1 (March 1997): 45–64; Neil MI Munro, Jane Duckett, Kate Hunt, and Matt Sutton, "Does China's Regime Enjoy 'Performance Legitimacy'? An Empirical Analysis Based on Three Surveys from the Past Decade," 2013, APSA 2013 Annual Meeting Paper, American Political Science Association 2013 Annual Meeting, https://ssrn.com/abstract=2302982; Tianjian Shi, "Cultural Values and Political Trust: A Comparison of the People's Republic of China and Taiwan," *Comparative Politics* 33, no. 4 (July 2001): 401; Zhengxu Wang, "Explaining Regime Strength in China," *China: An International Journal* 4, no. 2 (2006): 217–37; Dingxin Zhao, "The Mandate of Heaven and Performance Legitimation in Historical and Contemporary China," *American Behavioral Scientist* 53, no. 3 (2009): 416–33; on distributive justice, see Deborah Davis and Stevan Harrell, *Chinese Families in the Post-Mao Era*, vol. 17, University of California Press, 1993; Martin Whyte, *Myth of the Social Volcano: Perceptions of Inequality and Distributive Injustice in Contemporary China*, Stanford University Press, 2010; on procedural justice, see Pierre F. Landry, Deborah Davis, and Shiru Wang, "Elections in Rural China: Competition without Parties," *Comparative Political Studies* 43, no. 6 (2010): 763–90; Lianjiang Li, "The Empowering Effect of Village Elections in China," *Asian Survey* 43, no. 4 (2003): 648–62; Melanie Manion, "Democracy, Community, Trust: The Impact of Elections in Rural China," *Comparative Political Studies* 39, no. 3 (2006): 301–24.

the Chinese regime. Public opinion data show that the public views such punishment positively (Harvard Asia Programs Center for Business and Government 2016). This gives us reason to suspect that anti-corruption punishment may one day compete with other long-standing policies as the primary strategy for securing public support for the regime.

Data Sources

When I started this project in 2010, I was interested in understanding how ordinary people saw their relationship to higher-level government authorities beyond the grassroots officials and street-level bureaucrats within their communities. From talking with villagers in previous research, I knew that some could be critical of government authorities while others could be highly approving. But I was uncertain about what explained variation across communities and individuals. I also had the sense that citizen evaluations of higher-level government authorities had to do with their views of how higher levels interacted with the village officials that villagers could see on a daily basis.

At the time, there was also a lot of doubt about the accuracy of survey data on public opinion in authoritarian regimes. While this skepticism about survey responses in China has since been somewhat alleviated by research assessing the extent of political desirability bias among Chinese respondents, at the time I wanted to make sure I knew how ordinary people themselves spoke in conversation about government authorities. Rather than looking at their replies to close-ended questions using vocabulary and concepts generated from another context, I wanted to hear what was most salient to them about the behavior and characteristics of government authorities as it emerged in open-ended conversations. Preexisting ethnographic and qualitative data, however, on how citizens in authoritarian regimes talk about how they judge government authorities were scarce. Doing close-range fieldwork in authoritarian regimes requires permission from the government as well as trust from interview respondents, both of which can be hard to obtain for studies that ask questions about citizen evaluations of the government.

My research thus started with a long phase of open-ended, qualitative research, for which I was able to secure permissions through a network of contacts among Chinese academics. I decided to interview a random sample of households in three field sites scattered across rural China in very different regions – the mountainous interior region of Shaanxi province; a rural area several hours outside of Beijing; and a peri-urban region of coastal Fujian province in the south. In three village communities, I interviewed a random sample of households repeatedly over two years, 2010 and 2011. We talked about the challenges that they, their families, and their communities faced in their everyday lives. In these conversations, I did not start out by asking them how they felt about the government. Instead, we discussed the challenges they faced in their everyday lives, and I followed up on mentions of the government when they arose.

Although my follow-up questions were informed by existing theories of citizen evaluations, what was most surprising was that respondents stressed concerns that I had not previously considered based on my reading of existing theories of public opinion and political participation – concerns about corruption, the need for top-down supervision of local officials, and the desire for harsh punishment of misbehavior. These concerns generated the retributive justice model of citizen engagement proposed in this book.

While it is common to find batteries of questions measuring citizen perceptions of economic development, procedural justice, and distributive justice on public opinion surveys around the world, there are no such batteries measuring citizen perceptions of retributive justice. Although retributive justice has been discussed by philosophers and studied in laboratory settings by psychologists, empirical investigation outside the lab has been rare. Research on the role of retributive justice concerns on political attitudes and behavior is virtually nonexistent. To test these hypotheses, I thus implemented a series of original surveys and survey experiments. Specifically, I draw on a series of conjoint experiments conducted in 2016–17 (in collaboration with American and Chinese research assistants). Two of these were embedded in field surveys administered in person in rural Fujian and rural Beijing, and one was embedded in an original online survey of urban respondents.[61] These experiments assess the importance of retributive justice concerns for citizen evaluations of government relative to other criteria such as economic development and procedural justice.

In order to understand whether the findings from the survey experiments generalize to real-world circumstances and evaluate additional observable implications of the theory, I also draw on original datasets collected both before and after the current anti-corruption campaign launched in 2012. Observational data come from a nationally

---

[61] Conducted in collaboration with Minh Trinh and Shiyao Liu.

representative survey of China conducted in 2008 on actual bureaucratic institutions for top-down supervision and discipline,[62] regional field surveys in 2016–17, as well as additional conjoint experiments assessing the importance of retributive justice on tax compliance behavior. These analyses help to increase our confidence that retributive justice concerns are important across populations, time periods, and contexts. I also further evaluate the external validity of the argument by examining whether retributive justice concerns are salient beyond the context of China through a unique survey experiment administered to online respondents in fifty countries.[63]

BROADER IMPLICATIONS

Unless we start to pay attention to the fact that citizens have retributive justice concerns and that retributive justice is one of the fundamental expectations they have for government, we cannot fully explain the successes of authoritarian leaders and institutions or the failures of their democratic counterparts. A retributive justice model of citizen engagement has important implications for understanding democratic dissatisfaction, the conditions under which we might expect populism to increase, interventions promoting citizen participation and government accountability to fail, and state building to succeed in the absence of liberal democracy.

A Unified Framework for Understanding Democratic Dissatisfaction and Authoritarian Popularity

This book provides a theory for understanding when ordinary people are more likely to favor illiberal and authoritarian leaders, one that seeks to overcome the usual siloes that separate research on authoritarian regimes from scholarship on the United States and other democracies by providing a unified framework for understanding authoritarian popularity and democratic dissatisfaction. One main advantage of a unified framework is that it illuminates how citizen support of government authorities can fluctuate in both authoritarian and democratic regimes, even when the institutions do not change. Studies that focus only on democracies or only on authoritarian regimes tend to explain either persistence or

---

[62] Sampling excluded Xizang province (Tibet).
[63] Conducted in collaboration with the World Bank.

consolidation of the regime – more of the same – or to account for change going primarily in one direction (e.g., democratic backsliding or authoritarian breakdown). In contrast, a model of retributive justice helps us understand how citizens support leaders and regimes that credibly commit to upholding retributive justice and distrust leaders and regimes that fail to do so – regardless of what the rules governing access to power and leadership selection are.

Punitive Populism and the Rise of Illiberal and Authoritarian Leaders

Relatedly, retributive justice can help us explain when we are more likely to see increasing support for populist movements and illiberal policies. Case studies of anti-corruption programs from the 1990s and early 2000s show that campaigns involving severe and highly public punishments led to increased citizen support and political participation. In Hong Kong, the British colonial government instituted a wildly popular "guilty until proven innocent" standard for officials who were suspected of "unexplained enrichment."[64] Holmes finds in his examination of anti-corruption campaigns in Eastern Europe, the Soviet Union, and communist systems in Asia and Africa that the real purpose of these campaigns in communist systems was not to improve government performance but to boost regime legitimacy.[65] In Mozambique, these motivations led Machel to reinstitute the death penalty and flogging and possible punishments for corruption.[66]

A retributive justice argument posits that citizens want government authorities to punish wrongdoing by lower-level officials because such punishment indicates that government authorities are committed to upholding moral and social order. These concerns about order may be more salient when forces such as economic instability and immigration can make people less confident about whether everyone in society shares the same moral values and social norms.

In contrast, anti-corruption campaigns that do not result in indictments and sentencings are often viewed by citizens as "cheap talk" and lead to increased levels of disillusionment and distrust. Failures to address the

---

[64] Robert Klitgaard, *Controlling Corruption*, University of California Press, 1988.
[65] Leslie Holmes, *The End of Communist Power: Anti-Corruption Campaigns and Legitimation Crisis (Europe and the International Order)*, Oxford University Press, 1993, 204.
[66] Joseph Hanlon, *Mozambique: The Revolution under Fire*, Zed, 1985.

retributive justice concerns of citizens can lead to discontent with liberal democracy and pave the way to populist leaders and parties.[67] In his examination of new democracies, Holmes observes: "If citizens continually read and hear reports of corruption, they begin to lose faith in the democratization and marketization projects."[68] Smilov notes that in Eastern Europe, anti-corruption bodies and anti-corruption discourse have raised public awareness of corruption, but lack of action and improvement has in turn led to decreased voting in elections, lack of party membership, and declining party loyalty and discipline.[69] The rise of populist parties and protest then reinforce citizen perceptions that liberal democracy as a system is controlled by a corrupt political elite and is thus incapable of implementing retributive justice.

The Frequent Failure of "Transparency and Accountability" Interventions

A retributive justice theory of citizen engagement also helps us understand why providing citizens with information about government corruption and malfeasance fails to lead to increased participation and greater government accountability. Over the past ten years, there has been a tidal wave of interventions seeking to encourage citizens in developing contexts to hold their governments accountable for corruption and poor public goods provision by providing them with information about these problems and making it easier for them to monitor government performance. The consensus is that the evidence for impact is, at best, mixed.[70] Many of

---

[67] Martin Tisne and Daniel Smilov, *From the Ground Up. Assessing the Record of Anticorruption Assistance in Southeastern Europe*, Budapest: CEU University Press, 2004.

[68] Leslie Holmes, "Political Corruption in Central and Eastern Europe," in *Corruption in Contemporary Politics*, edited by Martin J. Bull and James L. Newell, Palgrave Macmillan, 2003, 193–206; Leslie Holmes, "*The End of Communist Power: Anti-Corruption Campaigns and Legitimation Crisis (Europe and the International Order)*," Oxford University Press, 1993, 204.

[69] Martin Tisne and Daniel Smilov, *From the Ground Up. Assessing the Record of Anticorruption Assistance in Southeastern Europe*, CEU University Press, 2004.

[70] Jonathan A. Fox, "Social Accountability: What Does the Evidence Really Say?" *World Development* 72 (2015): 346–61; John Gaventa and Rosemary McGee, "The Impact of Transparency and Accountability Initiatives," *Development Policy Review* 31 (July 2013): s3–28; Stephen Kosack and Archon Fung, "Does Transparency Improve Governance?" *Annual Review of Political Science* 17, no. 1 (May 11, 2014): 65–87; Lily L. Tsai, Varja Lipovsek, Benjamin S. Morse, and Guillermo Toral, "What Is the Evidence that Efforts to Promote International Norms and Standards for Transparency

us have been scratching our heads and wondering why information about corruption, malfeasance, and poor performance fail to galvanize action and make citizens outraged enough to go and complain to higher-level authorities.

A retributive justice model of citizen engagement provides an important part of the answer. If government authorities fail to uphold retributive justice and signal to citizens that they will punish corrupt agents, then it may seem irrational for citizens to make the effort to monitor local agents and flag potential misbehavior and wrongdoing to higher levels. Credible signals or commitments to retributive justice in the form of well-publicized punishments, anti-corruption investigations, and/or the establishment of top-down institutions for bureaucratic supervision and discipline may be a necessary precondition for these interventions to work.

Ironically, media coverage and information campaigns about government corruption and malfeasance may heighten citizen perceptions that the government lacks a commitment to retributive justice. Citizens may become more likely to search for signals about the moral character and intentions of politicians. Rather than taking more action themselves, they may instead become more likely to value and support leaders who appear to take these problems seriously and appear willing to punish wrongdoers severely, even at the expense of liberal values and the rule of law.

A New Look at State Building and Regime Consolidation

The production of retributive justice and moral order is a central function of the state and an important component of state building. Few regimes can purchase the acquiescence of all groups in society, or rely on constant coercion to repress protest. To understand stable regimes that are able to build effective institutions of governance, we need to know how government authorities persuade their citizens, at least at some minimal level, that they exercise political authority fairly, that citizens should comply with these institutions voluntarily, and that these institutions should govern citizen interactions with government officials and the political system.

and Accountability Have an Impact on Behaviors of Accountability Actors?" Evidence Review for the Transparency and Accountability Initiative, Massachusetts Institute of Technology Governance Lab (MIT GOV/LAB), Work in progress; World Bank Group, *Making Politics Work for Development: Harnessing Transparency and Citizen Engagement*, The World Bank, 2016.

State building, in short, entails the construction of a moral order. To maintain this moral order – and to show citizens the state's commitment to this order – authorities must show that they punish those who violate this order. In liberal democracies, punishment is ensured by the rule of law. Those who exercise their power wrongly or for private gain will be punished according to the law. Not all states, however, pursue retributive justice through the establishment of rule of law. Just as political systems do not all move in a linear fashion toward democracy, some have evolved alternative strategies for retributive justice. Unless we start to analyze how these other strategies work, we cannot fully understand authoritarian resilience and when, if ever, citizens demand a particular form of retributive justice over another.

Understanding how state strategies for retributive justice work can also reveal additional implications for governance and state building. Government authorities in weak states, for example, may choose to uphold retributive justice through "extreme sanctions," or severe punishments for malfeasance. Though this strategy may be a cost-saving measure for states with limited capacity, it can also act as a selection mechanism to weed out "bad type" officials who are primarily motivated by self-enrichment and material incentives.[71] When the costs of even being accused of misbehavior are so high, it becomes irrational for those seeking to maximize personal benefit to become public officials. For citizens in authoritarian and hybrid regimes who have no formal means of participating in the selection of officials, seeing government authorities implement this strategy of extreme sanctions may ease their concerns about what "type" of officials exist at both higher and lower levels. As a result, utilizing this strategy may lead to the citizen–government cooperation necessary for building new state institutions.

ROADMAP OF THE BOOK

Chapter 2 proposes a retributive justice theory of citizen engagement. This theory starts from the premise that people prefer government authorities

---

[71] Gabrielle S. Adams and Elizabeth Mullen, "Increased Voting for Candidates Who Compensate Victims Rather than Punish Offenders," *Social Justice Research* 26, no. 2 (2013): 168–92; Dena M. Gromet, "Restoring the Victim: Emotional Reactions, Justice Beliefs, and Support for Reparation and Punishment," *Critical Criminology* 20, no. 1 (March 19, 2012): 9–23; Dena M. Gromet and John M. Darley, "Political Ideology and Reactions to Crime Victims: Preferences for Restorative and Punitive Responses," *Journal of Empirical Legal Studies* 8, no. 4 (December 2011): 830–55.

who govern according to principles that have a moral basis, that we want more from government than simply deferring to elites with more power and resources. I argue that one fundamental expectation is for government authorities to provide retributive justice, or the use of punishment to uphold what is fair and right. Besides deterring future malfeasance, such punishment upholds the fundamental values of the political community and enables higher-level officials to show citizens they are moral leaders. Thus, when authoritarian politicians – both in robustly authoritarian regimes and in electoral democracies moving toward greater authoritarianism – successfully show citizens they are committed to retributive justice, they may enjoy a high level of public support and legitimacy and high levels of citizen engagement and voluntary compliance.

Chapter 3 illustrates the importance of retributive justice from the perspective of the state. Using the case of China, the chapter shows that Chinese rulers have long behaved as if addressing the public's concerns about retributive justice is important for their ability to maintain power. In fact, leaders may even foster such concerns in order to experience the bump in public support that comes from subsequently taking action to alleviate those concerns. In tracing the historical evolution of state strategies for retributive justice in China, we can see how state building involves not just resource extraction and the accumulation of coercive power but also the production of moral order. Government authorities and the public throughout the imperial and communist periods have consistently highlighted that retributive justice is and should be a core function of the state. Indeed, government authorities have at times taken active steps to encourage public outrage at the corruption and malfeasance of local state agents in order to then benefit from the implementation of retributive justice.

Chapter 4 turns to the perspective of ordinary citizens and examines the ways in which retributive justice concerns shape citizen attitudes and behavior toward government authorities. Drawing on qualitative research conducted with a random sample of households in three diverse communities across rural China, the chapter begins with three narratives that ordinary people frequently use to explain what they expect from government authorities and how they make decisions about whether to participate in local governance. These narratives help to generate specific hypotheses about retributive justice concerns and concretize the ways in which ordinary people speak about their desire for government authorities to uphold social order by punishing wrongdoers among government agents.

The chapter then tests whether the retributive justice concerns voiced by citizens in qualitative interviews indeed have a causal impact on citizen evaluations of government authorities. Through a series of experiments embedded in original, in-person field surveys administered in two rural regions of China, as well as an online survey of urban respondents, we see that citizens prefer government leaders who address citizen concerns about retributive justice by punishing corruption and malfeasance within the government. Even when government authorities fail on other dimensions, they can still garner approval from citizens when they show they are willing to engage in anti-corruption measures.

The next question is whether these findings apply to the real world. Do we see similar patterns between real-world institutions for top-down discipline and citizen evaluations of their actual officials? Does retributive justice affect behavioral outcomes? And are retributive justice concerns salient in countries other than China? Chapter 5 assesses the external validity of the causal relationships presented in Chapter 4 in several ways. It draws on original surveys conducted both before and after the launch of the current anti-corruption campaign in China to examine whether citizens in localities with stronger top-down institutions for bureaucratic discipline have more positive evaluations of local authorities, higher levels of participation, and higher willingness to engage in voluntary compliance. The chapter then expands the investigation beyond rural China to discuss findings showing that retributive justice concerns help account for voluntary compliance behaviors among urban Chinese as well as in countries beyond China.

The book concludes in Chapter 6 by turning a retributive justice lens on recent global trends in democratic backsliding. It discusses the conditions under which retributive justice concerns become more salient for ordinary citizens and make them more likely to support leaders who launch anti-corruption initiatives and promote "punitive populism." It reflects on the dangers of anti-corruption politics, the strategies that politicians use to promote the idea of the "benevolent dictator," and, finally, on lessons that liberal democrats can learn from successful authoritarians.

The main objective of this book is to show that citizens care deeply about retributive justice, sometimes more than they care about the provision of public services, economic development, procedural justice, or distributive justice. We may not always want citizens to care so much about retributive justice since these concerns pave the way for populist, authoritarian, and illiberal trajectories. But until we take these concerns seriously and develop theories that help us understand when and why these are concerns are most salient, we will not be able to know how best to work toward the political and social outcomes that we normatively desire.

2

A Retributive Justice Model of Citizen Engagement

This book examines the following question: When citizens look at the actions and policies of authoritarian leaders, what criteria do they use to evaluate these leaders and to decide whether they should engage with the political system? Existing scholarship on citizen evaluations of government in authoritarian regimes has focused either on performance or on procedural and distributive justice as the main principles by which citizens evaluate the fairness of their political leaders.[1] Regimes also vary in the degree to which they can satisfy concerns in different localities about economic performance, procedural justice, and distributive justice. Yet we do not always see unrest or even dissatisfaction in localities where the regime fails to deliver on these expectations. Why?

The main argument of this book is that citizens in nondemocratic and hybrid regimes may also view authorities as just, fair, and committed to the public good when they address citizen concerns about *retributive justice*. Government authorities uphold retributive justice when they affirm society's basic values by punishing wrongdoers who act against these values, especially wrongdoers among the government's own officials. Citizens who believe that government authorities have a commitment to retributive justice are likely to be more satisfied with

---

[1] Daniel Bell, *China's New Confucianism: Politics and Everyday Life in a Changing Society*, Princeton University Press, 2008; Robert Folger, Tom R. Tyler, Robert J. Boeckmann, Heather J. Smith, and Yuen J. Huo, "Social Justice in a Diverse Society," *Administrative Science Quarterly* 44, no. 4 (1999): 839; Robert G. Folger, *The Sense of Injustice: Social Psychological Perspectives*, Springer Science & Business Media, 2012; Tom R. Tyler, "Social Justice: Outcome and Procedure," *International Journal of Psychology* 35, no. 2 (2000): 117–25.

these authorities because they believe leaders have moral character and genuinely care about the public good. Top-down punishment of corruption and malfeasance can help signal to ordinary citizens that government authorities care about the public interest. Besides deterring future malfeasance, such punishment upholds the fundamental values of the political community and enables higher-level officials to show citizens they are moral leaders. As a result, citizens are more likely to believe that authorities will listen to them, participate through the formal channels provided by the government, and comply voluntarily with government regulations.

WHAT DO WE EXPECT FROM OUR GOVERNMENTS?

Citizens want governments to uphold justice in society.[2] We generally believe that authorities ought to govern according to principles that have a moral basis, that they should go beyond simply deferring to those with more power and resources.[3] Of course, our governments do not always meet these expectations. And when they fail, we may not have much power to do anything about it.

But all other things being equal, we prefer government authorities to uphold what we believe is fair and right. Paying attention to people's subjective judgments about what is just or fair is thus critical to understanding their evaluations of government and the actions they take to engage in politics and governance. Indeed, a large body of empirical research shows that people's judgments about what is just, fair, or deserved influence their political attitudes and behaviors.[4] Although we may disagree about whether specific policies or decisions meet our standards of justice and fairness, normative theorists as well as empirical scientists have identified a number of fundamental principles that human beings commonly use.

Two of these principles are distributive justice and procedural justice. As Chapter 1 discusses, most of the empirical research on citizen expectations

[2] Maryvonne Génaux, "Social Sciences and the Evolving Concept of Corruption," *Crime, Law and Social Change* 42, no. 1 (August 2004): 13–24; Bo Rothstein and Aiysha Varraich, *Making Sense of Corruption*, Cambridge University Press, 2017.

[3] Tom R. Tyler, Robert J. Boeckmann, Heather J. Smith, and Yuen J. Huo, *Social Justice in a Diverse Society*, 1st ed., Routledge, 1997.

[4] Tom R. Tyler, *Why People Obey the Law: Procedural Justice, Legitimacy, and Compliance*, Princeton University Press, 2006; Tom R. Tyler, Kenneth A. Rasinski, and Kathleen M. McGraw, "The Influence of Perceived Injustice on the Endorsement of Political Leaders," *Journal of Applied Social Psychology* 15, no. 8 (1985): 700–25; Tom R. Tyler, Robert J. Boeckmann, Heather J. Smith, and Yuen J. Huo, *Ibid*.

of government has focused almost exclusively on how our concerns about the fair distribution of resources and the existence of fair procedures for making decisions affects our political attitudes and behaviors.

The Concept of Retributive Justice

Political scientists, however, have been virtually silent on a third principle of social justice – *retributive justice*, the use of punishment to uphold what is fair and right. Part of this discomfort, as I note in the previous chapter, is because retributive justice sounds uncomfortably close to revenge. The two, however, are conceptually distinct (though revenge-takers may sometimes use principles of retributive justice to justify their actions). When we want revenge, we want to strike out at someone who has hurt us or someone who matters deeply to us. We conceptualize revenge as stemming from a passionate impulse coming from the primitive part of our brain responsible for automatic, self-preserving behaviors – an intense emotional reaction to anger, shame, or humiliation that happens without rational deliberation.[5] As Gollwitzer et al. show in experimental studies, people intuitively approve of personal retaliation, especially when they are forced to make quick, spontaneous judgments. Such findings substantiate a concern that our desire for punishment might result from intuitive responses rather than "reflected" or controlled judgments.[6]

Retributive justice, however, is something different. Punishment for retributive justice responds in a deliberated, principled fashion to the violation of moral norms.[7] It means that punishment is not only about deterring future wrongdoing but also about making sure that wrongdoers receive their "just deserts."[8] Retributively just authorities identify

---

[5] Jaak Panksepp, *Affective Neuroscience: The Foundations of Human and Animal Emotions*, Oxford University Press, 1998.

[6] Gollwitzer et al. provide experimental evidence that people intuitively approve of personal retaliation, especially when they are forced to make quick, spontaneous judgments. When an intuitive mindset is activated (which is more effective for people "low in need for cognition" (who do not particularly like to think or reflect), positive emotions and positive appraisals about personal retaliation are increased. People have instinctual approval for retaliation against wrongdoing. Mario Gollwitzer, Milena Meder, and Manfred Schmitt, "What Gives Victims Satisfaction When They Seek Revenge?" *European Journal of Social Psychology* 41, no. 3 (April 2011): 364–74.

[7] Morton Deutsch, Peter T. Coleman, and Eric C. Marcus, *The Handbook of Conflict Resolution: Theory and Practice*, John Wiley & Sons, 2011.

[8] John Rawls, *A Theory of Justice*, Cambridge University Press, 1971, 314–15; John Rawls, *A Theory of Justice, Revised Edition*, Cambridge University Press, 1999; Morton Deutsch, Peter T. Coleman, and Eric C. Marcus, *Ibid.*

wrongdoers, look retrospectively to evaluate their moral blameworthiness for their offenses, and carefully mete out punishment that is commensurate with the gravity of these offenses because it has been judged to be the right thing to do.[9]

Perhaps the clearest way to describe the relationship between retributive justice and revenge is as two sets of behavior that may intersect one another. It is theoretically possible that someone taking revenge may do so in a way that accords with these principles of retributive justice. This would mean that if someone blinded me in one eye, I would rationally consider the circumstances and whether the action was deliberate, judge whether society would think it fair to respond by blinding him in one eye, and then inflict this harm upon him as both revenge and retributive justice.

More commonly, however, we imagine revenge-takers as simply lashing out violently without caring about the effects of their actions on society and whether they are helping to reinstate order within their community or society. Indeed, cycles of blood feuds and vigilantism often undermine social stability rather than uphold it. This would be the area of revenge that does not intersect with retributive justice. And as the next section details, there are those who uphold retributive justice by supporting the punishment of wrongdoers – and even paying the costs of punishment – even when wrongdoers have caused them no personal harm or injury, beyond breaking society's rules. This would be the area of retributive justice that does not intersect with revenge.

Why is it morally necessary to punish those who harm others? Retributive justice, like procedural and distributive justice, is about understanding when there should and should not be inequalities in goods such as rights and liberties, powers and opportunities, income and wealth.[10] As Rawls argues in his treatise, *A Theory of Justice*, our basic natural duties

---

[9] Craig E. Smith and Felix Warneken, "Children's Reasoning about Distributive and Retributive Justice across Development," *Developmental Psychology* 52, no. 4 (April 2016): 613; see also Kevin M. Carlsmith and John M. Darley, "Psychological Aspects of Retributive Justice," *Advances in Experimental Social Psychology* 40 (2008): 193–236; Morton Deutsch, "A Framework for Thinking about Oppression and Its Change," *Social Justice Research* 19, no. 1 (March 2006): 7–41; Jeffrey Moriarty, "Against the Asymmetry of Desert," *Nous* 37, no. 3 (September 2003): 518–36; Jean Piaget, *The Moral Judgment of the Child*, Free Press, 1932; Bruce A. Marlowe and Alan S. Canestrari, *The Stages of the Intellectual Development of the Child*," Sage Publications, 2006, 98–106; John Rawls, *A Theory of Justice*, Cambridge University Press, 1971; Saul Smilansky, "The Paradox of Moral Complaint," *Utilitas* 18, no. 3 (September 21, 2006): 284–90; see also Samuel Scheffler, *Boundaries and Allegiances: Problems of Justice and Responsibility in Liberal Thought*, Oxford University Press on Demand, 2002.

[10] John Rawls, *A Theory of Justice*, Cambridge University Press, 1971.

forbid us to injure other people. Those who fail to fulfill these duties and commit these injuries ought to be punished. Punishment is not only important because it has instrumental benefits and constitutes a way of deterring potential criminals. In a well-functioning state and society, criminal law is not simply "a scheme of taxes and burdens designed to put a price on certain forms of conduct and in this way to guide men's conduct for mutual advantage." Rather, criminal law is essential because its existence declares to society that "[i]t would be far better if the acts proscribed by penal statutes were never done."[11] Punishment and criminal law, in other words, have expressive value – they are valuable because they express to society that rights are vindicated and wrongs are condemned.[12]

WHY DO CITIZENS CARE ABOUT RETRIBUTIVE JUSTICE?

Punishment of those who harm others ensures that the social and political order is maintained, and it communicates that authorities are maintaining this order. Because punishment of those who violate basic social values expressively restates the importance of those values to the public, it makes the institutions and organizations based on these values more stable and reduces the psychological discomforts produced by uncertainty.[13]

Thus, even those who are not the direct or immediate victims of wrongdoing want to punish rule breakers because they feel that these rule breakers threaten the stability of the social and political order. Sociologists such as Blau have noted that observers of wrongdoing desire punishment not because they believe it deters future violations but because it upholds, validates, and demonstrates the standards of behavior shared by the group.[14] Similarly, Durkheim notes that our desire to punish

---

[11] Herbert Lionel Adolphus Hart and Leslie Green, *The Concept of Law*, Oxford University Press, 2012; John Rawls, *Ibid.*, 314–15.

[12] Vincent Chiao, "What Is the Criminal Law For?" *Law and Philosophy* 35, no. 2 (April 12, 2016): 137.

[13] For example, Michael A. Hogg and Deborah I. Terry, "Social Identity and Self-Categorization Processes in Organizational Contexts," *Academy of Management Review* 25, no. 1 (January 2000): 121–40, cited in Tyler G. Okimoto, Michael Wenzel, and Michael J. Platow, "Restorative Justice: Seeking a Shared Identity in Dynamic Intragroup Contexts," in Mannix, E. A., Neale, M. A. and Mullen, E. (Eds.) *Fairness and Groups (Research on Managing Groups and Teams, Vol. 13)*, Emerald Group Publishing Limited, 2010, 205–42.

[14] See Linda Klebe Treviño, "The Social Effects of Punishment in Organizations: A Justice Perspective," *Academy of Management Review* 17, no. 4 (October 1992): 653.

criminals "comes from the social nature of the offended sentiments. Because they are found in all consciences, the infraction committed arouses in those who have evidence of it or who learn of its existence the same indignation."[15] When someone violates a community's basic values, everyone in the community reacts to the violation as a victim, regardless of who the direct victim is.

Empirical studies support these observations. Even when third-party observers witness an injustice, they feel an intuitive and affective impulse to implement punishment and restore justice despite the fact that they themselves are not the direct victims.[16] People indeed act as if they experience injustice as something that is not just done to an individual. Instead, they react as if the injustice is done to the entire community because the community's shared moral values and norms are being violated.[17] Piaget and others have shown that a desire to punish injustice and rule-breaking, even when one is not a direct victim, develops early in childhood.[18] Research in organizational behavior and management studies similarly shows that third-party observers are important contributors to upholding the norms of their organization. Even when observers can easily ignore the wrongdoing they witness, studies consistently show that observers punish people who mistreat others, even at personal cost to themselves.[19]

[15] Emile Durkheim, The *Division of Labour in Society* Free Press (first published 1893), Translated by George Simpson, 1964, 102; see Neil Vidmar, "Retributive Justice: Its Social Context," in *The Justice Motive in Everyday Life*, edited by Michael Ross and Dale T. Miller, Cambridge University Press, 2002, 291–313.

[16] Morton Deutsch, *Distributive Justice: A Social-Psychological Perspective*, Yale University Press, 1985, cited in Morton Deutsch, Peter T. Coleman, and Eric C. Marcus, *The Handbook of Conflict Resolution: Theory and Practice*, John Wiley & Sons, 2011, 51; see also Kevin M. Carlsmith and John M. Darley, "Psychological Aspects of Retributive Justice," 2008, 193–236; Kevin M. Carlsmith, John M. Darley, and Paul H. Robinson, "Why Do We Punish?: Deterrence and Just Deserts as Motives for Punishment," *Journal of Personality and Social Psychology* 83, no. 2 (2002): 284–99; N. T. Feather, "Judgments of Deservingness: Studies in the Psychology of Justice and Achievement," *Personality and Social Psychology Review* 3, no. 2 (May 21, 1999): 86–107; Neil Vidmar, "An Assessment of Public Opinion in Frontenac County Ontario Regarding R. v. Louise Reynolds," 2000. Superior Court of Ontario April 17, 2000.

[17] Morton Deutsch, Peter T. Coleman, and Eric C. Marcus, *The Handbook of Conflict Resolution: Theory and Practice*, John Wiley & Sons, 2011.

[18] Jean Piaget, "*The Moral Judgment of the Child*," Free Press, 1965; Craig E. Smith and Felix Warneken, "Children's Reasoning about Distributive and Retributive Justice across Development," *Developmental Psychology* 52, no. 4 (April 2016): 613–28.

[19] Wayne E. Baker and Nathaniel Bulkley, "Paying It Forward vs. Rewarding Reputation: Mechanisms of Generalized Reciprocity," *Organization Science* 25, no. 5 (October 2014): 1493–510; Ernst Fehr and Simon Gächter, "Cooperation and Punishment in Public Goods

In addition to collective benefits for society, reaffirmation of a community's basic values through punishing wrongdoers has psychological benefits. Upholding retributive justice by punishing wrongdoers can help to make people feel that the world is a just place where people get what they deserve. It helps people to feel like the world is predictable, and it reduces anxiety about uncertainty and things beyond one's control.[20] Seeing authorities punish wrongdoers, as Tyler et al. observe, "aids our psychological need to symbolically reassert the rules of society, standards that are important for defining social bonds, maintaining a just worldview, and reducing subjective uncertainty."[21] Failure to punish, on the

Experiments," *American Economic Review* 90, no. 4 (September 2000): 980–94; Daniel Kahneman, Jack L. Knetsch, and Richard H. Thaler, "Fairness and the Assumptions of Economics," *Journal of Business*, 59, no 4, pt. 2 (1986): S285–300; Deborah E. Rupp and Chris M. Bell, "Extending the Deontic Model of Justice: Moral Self-Regulation in Third-Party Responses to Injustice," *Business Ethics Quarterly* 20, no. 1 (January 23, 2010): 89–106; James R. Meindl and Melvin J. Lerner, "The Heroic Motive: Some Experimental Demonstrations," *Journal of Experimental Social Psychology* 19, no. 1 (January 1983): 1–20; Cynthia S. Wang, Niro Sivanathan, Jayanth Narayanan, Deshani B. Ganegoda, Monika Bauer, Galen V. Bodenhausen, and Keith Murnighan, "Retribution and Emotional Regulation: The Effects of Time Delay in Angry Economic Interactions," *Organizational Behavior and Human Decision Processes* 116, no. 1 (September 2011): 46–54.

[20] Emile Durkheim, *The Division of Labour in Society* Free Press (first published 1893), Translated by George Simpson 1964; Tyler G. Okimoto, Michael Wenzel, and N. T. Feather, "Retribution and Restoration as General Orientations Towards Justice," *European Journal of Personality* 26, no. 3 (May 2012): 255–75; Linda Klebe Treviño, "The Social Effects of Punishment in Organizations: A Justice Perspective," *Academy of Management Review* 17, no. 4 (October 1992): 653; Tom R. Tyler and Robert J. Boeckmann, "Three Strikes and You Are Out, but Why? The Psychology of Public Support for Punishing Rule Breakers," *Law & Society Review* 31, no. 2 (1997): 237; Neil Vidmar, "Retributive Justice: Its Social Context," in *The Justice Motive in Everyday Life*, edited by Michael Ross and Dale T. Miller, Cambridge University Press, 2002, 291–313.

[21] S. Alexander Haslam, Craig Mcgarty, and John C. Turner, "Salient Group Memberships and Persuasion: The Role of Social Identity in the Validation of Beliefs," in *What's Social about Social Cognition? Research on Socially Shared Cognition in Small Groups*, edited by Judith L. Nye and Aaron M. Brower, 29–56, SAGE Publications, 1996; Michael A. Hogg, "Group Cohesiveness: A Critical Review and Some New Directions," *European Review of Social Psychology* 4, no. 1 (January 1993): 85–111; Tyler G. Okimoto, Michael Wenzel, and N. T. Feather, "Retribution and Restoration as General Orientations Towards Justice," *European Journal of Personality* 26, no. 3 (May 2012): 255–75; John C. Turner, "The Analysis of Social Influence," in J. C. Turner, M. A. Hogg, P. J. Oakes, S. D. Reicher, & M. S. Wetherell (Eds.), *Rediscovering the Social Group: A Self-Categorization Theory*, Blackwell, 1987, 68–88; for example, Barbara Reichle, Angela Schneider, and Leo Montada, "How Do Observers of Victimization Preserve Their Belief in a Just World Cognitively or Actionally?" in *Responses to Victimizations and Belief in a Just World*, edited by Leo Montada and Melvin J. Lerner, 55–64, Springer US, 1998.

other hand, leaves the group's belief systems and norms open to question and may be viewed as degrading to those who were hurt by the misconduct.[22]

In social psychology, retributive justice plays an important role in terror management theory, which proposes that people need cultural values, symbols, and rules to help them deal with existential anxiety and the terror of death. Their psychological defense system consists of cultural world views that provide an explanation for existence and standards through which they can attain a sense of personal significance and worth. If those who violate these cultural values are not punished, the absence of retribution implies that either the world is not just or that they are not of any inherent value.[23] Hirschberger et al. tested this theory through experiments that manipulated the salience of concerns about death and eradication among Israelis, Palestinian Muslim citizens of Israel, and South Koreans. When participants had stronger existential fears, they were more likely to support military interventions even when informed by military experts that the deterrence benefit was low or ambiguous. Hirschberger et al. argue that at least part of this support for political violence comes from the protection from psychological anxiety that retribution for perceived injustices provides.[24] Similarly, Ginges and Atran conducted a series of experiments with Nigerian, American, and Israeli participants, which suggest that participants do not calculate expected utilities and instead use deontological reasoning to determine whether or not to support war.[25]

---

[22] Dale T. Miller and Neil Vidmar, "The Social Psychology of Punishment Reactions," in *The Justice Motive in Social Behavior: Adapting to Times of Scarcity and Change*, edited by Melvin J. Lerner and Sally C. Lerner, 145–72, Springer US, 1981.

[23] Pelin Kesebir and Tom Pyszczynski, "The Role of Death in Life: Existential Aspects of Human Motivation," in R. M. Ryan (Ed.), *Oxford Library of Psychology. The Oxford Handbook of Human Motivation*, Oxford University Press, 2012, 43–64; Tom Pyszczynski, Sheldon Solomon, and Jeff Greenberg, "Thirty Years of Terror Management Theory," 2015, 1–70. https://doi.org/10.1016/bs.aesp.2015.03.001

[24] Gilad Hirschberger, Tom Pyszczynski, and Tsachi Ein-Dor, "Why Does Existential Threat Promote Intergroup Violence? Examining the Role of Retributive Justice and Cost-Benefit Utility Motivations," *Frontiers in Psychology* 6 (November 20, 2015), https://www.frontiersin.org/articles/10.3389/fpsyg.2015.01761/full; Gilad Hirschberger, Tom Pyszczynski, Tsachi Ein-Dor, Tal Shani Sherman, Eihab Kadah, Pelin Kesebir, and Young Chin Park, "Fear of Death Amplifies Retributive Justice Motivations and Encourages Political Violence," *Peace and Conflict: Journal of Peace Psychology* 22, no. 1 (February 2016): 67–74.

[25] J. Ginges and S. Atran, "War as a Moral Imperative (Not Just Practical Politics by Other Means)," *Proceedings of the Royal Society B: Biological Sciences* 278, no. 1720 (October 7, 2011): 2930–38.

Retributive Justice Concerns versus Utility Motivations for Punishment

Though people likely want the authorities to punish wrongdoers for a range of reasons – deterrence of future wrongdoing, incapacitation of the dangerous, reformation of the misguided – there is widespread agreement across multiple fields of study that authorities should and do use retributive justice as the primary principle for the punishment of wrongdoing.[26] In his history of punishment in the Western world, Friedland shows that deterrence has not always been central to justifying criminal punishment. Instead, public punishment has been motivated more strongly and consistently throughout European history by the desire to repair the damage to the community that a crime creates. Public executions in early modern France through to the Enlightenment were not designed to deter future criminals by instilling fear into the hearts of citizens and making them think twice about the benefits of rule-breaking. Audiences participating in the spectacle of capital punishment in fact showed little fear of graphic punishments: "Far from being 'terrified' by the example of what they saw, audiences willingly participated in public executions as a means of overcoming the fact of the crime itself and healing from the wound inflicted by the offense." The importance of retributive justice in upholding society's moral values also extended to less spectacular punishments: "Even in the case of executions of justice in which the offender was merely humiliated or banished rather than killed, the ritual had more to do with the marginalization of the criminal and the reaffirmation of social norms than with exemplary deterrence."[27]

Survey research and lab experiments also suggest that individuals desire to see wrongdoers punished in order to protect the moral values of the community rather than for instrumental benefits such as the deterrence of other potential wrongdoers.[28] Even when punishments have no

---

[26] Vincent Chiao, "What Is the Criminal Law For?" *Law and Philosophy* 35, no. 2 (April 12, 2016): 137–63; Morton Deutsch, Peter T. Coleman, and Eric C. Marcus, *The Handbook of Conflict Resolution: Theory and Practice*, John Wiley & Sons, 2011.

[27] Paul Friedland, *Seeing Justice Done: The Age of Spectacular Capital Punishment in France*, Oxford University Press, 2012.

[28] Geoffrey P. Goodwin and Dena M. Gromet, "Punishment," *Wiley Interdisciplinary Reviews: Cognitive Science* 5, no. 5 (September 2014): 561–72; Dena M. Gromet and John M. Darley, "Political Ideology and Reactions to Crime Victims: Preferences for Restorative and Punitive Responses," *Journal of Empirical Legal Studies* 8, no. 4 (December 2011): 830–55; Dena M. Gromet and John M. Darley, "Restoration and Retribution: How Including Retributive Components Affects the Acceptability of Restorative Justice Procedures," *Social Justice Research* 19, no. 4 (November 27, 2006): 395–432.

other purpose but to ensure that offenders are given some type of "morally proportional consequence" for their wrongdoing, people still believe that punishments should take place, and they are willing to pay a cost for such punishments.[29] If deterrence were the primary motivation for punishment, then individuals would decide on the ideal punishment based entirely on its effects on would-be offenders. Instead, participants of lab experiments look backward at the magnitude of harm done, the offender's motivations, and extenuating circumstances as important when determining punishment – considerations that are consistent with retributive justice motivations for punishment.[30] Studies of children show that people make judgments about what constitutes fair punishment based largely on the rule breaker's motives rather than the impacts of the rule-breaking. Children as young as age five view attempted-but-failed transgressions as more deserving of punishment than accidental transgressions.[31]

By looking backward at people's moral blameworthiness for past offenses, retributive justice contrasts with consequentialist or instrumental theories of punishment that are grounded in the potentially beneficial future consequences of punishment such as the deterrence of other potential rule breakers.[32] Other experiments show that people pay to punish

---

[29] Kevin M. Carlsmith, John M. Darley, and Paul H. Robinson, "Why Do We Punish?: Deterrence and Just Deserts as Motives for Punishment," *Journal of Personality and Social Psychology* 83, no. 2 (2002): 284–99; John M. Darley, Kevin M. Carlsmith, and Paul H. Robinson, "Incapacitation and Just Deserts as Motives for Punishment," *Law and Human Behavior* 24, no. 6 (2000): 659–83; Ernst Fehr and Urs Fischbacher, "Third-Party Punishment and Social Norms," *Evolution and Human Behavior* 25, no. 2 (March 2004): 63–87; Ernst Fehr and Simon Gächter, "Cooperation and Punishment in Public Goods Experiments," *American Economic Review* 90, no. 4 (September 2000): 980–94; Robert J. MacCoun, "Drugs and the Law: A Psychological Analysis of Drug Prohibition," *Psychological Bulletin* 113, no. 3 (1993): 497; Tyler G. Okimoto and Michael Wenzel, "Punishment as Restoration of Group and Offender Values Following a Transgression: Value Consensus through Symbolic Labelling and Offender Reform," *European Journal of Social Psychology* 39, no. 3 (April 2009): 346–67; Phoebe C. Ellsworth and Lee Ross, "Public Opinion and Capital Punishment: A Close Examination of the Views of Abolitionists and Retentionists," *Crime & Delinquency* 29, no. 1 (January 5, 1983): 116–69; Tom R. Tyler, *Why People Obey the Law*, Princeton University Press, 2006.

[30] Geoffrey P. Goodwin and Dena M. Gromet, "Punishment," *Wiley Interdisciplinary Reviews: Cognitive Science* 5, no. 5 (September 2014): 562.

[31] Fiery Cushman, Rachel Sheketoff, Sophie Wharton, and Susan Carey, "The Development of Intent-Based Moral Judgment," *Cognition* 127, no. 1 (April 2013): 6–21, cited in Craig E. Smith and Felix Warneken, "Children's Reasoning about Distributive and Retributive Justice across Development," Developmental Psychology 52, no. 4 (April 2016): 613–28.

[32] Geoffrey P. Goodwin and Dena M. Gromet, "Punishment," *Wiley Interdisciplinary Reviews: Cognitive Science* 5, no. 5 (September 2014): 561.

others who do not contribute to a public good, even when there is no future benefit to the punishment. Nadelhoffer et al., for example, show that people still desire such punishment even when the game's procedures guarantee that the potential recipient will never even know of the punishment or its absence.[33] Survey research indicates that death penalty supporters do not change their level of support when informed that the death penalty has no deterrent effect.[34]

In sum, both normative and empirical studies of retributive justice suggest that punishment of wrongdoers affirms the social order and society's shared moral values. Punishment provides "order, structure, and emotional security by implying that behavior is related to outcomes."[35] People believe that retributive justice and punishment are essential for maintaining social order, and they care deeply about whether government authorities uphold retributive justice by punishing wrongdoers, especially those within the government itself.

THE STATE AS A PUNISHER OF FIRST RESORT

Citizens usually hope that the state will be the punisher of first resort and the primary upholder of retributive justice.[36] Government authorities are expected to have this responsibility for three reasons. First, people see

---

[33] Thomas Nadelhoffer, Saeideh Heshmati, Deanna Kaplan, and Shaun Nichols, "Folk Retributivism and the Communication Confound," *Economics and Philosophy* 29, no. 2 (July 11, 2013): 235–61.

[34] Robert M. Bohm, "Retribution and Capital Punishment: Toward a Better Understanding of Death Penalty Opinion," *Journal of Criminal Justice* 20, no. 3 (January 1992): 227–36, cited Peter Liberman, "Retributive Support for International Punishment and Torture," *Journal of Conflict Resolution* 57, no. 2 (2013): 285–306; Phoebe C. Ellsworth and Lee Ross, "Public Opinion and Capital Punishment: A Close Examination of the Views of Abolitionists and Retentionists," *Crime & Delinquency* 29, no. 1 (January 5, 1983): 116–69; Phoebe C. Ellsworth and Samuel R. Gross, "Hardening of the Attitudes: Americans' Views on the Death Penalty," *Journal of Social Issues* 50, no. 2 (July 1994): 19–52; Samuel R. Gross and Phoebe C. Ellsworth, "Second Thoughts: Americans' Views on the Death Penalty at the Turn of the Century," *SSRN Electronic Journal*, 2001. http://dx.doi.org/10.2139/ssrn.264018; Tom R. Tyler and Renee Weber, "Support for the Death Penalty; Instrumental Response to Crime, or Symbolic Attitude?" *Law & Society Review* 17, no. 1 (1982): 21.

[35] Melvin J. Lerner, "The Belief in a Just World," in *The Belief in a Just World*, 9–30, Springer US, 1980, cited in Gilad Hirschberger, Tom Pyszczynski, and Tsachi Ein-Dor, "Why Does Existential Threat Promote Intergroup Violence? Examining the Role of Retributive Justice and Cost-Benefit Utility Motivations," *Frontiers in Psychology* 6 (November 20, 2015). https://www.frontiersin.org/articles/10.3389/fpsyg.2015.01761/full

[36] Thanks to Aidan Miliff for suggesting this term.

injustice as something that the community as a whole – and in particular, the leadership of the community – has a responsibility to address. Given the various religious, social, and political cleavages that exist in all societies, the state has to be, as Hegel notes, the "institutional voice of the community's shared moral values" and the "citizenry's moral representative."[37] The set of core moral values may be minimal (preventing theft and violence to others) but often encompasses more, depending on the strength of national identity and the degree of social homogeneity. Upholding retributive justice through punishment maintains social order and "reaffirms moral and civic standards."[38] After the violation of a moral rule, the rule is necessarily weakened and called into question unless "another action is taken to reestablish the validity of the moral rules."[39] When authorities uphold retributive justice by punishing wrongdoers, they create common knowledge among members of a community that even though the rule was broken, it remains valuable and legitimate.

Second, people may also expect the state to take responsibility for retributive justice because the state is often the only actor with enough power to implement the punishment.[40] It is up to the state and its exercise (ideally, monopoly) of coercion to affirm the importance of its values by punishing actions that call those values into question. Hampton explains: "Serious crimes represent serious attacks on those moral views, and in particular, on the conception of worth animating those views, and thus the state is the only institution that can speak and act on behalf of the community against the diminishment accomplished by the crime."[41]

Third, under ideal circumstances, citizens want a retributively just state to have exclusive responsibility for punishing wrongdoers in order to channel people's primitive instincts for revenge. Again, the emotional

---

[37] See Jean Hampton, "Correcting Harms vs. Righting Wrongs: The Goal of Retribution," *UCLA Law Review*, 39, no. 6 (1992): 1659–1702., cited in Colleen Murphy, "Transitional Justice, Retributive Justice and Accountability for Wrongdoing," in Claudio Corradetti and Nir Eisikovits (Eds.), *Theorizing Transitional Justice*, Routledge, 2015, 59–68; G. W. F. Hegel, *Elements of the Philosophy of Right*, edited by Allen W. Wood, Cambridge University Press, 1991.

[38] Noam Schimmel, "The Moral Case for Restorative Justice as a Corollary of the Responsibility to Protect: A Rwandan Case Study of the Insufficiency of Impact of Retributive Justice on the Rights and Well-Being of Genocide Survivors," *Journal of Human Rights* 11, no. 2 (April 2012): 161–88.

[39] Morton Deutsch, Peter T. Coleman, and Eric C. Marcus, *The Handbook of Conflict Resolution: Theory and Practice*, John Wiley & Sons, 2011.

[40] Jean Hampton, "Correcting Harms vs. Righting Wrongs: The Goal of Retribution," *UCLA Law Review*, 39, no. 6 (1992): 1659–1702.

[41] Ibid.

desire for revenge should not be confused with a moral commitment to retributive justice. As Panksepp and Biven note, the desire to get even is hardwired and part of our instinct for self-preservation. Revenge is motivated by an individual's biological instincts.[42] Retributive justice, however, is a duty and moral commitment to a community. Emotional and psychological needs for revenge that are not governed by formal institutions of retributive justice can devolve into vigilantism, blood feuds, and violence that spiral out of control. Such violence usually undermines rather than upholds the social order. As Gollwitzer et al. observe, " [i]n most countries, the right to retaliate has been taken away from the individual and given exclusively to the state – apparently in order to channel the 'retributive instinct.'"[43] The idea of punishment by the state as a means for moral retribution has been a fundamental principle in the construction of judicial and legal systems in modern Western civilizations.[44]

Empirical research also documents how people expect their leaders to use punishment and sanctioning to address injustice. Experiments in behavioral economics, for example, indicate that ordinary individuals reward leaders who punish wrongdoers. Barclay finds that punishers in public goods games acquire reputational benefits from other players who indirectly benefit from the punishment.[45] Ellickson notes that individuals hold punishers in higher esteem than nonpunishers because by imposing sanctions, punishers signal that they value the group's rules, norms, and identity.[46] Adams and Mullen provide experimental evidence that American citizens are more likely to vote for politicians who punish

---

[42] Jaak Panksepp and Lucy Biven, *The Archaeology of Mind: Neurorevolutionary Origins of Human Emotions*, W. W. Norton, 2012.

[43] Mario Gollwitzer, Milena Meder, and Manfred Schmitt, "What Gives Victims Satisfaction When They Seek Revenge?" *European Journal of Social Psychology* 41, no. 3 (April 2011): 364–74; *Furman* v. *Georgia 1972*, cited in Neil Vidmar, "Retributive Justice: Its Social Context," in *The Justice Motive in Everyday Life*, edited by Michael Ross and Dale T. Miller, 291–313, Cambridge University Press, 2002.

[44] David Santos and Reynaldo G. Rivera, "The Accessibility of Justice-Related Concepts Can Validate Intentions to Punish," *Social Influence* 10, no. 3 (July 3, 2015): 180–92.

[45] Pat Barclay, "Reputational Benefits for Altruistic Punishment," *Evolution and Human Behavior* 27, no. 5 (September 2006): 325–44, cited in Gabrielle S. Adams and Elizabeth Mullen, "Increased Voting for Candidates Who Compensate Victims Rather than Punish Offenders," *Social Justice Research* 26, no. 2 (2013): 168–92.

[46] R. C. Ellickson, "The Market for Social Norms," *American Law and Economics Review* 3, no. 1 (January 2001): 1–49; D. C. Feldman, "The Development and Enforcement of Group Norms," *Academy of Management Review* 9, no. 1 (January 1, 1984): 47–53, cited in Gabrielle S. Adams and Elizabeth Mullen, "Increased Voting for Candidates Who Compensate Victims Rather than Punish Offenders," *Social Justice Research* 26, no. 2 (2013): 168–92.

domestic and international actors who violate basic moral values, arguing that "an individual's response to transgressions should influence others' perceptions of that individual including their willingness to select that individual for a leadership position."[47] Liberman finds that people who value retributive justice are more likely to support leaders who torture detained terrorists and who use military force against states that have violated international norms.[48]

The state's commitment to implementing retributive justice to uphold a social and moral order can be essential to their legitimacy. Sociologists studying state–society relations in Norway use the concept of congruence to describe state behavior that conformed to society's definitions of the moral use of power.[49] In China, the term *hefaxing* emerged during the Tang and Song dynasties from the seventh to the thirteenth century AD to refer to conformity to both moral and statutory laws.[50] As Gilley notes, "Legitimacy, then, is rightful rule, where rightfulness entails meeting the shared moral standards of a political community. . . . This means that the state has acquired and exercises political power in a way that accords with a political community's laws, rules, and customs."[51]

RETRIBUTIVE JUSTICE AND PUNISHMENT OF CORRUPTION

The first and most important signal of a government's commitment to retributive justice is whether it will punish its own: Citizens want to make sure that government authorities punish their own officials for corruption and malfeasance. In every organization, members expect leaders to enforce the rules impartially. Rothstein and Varraich illustrate the universal nature of this expectation through an analogy to football leagues. League authorities have to uphold a set of rules everyone is willing to accept; otherwise there is no point in participating or watching the game.

---

[47] Gabrielle S. Adams and Elizabeth Mullen, "Increased Voting for Candidates Who Compensate Victims Rather than Punish Offenders," *Social Justice Research* 26, no. 2 (2013): 168–92.

[48] Peter Liberman, "Retributive Support for International Punishment and Torture," *Journal of Conflict Resolution* 57, no. 2 (2013): 285–306.

[49] The term developed by sociologists studying this phenomenon, first in Norway, was "congruence," meaning that the state's moral relationship to society mirrored the moral uses of power within that society. Cited in Bruce Gilley, *The Right to Rule: How States Win and Lose Legitimacy*, Columbia University Press, 2009.

[50] Bruce Gilley, *The Right to Rule: How States Win and Lose Legitimacy*, Columbia University Press, 2009.

[51] Ibid.

Agents of the organization – officials, referees, league managers – have to follow these rules, and fans and players expect league authorities to punish those who break the rules. This expectation is not cultural – the importance of enforcing the rules impartially seems to be universally understood and accepted.[52]

Citizen expectations of retributive justice can be a crucial reason for why anti-corruption initiatives are popular with citizens and thus useful for governments who might otherwise be underperforming in terms of economic development, democratic reforms, and social welfare provision. When government authorities take measures to sanction their agents for corruption and malfeasance, citizens are more likely to view them as benevolent, just, and morally committed. This belief in the government's good intentions can help to stave off dissatisfaction and frustration with other aspects of governance, making it a common strategy for leaders who seek to consolidate power and mobilize public support.

Political leaders know that widespread corruption has a negative effect on citizen trust and engagement. Facing growing discontent just before the fall of communism, the general secretary of Czechoslovakia noted in 1988:

Leading the drive for renewal means being in the forefront of struggle with reprehensible things in our society like corruption. ... The conflict between one's words and actions has unfavourable ideological, moral and political repercussions and generates distrust not only of the state and economic bodies, but also of the party and socialism generally. ... Therefore, what the party, its bodies and organisations and every Communist should do in the first place is to consistently and uncompromisingly battle against such behavior, which is incompatible with socialist moral values.[53]

The failure of this and other Eastern European regimes to address citizen expectations to uphold retributive justice played a large role in the fall of communism.

When the government's own agents violate social and political order by abusing the power of their offices to pursue their private interests at the expense of the public interest, it becomes a particularly important test of how committed to upholding retributive justice government authorities really are. If they make an exception for their own, then citizens are likely

---

[52] Bo Rothstein and Aiysha Varraich, *Making Sense of Corruption*, Cambridge University Press, 2017.
[53] As cited in Stephen Holmes, "Crime and Corruption after Communism. Introduction," *East European Constitutional Review* 6, no. 4 (1997): 7.

to view their commitments to justice and order as empty words, which can lead to cynicism, distrust, and an erosion of legitimacy. In the case of China, for example, survey data show that both rural and urban citizens prioritize the punishment of government corruption over corruption and wrongdoing by businesses, the media, and academic institutions. Fifty-two percent of respondents in a 2016 survey thought the government should focus on punishing government corruption, cronyism, and collusion, while only 14 percent thought the government should focus on punishing business corruption.[54]

As a violation of fundamental public values, government corruption leads all members of the public to see themselves as victims. Citizens want government leaders to sanction delinquent officials, not only to deter malfeasance by other officials, but also because after such a violation is committed by agents of the government, citizens need government leaders to reaffirm their commitment to the public interest. Punishment communicates that the corrupt official's actions are not representative of the government as a whole.[55] Such punishment distances these "bad" officials from the otherwise "good" political system in the eye of citizens.[56]

Punishment of misbehaving officials can also be important to citizens because retributive justice can alleviate the status concerns of victims, that is, whether they are respected and valued members of the polity. When wrongdoing goes unpunished, it can signal to citizens that they are less important than the wrongdoers, that government officials are a privileged class. Punishment of the wrongdoers restores the status that citizens feel

---

[54] Harvard Asia Programs Center for Business and Government, 2016 年中国居民评价政府及政府公共 务研究报告 [Research Report on the Evaluation of Government and Public Service Provided by Government by Chinese Residents (2016)], Technical report, 40.

[55] Robert J. Bies, "The Predicament of Injustice: The Management of Moral Outrage," *Research in Organizational Behavior*, 9 (1987): 289–319; Antony Duff, *Punishment, Communication, and Community*, Oxford University Press, 2001; Tyler G. Okimoto and Michael Wenzel, "Punishment as Restoration of Group and Offender Values Following a Transgression: Value Consensus through Symbolic Labelling and Offender Reform," *European Journal of Social Psychology* 39, no. 3 (April 2009): 346–67.

[56] Leon Festinger, "Informal Social Communication," *Psychological Review* 57, no. 5 (1950): 271–82; Norbert L. Kerr, Robert W. Hymes, Alonzo B. Anderson, and James E. Weathers, "Defendant-Juror Similarity and Mock Juror Judgments," *Law and Human Behavior* 19, no. 6 (1995): 545; John M. Levine, "Reaction to Opinion Deviance in Small Groups," *Psychology of Group Influence* 2 (1989): 187–231; Jose M. Marques, Vincent Y. Yzerbyt, and Jacques-Philippe Leyens, "The 'Black Sheep Effect': Extremity of Judgments Towards Ingroup Members as a Function of Group Identification," *European Journal of Social Psychology* 18, no. 1 (January 1988): 1–16.

they should have and reassures them that they are not "suckers" for following the rules of the state.[57]

Here again, it is important to note that there are two distinct ways in which citizens might care about not being suckers – one that has to do with utility motivations and one that has to do with retributive justice motivations. Utility motivations for the punishment of officials are rooted in rational calculations about the costs and benefits of contributing to collective goods. As Levi points out, one reason that punishment of misbehavior is important is to demonstrate to citizens that authorities will ensure that others will also make their legally required contributions to the public good.[58] Levi and Sacks note that the most important use of coercion by the state is not directly against an individual as a negative incentive for compliance but against others as an assurance that the individual will not be the only who complies.[59] In other words, it would be rational for me not to pay my taxes if no one else pays their taxes because then I will lose my tax money without gaining any roads, schools, or other public goods. In addition to punishment of free riders among my fellow citizens, however, I may also rationally want to see punishment of government officials who engage in corruption because I see them as stealing my tax money. In this account, I do not want to be a sucker in the sense of that it is irrational to give my money away for no reason. Punishing corrupt officials may increase my beliefs that officials remaining in office will be more honest in the sense of stealing less public money, which will make me more likely to comply with government regulations.

[57] Heider Fritz, "The Psychology of Interpersonal Relations," *The Journal of Marketing* 56 (1958): 322; Arie Nadler and Nurit Shnabel, "Instrumental and Socioemotional Paths to Intergroup Reconciliation and the Needs-Based Model of Socioemotional Reconciliation," in A. Nadler, T. E. Malloy, & J. D. Fisher (Eds.) *The Social Psychology of Intergroup Reconciliation*, 2008, 37–56, Oxford University Press. https://doi.org/10.1093/acprof:oso/9780195300314.003.0003; Neil Vidmar and Dale T. Miller, "Socialpsychological Processes Underlying Attitudes toward Legal Punishment," *Law & Society Review*, 14, no. 3 (Spring 1980): 565–602, https://doi.org/10.2307/3053193; On this point, see also citations in Morton Deutsch, Peter T. Coleman, and Eric C. Marcus, *The Handbook of Conflict Resolution: Theory and Practice*, John Wiley & Sons, 2011.

[58] Margaret Levi, *Of Rule and Revenue*, vol. 13, University of California Press, 1989, 54; Margaret Levi and Institut Universitaire Européen Centre Robert Schuman, *A State of Trust*, Citeseer, 1996; Margaret Levi, *Consent, Dissent, and Patriotism*, Cambridge University Press, 1997.

[59] Margaret Levi and Audrey Sacks, "Legitimating Beliefs: Sources and Indicators," *Regulation & Governance* 3, no. 4 (2009): 311–33.

Retributive justice motivations for punishing corrupt officials, however, are rooted in moral commitments and psychological concerns about status. We may want to punish corrupt officials simply because they deserve it – and our government also says they deserve it. If corrupt officials can get away with corruption – or wrongdoing that involves abuse of power without stealing from public coffers, for example, threatening to arrest a personal enemy – we may begin to think that public officials are a privileged class and that we as ordinary citizens are the underclass and somehow entitled to fewer rights and privileges. We may not only be offended – but if we have been obediently following the government's laws and policies while assuming that they are also committed to same moral values, we may feel angry and humiliated for being suckers in what has now been revealed to be a sham and grow to resent those in government.[60] In this account, I do not want to be a sucker in the sense that I do not want to feel that the political class thinks of me as stupid and treats me with disrespect. As Levi notes, we need "accepted justifications for government and its actions, justifications based on widely shared moral principles and beliefs."[61]

The act of punishing corruption is a way of taking these justifications beyond empty words – it expresses the government's moral commitments through action, embodying and performing them in the real world. Retributive punishment thus helps to restore our sense of status in the political community by humiliating the malfeasant official. It is the government acknowledging that corrupt officials are the underclass, and that we as rule-abiding members of the political community have higher status. As Tyler notes, retributive justice can serve "a leveling goal by demeaning and disempowering the offender."[62] Without this "re-leveling," our anger

---

[60] Tyler G. Okimoto and Michael Wenzel, "Punishment as Restoration of Group and Offender Values Following a Transgression: Value Consensus through Symbolic Labelling and Offender Reform," *European Journal of Social Psychology* 39, no. 3 (April 2009): 346–67.

[61] Margaret Levi, "Trustworthy Government and Legitimating Beliefs," in *Political Legitimacy: NOMOS LXI*, edited by Jack Knight and Melissa Schwartzberg. NYU Press, 2019, 362–384.

[62] Robert J. Bies and Thomas M. Tripp, "Beyond Distrust: 'Getting Even' and the Need for Revenge," in *Trust in Organizations*, edited by R. M. Kramer and T. R. Tyler, Sage Publications, 246–60, 1996, https://us.sagepub.com/en-us/nam/trust-in-organizations/book4948#preview; Dale T. Miller, "Disrespect and the Experience of Injustice," *Annual Review of Psychology* 52, no. 1 (February 2001): 527–53; Neil Vidmar, "Retributive Justice: Its Social Context," in *The Justice Motive in Everyday Life*, edited by Michael Ross and Dale T. Miller, 291–313, Cambridge University Press, 2002.

and offense may continue to rankle, and public support for government authorities may erode.[63]

In sum, we often want punishment because we believe that punishing wrongdoing is the moral thing to do, even if the punishment takes place secretly or has no impact on deterring future corruption. Our desire for retributive justice means that as long as I know that authorities have punished the corrupt official – *even if no one else knows the punishment has taken place and the incidence of corruption does not change* – I will feel that authorities care about upholding justice. Knowing that authorities are retributively just may make me feel more secure about social order and more likely to support and engage with authorities and comply with their demands – even if actual levels of corruption do not change.

Given our desire for retributive justice, it is not surprising that one strategy of populist leaders is to promise the public severe punishments for corruption and crime. Studies of anti-corruption campaigns suggest that it is not the campaign itself but punishment of misbehaving officials that increases citizen beliefs in the morality and responsiveness of government authorities. Sampson, for example, notes: "[C]orruption arrests and indictments are not just 'law enforcement'. They are 'signals' by the authorities that they are doing something about corrupt behavior." In his study of Romania's anti-corruption initiatives in the postcommunist period, he notes that these signals are sent to the public and "can raise or lower Romania's complex intersection of government claims that morality is being safeguarded, citizen demands for justice, and political jockeying for power." In contrast, "anti-corruption rituals" such as press conferences, statistical presentations, and the establishment of anti-corruption agencies without any actual punishment can have negative effects on citizen evaluations of government.[64]

---

[63] Morton Deutsch, Peter T. Coleman, and Eric C. Marcus, *The Handbook of Conflict Resolution: Theory and Practice*, John Wiley & Sons, 2011.

[64] Sampson contrasts the "anti-corruption rituals" such as press conferences, statistical presentations, opening of anti-corruption units with actual punishment of corrupt officials: "In this context, corruption arrests and indictments are not just 'law enforcement'. They are 'signals' by the authorities that they are doing something about corrupt behavior." These signals are sent to the public and "can raise or lower Romania's complex intersection of government claims that morality is being safeguarded, citizen demands for justice, and political jockeying for power." Steven Sampson, "Integrity Warriors: Global Morality and the Anti-Corruption Movement in the Balkans," in *Corruption: Anthropological Perspectives*, edited by Dieter Haller and Cris Shore, Pluto Press, 2005, 103–130; see also L. V. Akker, Leonie Heres, Karin Lasthuizen, and F. E. Six, "Ethical Leadership and Trust: It's All about Meeting Expectations," *International Journal of Leadership Studies* 5, no. 2, 2009, 102–122, http://www.regent.edu/acad/global/publica

RETRIBUTIVE JUSTICE AND CITIZEN ENGAGEMENT
WITH GOVERNMENT AUTHORITIES

Whether or not government authorities uphold retributive justice can play an important role in whether citizens decide to engage with government authorities in order to address issues of public concern, influence public decisions, and contribute to government efforts to provide public goods. Given how deeply people can care about whether government authorities punish wrongdoing, especially among their own agents, evidence of government commitment to punishing corruption and malfeasance is likely to affect citizen evaluations of government and their engagement with government authorities – how likely they are to participate in selecting government officials, monitoring government behavior, providing feedback to government, and cooperating with government in organizing and providing public goods. Understanding when citizens engage (and disengage) from interaction with government is important, not only because citizen engagement can provide authorities with information about their needs and preferences, but also because the more citizens interact with authorities and their institutions, the more robust and established these authorities and institutions can become.[65] In contrast, citizens who disengage from interaction with government authorities and institutions are or can become alienated from the political system.

Sanctioning Government Agents and Evaluating the Moral Character of Principals

The first part of a retributive justice theory of citizen engagement posits that citizens pay attention to whether government authorities are sanctioning misbehaving officials – and that what they see shapes their evaluations of the moral character of authorities. Authorities have an obligation to punish

---

tions/ijls/new/vol5iss2/IJLS_vol5_iss2_akker_ethical_leadership.pdf; Michael E. Brown, Linda K. Treviño, and David A. Harrison, "Ethical Leadership: A Social Learning Perspective for Construct Development and Testing," *Organizational Behavior and Human Decision Processes* 97, no. 2 (July 2005): 117–34; Linda Klebe Treviño, Laura Pincus Hartman, and Michael Brown, "Moral Person and Moral Manager: How Executives Develop a Reputation for Ethical Leadership," *California Management Review* 42, no. 4 (July 2000): 128–42; Linda Klebe Treviño, Michael Brown, and Laura Pincus Hartman, "A Qualitative Investigation of Perceived Executive Ethical Leadership: Perceptions from Inside and Outside the Executive Suite," *Human Relations* 56, no. 1 (January 22, 2003): 5–37.

[65] Samuel P. Huntington, *Political Order in Changing Societies*, Yale University Press, 1968.

those who violate the basic moral values of the community. Authorities who fulfill this obligation are more likely to be viewed as morally good and benevolent. Failure of authorities to punish wrongdoers can raise concerns with the moral character of the leaders themselves.

Extensive research on firms and other organizations is consistent with this argument. In firms, when supervisors are seen to punish deviations to organizational values, principles, and standards, their employees evaluate their moral character more positively and express higher levels of trust in them.[66] When company leaders adhere to a set of values, norms, and principles that are shared by their followers, and they punish violations to these norms, employees are more likely to view these leaders as having integrity and benevolent intentions.[67]

Institutions for punishment and sanctioning of misbehavior provide important information to followers about the nature of their community and leadership. Treviño et al., for example, observe that followers look carefully at rewards and punishment within an organization.[68] They note

---

[66] Michael E. Brown, Linda K. Treviño, and David A. Harrison, "Ethical Leadership: A Social Learning Perspective for Construct Development and Testing," *Organizational Behavior and Human Decision Processes* 97, no. 2 (July 2005): 117–34; Karin M. Lasthuizen, "Leading to Integrity: Empirical Research into the Effects of Leadership on Ethics and Integrity," 2008, https://research.vu.nl/en/publications/leading-to-integrity-empirical-research-into-the-effects-of-leade; Linda Klebe Treviño, Laura Pincus Hartman, and Michael Brown, "Moral Person and Moral Manager: How Executives Develop a Reputation for Ethical Leadership," *California Management Review* 42, no. 4 (July 2000): 128–42; Linda Klebe Treviño, Michael Brown, and Laura Pincus Hartman, "A Qualitative Investigation of Perceived Executive Ethical Leadership: Perceptions from Inside and Outside the Executive Suite," *Human Relations* 56, no. 1 (January 22, 2003): 5–37.

[67] Linda Klebe Treviño and Gail A. Ball, "The Social Implications of Punishing Unethical Behavior: Observers' Cognitive and Affective Reactions," *Journal of Management* 18, no. 4 (December 30, 1992): 751–68; see also Roger C. Mayer, James H. Davis, and F. David Schoorman, "An Integrative Model of Organizational Trust," *Academy of Management Review* 20, no. 3 (July 1995): 718; Holly H. Brower, F. David Schoorman, and Hwee Hoon Tan, "A Model of Relational Leadership," *The Leadership Quarterly* 11, no. 2 (June 2000): 227–50; Graham Dietz and Deanne N. Den Hartog, "Measuring Trust Inside Organisations," edited by Karin Sanders, *Personnel Review* 35, no. 5 (September 2006): 557–88; Roy J. Lewicki, Edward C. Tomlinson, and Nicole Gillespie, "Models of Interpersonal Trust Development: Theoretical Approaches, Empirical Evidence, and Future Directions," *Journal of Management* 32, no. 6 (December 2006): 991–1022; Linda Klebe Treviño, Michael Brown, and Laura Pincus Hartman, "A Qualitative Investigation of Perceived Executive Ethical Leadership: Perceptions from Inside and Outside the Executive Suite," *Human Relations* 56, no. 1 (January 22, 2003): 5–37.

[68] Richard D. Arvey and Allen P. Jones, "The Use of Discipline in Organizational Settings: A Framework for Future Research," *Research in Organizational Behavior*, 7, 1985, 367–408; Ruth Kanfer, "Motivation Theory and Industrial and Organizational

that institutions for oversight and appropriate punishment are social phenomena that can influence the cognitions and actions of observers because they provide social information that helps individuals make sense of the situation and its implications for them and their group. Observers view oversight and punishment as positive outcomes that support the group and its values.[69]

These studies suggest that followers actively pay attention to whether leaders sanction misbehaving agents. How principals use punishment to sanction misbehaving agents can have a large effect on whether members of their organization believe both the principals and the organization itself to be just or unjust.[70] Hamilton finds that workers in a firm hold their co-workers responsible for their deeds, but they hold higher-level managers responsible not only for their specific deeds but also for a broad range of problems that may arise within their team.[71] Schultz, Jaggi, and Schleifer note that a leader may be held responsible for the misconduct of lower-level workers, especially if the leader could have prevented the misconduct.[72] When the principal fails to monitor agents and impose punishment when observers believe that it is deserved, observers react negatively.[73]

Psychology," *Handbook of Industrial and Organizational Psychology* 1, no. 2 (1990): 75–130; Linda Klebe Treviño, "The Social Effects of Punishment in Organizations: A Justice Perspective," *Academy of Management Review* 17, no. 4 (October 1992): 653.

[69] Linda Klebe Treviño and Gail A. Ball, "The Social Implications of Punishing Unethical Behavior: Observers' Cognitive and Affective Reactions," *Journal of Management* 18, no. 4 (December 30, 1992): 651.

[70] Jerald Greenberg, "Organizational Justice: Yesterday, Today, and Tomorrow," *Journal of Management* 16, no. 2 (June 30, 1990): 399–432, cited in Linda Klebe Treviño, "The Social Effects of Punishment in Organizations: A Justice Perspective," *Academy of Management Review* 17, no. 4 (October 1992): 647–676.

[71] V. Lee Hamilton, "Who Is Responsible? Toward a Social Psychology of Responsibility Attribution," *Social Psychology* 41, no. 4 (December 1978): 316, cited in Linda Klebe Treviño, "The Social Effects of Punishment in Organizations: A Justice Perspective," *Academy of Management Review* 17, no. 4 (October 1992): 647–676.

[72] Thomas R. Shultz, Christine Jaggi, and Michael Schleifer, "Assigning Vicarious Responsibility," *European Journal of Social Psychology* 17, no. 3 (July 1987): 377–80. See also Linda Klebe Treviño, "The Social Effects of Punishment in Organizations: A Justice Perspective," *Academy of Management Review* 17, no. 4 (October 1992): 647–676. Furthermore, people may hold higher-status actors to a higher standard of responsibility because the misconduct of higher-status actors is less likely to be viewed as coerced and thus more likely to be viewed as intentional. Thus, observers may judge the misconduct of organizational members of higher status more harshly than they judge the misconduct of lower-status organizational members. V. Lee Hamilton, "Who Is Responsible? Toward a Social Psychology of Responsibility Attribution," *Social Psychology* 41, no. 4 (December 1978): 316.

[73] Linda Klebe Treviño, "The Social Effects of Punishment in Organizations: A Justice Perspective," *Academy of Management Review* 17, no. 4 (October 1992): 667.

Moral Character Evaluations and Citizen Engagement

The second part of a retributive justice theory of engagement builds on literature that shows moral character evaluations affect citizen support for government and their political behavior. Political scientists have paid increasing attention to how citizen evaluations of moral character affect their support for political leaders and their decisions to participate in politics and governance. Fearon, for example, argues that democratic elections are not necessarily effective mechanisms for making politicians accountable to citizens by enabling voters to sanction poor performers. Rather, elections contribute to government performance and responsiveness to citizen input because they act as a selection mechanism for "good type" officials – they enable voters to select candidates into office that they believe to have moral character and good intentions. Such officials perform well, not because they fear being voted out of office, but because they have internal motivations for responding to citizen concerns and a moral character that makes them less responsive to material inducements and self-enrichment at the expense of others.[74] Voters thus care about elections because they care about selecting public officials with moral character and intrinsic motivations for acting in the public good.

The emphasis of this retributive justice theory of citizen engagement on citizen evaluations of the moral character of government officials also builds on empirical research on the importance of "warmth" in evaluations of election candidates by voters. A large body of work has shown that voters in the United States judge politicians primarily on the basis of perceived competence and "warmth," a multidimensional concept combining likability, friendliness, and moral character. Studies show that warmth and competence are the primary components of people's judgments of others generally,[75] and citizen evaluations of political leaders specifically.[76]

---

[74] James D. Fearon, "Electoral Accountability and the Control of Politicians: Selecting Good Types versus Sanctioning Poor Performance," in Adam Przeworski, Susan C. Stokes, and Bernard Manin (Eds.), *Democracy, Accountability, and Representation*, Cambridge University Press, 1999, 55–97.

[75] See Robert P. Abelson, Donald R. Kinder, Mark D. Peters, and Susan T. Fiske, "Affective and Semantic Components in Political Person Perception," *Journal of Personality and Social Psychology* 42, no. 4 (1982): 619–30; Donald R. Kinder, Mark D. Peters, Robert P. Abelson, and Susan T. Fiske, "Presidential Prototypes," *Political Behavior* 2, no. 4 (1980): 315–37.

[76] Bogdan Wojciszke and Bożena Klusek, "Moral and Competence-Related Traits in Political Perception," *Polish Psychological Bulletin*, 27, no. 4 (1996): 319–324.

Experimental research shows that increased warmth perceptions predict the conferral of status and an increased probability of voting for a particular election candidate.[77]

The problem, of course, is that moral character is conceptually quite different from friendliness and likability. We can rate someone as very friendly, even likable, yet also consider them immoral. When existing studies lump these qualities together, it is difficult to identify the exact relationship between moral character evaluations and citizen support of political leaders.

One notable exception is experimental work by Adams and Mullen, with American university students showing that participants are more likely to vote for politicians who punish transgressions that violate basic social norms such as the Darfur human rights crisis and domestic violence. When they measure perceptions of moral character separately from the other components of "warmth," they find that punishment of violations leads to increased voting for a candidate through increased perceptions of moral character specifically. Little of the effect of punishment on support for political leaders goes through increased perceptions of their competence.[78]

Work in social psychology also shows that citizens in the United States are more likely to support government policies and authorities when they have positive evaluations of the moral character of authorities.[79] Good intentions are important. Tyler and Degoey find that trust in the benevolence of authorities and their moral character is what shapes the willingness of individuals to accept their decision – not confidence in their competence.[80] Smith and Tyler find that when

---

[77] Donald R. Kinder, Mark D. Peters, Robert P. Abelson, and Susan T. Fiske, "Presidential Prototypes," *Political Behavior* 2, no. 4 (1980): 315–37; Larissa Z. Tiedens, "Anger and Advancement versus Sadness and Subjugation: The Effect of Negative Emotion Expressions on Social Status Conferral," *Journal of Personality and Social Psychology* 80, no. 1 (2001): 86–94; Robert P. Abelson, Donald R. Kinder, Mark D. Peters, and Susan T. Fiske, "Affective and Semantic Components in Political Person Perception," *Journal of Personality and Social Psychology* 42, no. 4 (1982): 619–30.

[78] Gabrielle S. Adams and Elizabeth Mullen, "Increased Voting for Candidates Who Compensate Victims Rather than Punish Offenders," *Social Justice Research* 26, no. 2 (2013): 168–92; see also Linda Klebe Treviño, "The Social Effects of Punishment in Organizations: A Justice Perspective," *Academy of Management Review* 17, no. 4 (October 1992): 647–76.

[79] Tom R. Tyler, "Trust and Democratic Governance," in *Trust and Governance*, edited by Valerie Braithwaite and Margaret Levi, vol. 1, 269–294, Russell Sage Foundation New York, 1998.

[80] Tom R. Tyler and Peter Degoey, "Trust in Organizational Authorities: The Influence of Motive Attributions on Willingness to Accept Decisions," in *Trust in Organizations: Frontiers of Theory and Research*, edited by Roderick M. Kramer and Tom R. Tyler, 16–38, Sage, 1996.

people identify with legislators, they are more likely to evaluate decisions by Congress by asking, "Do I trust the motives of the decision makers?"[81] When citizens believe that officials are morally motivated, they may continue to support those officials even when they disagree with particular decisions. Research from social psychology shows that when people believe that a decision maker has good intentions, they are more likely to judge bad side effects from his or her decisions as unintentional.[82] Hibbing and Theiss-Morse similarly observe in their study of citizen attitudes toward participation and engagement in the United States that "[p]eople know that many problems are beyond the control of elected officials and that others are devilishly difficult. But while they may not demand solutions to these problems, they do demand respect, sensitivity, and understanding."[83]

The Relationship between Punishing Corruption and Citizen Engagement

A retributive justice theory of citizen engagement thus argues that citizens care deeply about whether government authorities uphold retributive justice by punishing corruption and wrongdoing among government officials – and that their retributive justice concerns influence their support for the government, their trust in institutions, and their participation in politics and governance. This is why we see that anti-corruption campaigns from the latter part of the twentieth century resulted in higher levels of public support and citizen engagement when they involved public (and sometimes draconian) punishments – but disillusionment and disengagement when such initiatives did not result in indictments and sentencings.

Studies of successful anti-corruption campaigns observe that they often begin with a stage of well-publicized indictments and punishments. This initial stage of the campaign is then followed by a wave of increased citizen participation, both on anti-corruption but interestingly, on other issues as

[81] Heather J. Smith and Tom R. Tyler, "Justice and Power: When Will Justice Concerns Encourage the Advantaged to Support Policies Which Redistribute Economic Resources and the Disadvantaged to Willingly Obey the Law?" *European Journal of Social Psychology* 26, no. 2 (March 1996): 171–200.

[82] Andrew E. Monroe and Glenn D. Reeder, "Motive-Matching: Perceptions of Intentionality for Coerced Action," *Journal of Experimental Social Psychology* 47, no. 6 (November 2011): 1255–61.

[83] John R. Hibbing and Elizabeth Theiss-Morse, *Stealth Democracy: Americans' Beliefs about How Government Should Work*, Cambridge University Press, 2002, 154.

well. Holmes finds in his examination of anti-corruption campaigns in Eastern Europe, the Soviet Union, and communist systems in Asia and Africa that the real purpose of these campaigns in communist systems was not to improve government performance but to boost regime legitimacy.[84] For this reason, Machel in Mozambique reinstituted the death penalty and flogging and possible punishments for corruption. In Hong Kong, the British colonial government instituted a "guilty until proven innocent" standard in 1971 for officials who were suspected of "unexplained enrichment."[85] In Manion's study of China's anti-corruption efforts in the 1980s, she observes that citizens participate in reporting corruption to the government at higher levels during campaigns that publicize actual punishment.[86] Larmour's study of the military coup in Fiji observes that after an initial wave of bureaucratic purges and punishments, citizens flooded into government offices with public complaints and citizen feedback on a variety of matters, ranging from petty bribery to discrimination, and the provision of public services. He quotes the *Fiji Times* as noting "wryly" that the anti-corruption unit has been a "spectacular success – at receiving complaints," not necessarily about corruption.[87]

Conversely, citizens are more likely to disengage from formal channels of participation when authorities fail to sanction misbehaving government officials. In looking back over the wave of anti-corruption initiatives in the 1990s and 2000s, Andersson and Heywood observe that few of them have had discernible effects on reducing corruption.[88] The failure of political leaders to uphold retributive justice by implementing punishments for corrupt officials has resulted in disillusionment and lower

---

[84] Leslie Holmes argues that the real purpose of anticorruption campaigns in communist systems is to boost regime legitimacy. Leslie Holmes, *The End of Communist Power: Anti-Corruption Campaigns and Legitimation Crisis (Europe and the International Order)*, Oxford University Press, 1993.

[85] Joseph Hanlon, *Mozambique: The Revolution under Fire*, Zed, 1985, 144, 208, cited in Leslie Holmes, *The End of Communist Power: Anti-Corruption Campaigns and Legitimation Crisis (Europe and the International Order)*, Oxford University Press, 1993, 234; On Hong Kong, see Robert Klitgaard, *Controlling Corruption*, University of California Press, 1988.

[86] Melanie Manion, *Corruption by Design*, Harvard University Press, 2009.

[87] Peter Larmour, "Populist Anti-Corruption and Military Coups: The Clean-up Campaign in Fiji 2006–07," in *Governments, NGOs and Anti-Corruption*, edited by Luís de Sousa, Barry Hindess, and Peter Larmour, 146–58, Routledge, 2012, citing *Fiji Times*, February 2, 2007.

[88] Staffan Andersson and Paul M. Heywood, "The Politics of Perception: Use and Abuse of Transparency International's Approach to Measuring Corruption," *Political Studies* 57, no. 4 (December 2009): 746–67.

trust in government, which has sometimes led to the rise of populist leaders and parties and discontent with liberal democracy.[89] Holmes observes, for example, of new democracies: "If citizens continually read and hear reports of corruption, they begin to lose faith in the democratization and marketization projects."[90] Smilov notes that in Eastern Europe, anti-corruption bodies and anti-corruption discourse have raised public awareness of corruption, but lack of action and improvement has in turn led to decreased voting in elections, lack of party membership, and declining party loyalty and discipline. The rise of populist parties and protest then reinforce citizen perceptions that liberal democracy as a system is controlled by a corrupt political elite and is thus incapable of implementing retributive justice.[91]

When people expect their leaders to punish wrongdoing and leaders fail to do so, there is also microlevel evidence that this failure to punish can lead to disengagement and disillusionment. Studies in organizational behavior show that failure to punish misconduct can lead to lower participation in the group or organization. Greenberg notes that an inability to redress injustice leads to feelings of powerlessness and lack of efficacy.[92] Utne and Kidd suggest that individuals who feel powerless to act will not take action to redress injustice even when they have motivation to do so.[93] Studies of organizational citizenship behaviors (OCBs) have also suggested that discretionary and voluntary behaviors of an organization's members, such as civic participation and voluntary contributions to the collective good, depend on the trust of subordinates in the leaders of the organization.[94]

---

[89] Martin Tisne and Daniel Smilov, *From the Ground Up. Assessing the Record of Anticorruption Assistance in Southeastern Europe*, CEU University Press, 2004.

[90] Leslie Holmes, "Political Corruption in Central and Eastern Europe," in *Corruption in Contemporary Politics*, edited by Martin J. Bull and James L. Newell, 204, Palgrave Macmillan, 2003.

[91] Daniel Smilov, "Anti-Corruption Bodies as Discourse-Controlling Instruments: Experiences from South-East Europe," in *Governments, NGOs and Anti-Corruption*, edited by Luís de Sousa, Barry Hindess, and Peter Larmour, 111–27, Routledge, 2012.

[92] Gerald R. Greenberg, "Left Dislocation, Topicalization, and Interjections," *Natural Language and Linguistic Theory* 2, no. 3 (September 1984): 283–87.

[93] Mary Kristine Utne and Robert F. Kidd, "Equity and Attribution," in *Justice and Social Interaction*, edited by Gerold Mikula, Springer-Verlag, 1980, 63–93.

[94] Thomas S. Bateman and Dennis W. Organ, "Job Satisfaction and the Good Soldier: The Relationship between Affect and Employee 'Citizenship'," *Academy of Management Journal* 26, no. 4 (December 1983): 587–95; Gary Yukl, "Managerial Leadership: A Review of Theory and Research," *Journal of Management* 15, no. 2 (1989): 251–89; see also Arthur P. Brief and Stephan J. Motowidlo, "Prosocial Organizational Behaviors," *Academy of Management Review* 11, no. 4 (October 1986): 710–25; Dennis W. Organ, "A Restatement of the Satisfaction-Performance Hypothesis," *Journal of*

When leaders fail to live up to their obligations to punish wrongdoers within the organization, there is also evidence that members switch from thinking of themselves as citizens of the organization, with duties to contribute to the collective good, to individual actors engaged in a commercial transaction with other members as well as the organization's leaders. Research on firms suggests that when the trust of subordinates is violated by perceived unfairness on the part of leaders, subordinates are more likely to think of their relationship as a rigid, self-interested exchange between themselves and the leaders and thus to be less willing to engage in civic, collectively oriented behaviors.[95]

These findings are consistent with a recent argument made by Persson et al. that in political systems characterized by widespread corruption, it simply makes sense for everyone in the system to act in a self-interested manner. In systems where corruption is a collective action and coordination problem, there is no point for citizens to act as principled principals holding elected officials accountable. Instead, what makes the most sense in this equilibrium is to avoid being the "sucker" in the corruption game.[96] Thus, in places like Kenya and the Philippines, where corruption is pervasive, citizens resign themselves to the fact that the relationship between citizens and government is one based on self-interested exchange. Elections become monetized, and votes can be bought and sold. People with more money can buy more attention from government officials, and people with less

Management 14, no. 4 (1988): 547–57; Dennis W. Organ, "The Motivational Basis of Organizational Citizenship Behavior," *Research in Organizational Behavior* 12, no. 1 (1990): 43–72; Mel Schnake, "Organizational Citizenship: A Review, Proposed Model, and Research Agenda," *Human Relations* 44, no. 7 (1991): 735–59; C. Ann Smith, Dennis W. Organ, and Janet P. Near, "Organizational Citizenship Behavior: Its Nature and Antecedents," *Journal of Applied Psychology* 68, no. 4 (1983): 653–63.

[95] Dennis W. Organ and Mary Konovsky, "Cognitive versus Affective Determinants of Organizational Citizenship Behavior," *Journal of Applied Psychology* 74, no. 1 (1989): 157–64. Punishment is generally a private event conducted without direct observers, making observers' attributions highly subject to bias and error. Observers may fill knowledge gaps with assumptions, preconceptions, and information derived through the grapevine. Sally M. Lloyd-Bostock, *Attributions of Cause and Responsibility as Social Phenomena*, Academic Press, 1983; Linda Klebe Treviño, "The Social Effects of Punishment in Organizations: A Justice Perspective," *Academy of Management Review* 17, no. 4 (October 1992): 647–76. Because most observers do not directly observe the punishment incident, their knowledge of the punishment process is limited.

[96] Anna Persson, Bo Rothstein, and Jan Teorell, "Why Anticorruption Reforms Fail-Systemic Corruption as a Collective Action Problem," *Governance* 26, no. 3 (July 2013): 454–55.

money have to resign themselves to being ignored or worse, experiencing predation.

THE IMPORTANCE OF RETRIBUTIVE JUSTICE UNDER CONDITIONS OF UNCERTAINTY

When might we expect government sanctioning of misbehaving officials to have a stronger impact on the retributive justice concerns of citizens and their engagement in politics and governance? Based on the research from sociology and psychology discussed earlier, retributive justice concerns may be more salient for people who feel powerless and uncertain. As Gilley notes, "Predictability is a great moral good for individuals seeking to plan their lives, even if it may entrench some injustices. . . . It is clear that rules serve a great moral purpose in most societies."[97]

This desire for predictability, and its moral valence, is especially important because it helps account for why populism and anti-corruption initiatives resonate so strongly at certain times and with certain people, even when levels of corruption have not changed. Government actions to uphold retributive justice can alleviate or redirect anxiety resulting from threats to the social and political order, even when such threats are unrelated to corruption. These threats may be real (the spread of drug addiction, increasing levels of unemployment) or perceived (e.g., due to political elites and media coverage increasing the salience of crime, without a concomitant rise in crime rates). By increasing uncertainty about the existence of order and stability, these phenomena can magnify the concerns that citizens have about retributive justice and strengthen the role that retributive justice evaluations play in their attitudes toward government authorities and their decisions to engage in politics and governance. This section thus discusses contextual and individual factors that may increase uncertainty and perceptions of social disorder, thereby making citizens more vulnerable to political leaders who decide to mobilize public support through populist strategies.

Contextual Factors

Social and demographic changes that lead to more ethnic diversity, social heterogeneity, rising inequality, and economic instability can make people

---

[97] Bruce Gilley, *The Right to Rule: How States Win and Lose Legitimacy*, Columbia University Press, 2009.

less confident about whether everyone in society shares a set of fundamental moral values and social norms. Stinchcombe et al. hypothesize that this increased uncertainty has been correlated with increasing support for the death penalty as people feel the need to reinstate clear and dominant social norms.[98] Hirschberger et al. observe that people especially want validation of their cultural views and values in contexts with high risk and uncertainty.

In the United States, rising inequality and disparity in opportunities for economic and social mobility has also led people to gravitate toward politicians who emphasize the importance of moral order, even when those politicians propose policies that undermine their objective economic interests. In his study of recent US elections, Enke uses text analysis of over 17,000 campaign documents to categorize the type of moral values espoused by different candidates. He finds that Trump was more likely than Clinton to use political rhetoric emphasizing respect for social order and other communalist values, and that voters who hold these values were more likely to vote for him. They suggest that these findings may explain voting patterns in the United States and Europe that show a strong rural–urban divide in voting and pronounced support for right-wing parties not among the very poor, but among the working class. Working class voters might have voted for Trump (and against their material interests) because their experience with job losses and other disruptions due to declines in domestic manufacturing might create intense feelings of uncertainty and make them more likely to value social order and other communal values, despite their not being the poorest group in society.

Another important contextual factor that may increase uncertainty and a sense of powerlessness is bureaucratic opacity. People often feel more powerless when they cannot understand how or whether the state and bureaucracy are responding efficiently to solving their problems. Even in a consolidated democracy like the United States with institutions that are considered procedurally just, Tyler argues that frustration with the slow pace of bureaucracy in the criminal justice system and its ability to solve complex social and political problems efficiently is correlated with increasing desire for punishment and retributive justice.[99]

---

[98] Arthur L. Stinchcombe, Rebecca Adams, Carol A. Heimer, Kim Lane Scheppele, Tom W. Smith, and D. Garth Taylor, *Crime and Punishment: Changing Attitudes in America*, Jossey-Bass, 1980.

[99] Tom R. Tyler, Robert J. Boeckmann, Heather J. Smith, and Yuen J. Huo, *Social Justice in a Diverse Society*, 1st ed., Routledge, 1997.

In nondemocratic and hybrid regimes, the lack of guaranteed civil liberties and individual rights is a powerful aspect of the political context that creates widespread political fear and uncertainty.[100] Under these conditions, people may feel that it is irrational to participate in formal channels for citizen input and complaints unless they have some indication that government authorities are motivated at least in part by a commitment to the public good. Without any indication that there are actors within the government who may respond positively to citizen input, such an action may be useless, or worse, may subject citizens to the possibility of retaliation.

Another characteristic of many nondemocratic and hybrid regimes that may make retributive justice concerns more salient for people in these regimes is the lack of reliable institutions for selecting "good type" officials, that is, individuals with moral character and good intentions. These regimes often lack reliable bureaucratic selection mechanisms, such as meritocratic civil service exams, and/or democratic selection mechanisms in the form of free and fair elections that enable citizens to be confident that the people in office have intrinsic motivations for acting on behalf of the public interest, independent of whether they have formal incentives to do so (Fearon 1999). Without these institutions for selecting good types into office, punishment and retributive justice may be particularly important to citizens who are trying to assess whether there are good types among bureaucratic principals at higher levels. If citizens are confident that there are at least some government authorities who seem to be good types, these good types may offer some protection against the general uncertainty in the political environment. Beliefs in retributive justice might thus offset perceptions of general political uncertainty created by the macro-institutional context. Moreover, if there are indeed good types in office at higher levels, and these good-type officials are willing to punish corruption severely at lower levels, the risk of these severe punishments can make public office much less attractive to "bad types" who are primarily motivated by self-enrichment. Such bad types may select out of public office, thus increasing the number of good-type officials at lower levels.

Finally, retributive justice and citizen perceptions of the moral character of government officials may of course be particularly salient in

[100] Lily L. Tsai and Yiqing Xu, "Outspoken Insiders: Political Connections and Citizen Participation in Authoritarian China," *Political Behavior* 40, no. 3 (September 11, 2018): 629–57.

contexts where the media and public discourse has focused on corruption as a critical issue. As Andersson and Heywood note, "[i]n such a context, when the trustworthiness of candidates becomes more important than what they are actually saying, political judgments cease to be about political choices as opposed to moral judgments."[101] In these contexts, citizen evaluations of politicians and government officials are even less likely to focus on programmatic concerns and more likely to focus on signals about moral character and intentions.

Individual Factors

Individual-level characteristics can of course also affect how salient retributive justice concerns are. An individual's socioeconomic status or political and social connections can shield him or her from societal-level upheavals so that individuals within the same society vary in their concerns for retributive justice. The well connected and the privileged may already feel efficacious about their ability to influence decision makers, and they may already be relatively engaged in politics and governance or have less of a need to participate given other means for pursuing their interests.[102] They may also already have positive perceptions of the state's

---

[101] Paul Heywood and Ivan Krastev, "Political Scandals and Corruption," in *Developments in European Politics*, edited by Paul M. Heywood, Erick Jones, Martin Rhodes, Ulrich Sedelmeier, Palgrave Macmillan, 2006, 157–77, quoted in Paul M. Heywood and Staffan Andersson, "Anti-Corruption as a Risk to Democracy: On the Unintended Consequences of International Anti-Corruption Campaigns," in *Governments, NGOs and Anti-Corruption*, edited by Luís de Sousa, Peter Larmour, and Barry Hindess, Routledge, 2012, 33–50.

[102] Yuen Yuen Ang and Nan Jia, "Perverse Complementarity: Political Connections and the Use of Courts among Private Firms in China," *The Journal of Politics* 76, no. 2 (April 2014): 318–32; Lianjiang Li and Kevin J. O'Brien, "Villagers and Popular Resistance in Contemporary China," *Modern China* 22, no. 1 (January 19, 1996): 28–61; Gang Guo, "Retrospective Economic Accountability under Authoritarianism," *Political Research Quarterly* 60, no. 3 (September 2, 2007): 378–90. It is important to note the growing research suggesting that political connections provide important resources for participation in transitional systems and developing contexts highlight the importance of political connections for civic and political engagement. For example, Catherine Boone, "Decentralization as Political Strategy in West Africa," *Comparative Political Studies* 36, no. 4 (2003): 355–80; Richard C. Crook, James Manor, and A. Sinha, "Democracy and Decentralization in South Asia and West Africa: Participation, Accountability and Performance," Comparative Political Studies 33, no. 1 (2000): 144–47; M. Kent Jennings, "Political Participation in the Chinese Countryside," *American Political Science Review* 91, no. 2 (June 1, 1997): 361–72. Duara notes that throughout the developing world, ordinary people often need the help of a broker who has political connections in order to access the government. Prasenjit Duara, "Superscribing Symbols:

commitment to retributive justice. For these individuals, government actions to punish corruption may not have much impact on their level of participation and engagement.

There is also research showing that individuals can vary in their psychological predispositions for obedience and submissiveness.[103] Such theories are unlikely to account for cross-national variation in authoritarian popularity and the salience of retributive justice as there is little reason to think that individuals with authoritarian personalities are more likely to be born in certain countries. These theories are also limited in their ability to explain variation in authoritarian popularity in the same country over time.[104] But personality traits may help to account for variation across individuals within the same society.

A TYPOLOGY OF STATE APPROACHES TO RETRIBUTIVE JUSTICE

Government authorities pursue a wide variety of strategies for upholding retributive justice through sanctioning corruption and malfeasance among their agents. These strategies range from setting up supreme audit institutions and courts at the national levels to inspector general offices and personnel departments in local governments to mass mobilization campaigns and state-sanctioned vigilantism. These strategies vary across countries but can also vary within a country, across regions and localities. According to a retributive justice theory of citizen engagement, all of these strategies may affect citizen engagement, but different strategies for retributive justice may have different implications for who engages and with which government authorities they engage. This section thus proposes a typology of government strategies for retributive justice

The Myth of Guandi, Chinese God of War," *The Journal of Asian Studies* 47, no. 4 (November 1988): 778. Krishna finds that the existence of new, noncaste-based village leaders increase levels of political participation in villages with high social capital by providing political information and direction. Anirudh Krishna, "Enhancing Political Participation in Democracies: What Is the Role of Social Capital?" *Comparative Political Studies* 35, no. 4 (2002): 437–60; Anirudh Krishna, "Gaining Access to Public Services and the Democratic State in India: Institutions in the Middle," *Studies in Comparative International Development* 46, no. 1 (2011): 98–117.
[103] Marc J. Hetherington and Jonathan D. Weiler, *Authoritarianism and Polarization in American Politics*, Cambridge University Press, 2009.
[104] Larry M. Bartels, J. Eric Oliver, and Wendy M. Rahn, "Rise of the Trumpenvolk: Populism in the 2016 Election," *The ANNALS of the American Academy of Political and Social Science* 667, no. 1 (2016): 189–206, https://doi.org/10.1177/0002716216662639.

organized along two dimensions: level of institutionalization and level of centralization.

Level of Institutionalization

The first dimension is the level of institutionalization, or the extent to which retributive justice is pursued through formal institutions. Do government authorities pursue retributive justice primarily through formal, standardized channels such as bureaucratic agencies and courts? Do fixed rules and procedures govern how corrupt officials are investigated and punished? Or do authorities pursue retributive justice through ad hoc methods such as periodic campaigns and purges, which are organized at the discretion of political leaders and in response to particular situations or cases at hand?

The rule of law, of course, is one important approach to pursuing retributive justice through formal institutions. In systems with rule of law, government authorities are bound to punish corruption and malfeasance among state agents. Formal channels for public oversight and checks and balances ensure that they do so.

Another example of a highly institutionalized strategy for retributive justice is formal anti-corruption agencies. In the United States, for example, the Federal Bureau of Investigation (FBI)'s Public Corruption program works with the Department of Justice, inspector general offices, the internal affairs offices of law enforcement agencies, and local prosecutors to detect and investigate corruption from both citizens and other actors within government. Such agencies can work to uphold retributive justice in systems even without the rule of law if top leaders are committed to upholding social order.[105]

In developing contexts, anti-corruption agencies with wide-ranging powers are more common. Many countries have institutions such as comptroller generals, ombudsman offices, and government audit offices. Hong Kong's Independent Commission Against Corruption (ICAC) is an oft-cited archetypal example. Established in 1974 by the British colonial governor, the ICAC was formed as an independent statutory body outside

---

[105] Plato makes a similar point in the *Republic* when he notes that in poorly run states there is no point in creating legislation against corruption because they cannot implement it, while in well-run states, legislation against corruption is unnecessary because retributive justice will be inherent in "the practices already established." Plato, *The Republic*, edited by Allan Bloom and Adam Kirsch, Basic Books, 2016.

the government, civil service, and police force and reported directly to the governor. Between 1974 and 1976, it investigated more than a thousand cases of corruption and successfully convicted hundreds of corrupt officials in public offices and the police force, often with severe punishments, leading to Hong Kong being regarded as one of the least corrupt cities by the 1990s.[106] Singapore has also established similar institutions, and initiatives to establish independent public audit bodies were a high priority for Central and Eastern European countries after the fall of communism, with a region-wide consortium of country-level bodies, the European Organisation of Supreme Audit Institutions (EUROSAI), established in 1990.

More recently, in Brazil the judiciary and prosecutor's offices at both federal and state levels have become more autonomous and powerful anti-corruption actors over the last decade. In Rwanda, Kagame has established the Office of the Ombudsman, which conducts regular audits of government offices and ensures asset declarations by public officials and their families.[107] By 2007, the OMB had dismissed more than 500 members of the judiciary for corruption and incompetence, 62 police officers for soliciting bribes, and thousands of public sector employees.[108]

Anti-corruption agencies in developing contexts often fall in the middle of the spectrum. They are legal entities, but the extent to which their activities are rule-bound varies. Some may have detailed rules. But others have broad discretion governed only by broad principles.

Even less institutionalized are approaches at the extreme end of the spectrum such as mass campaigns and even state-sanctioned violence. The current anti-drug, anti-corruption campaign initiated by President Duterte in the Philippines, for example, has encouraged the participation

---

[106] Ray Yep, "The Crusade against Corruption in Hong Kong in the 1970s: Governor MacLehose as a Zealous Reformer or Reluctant Hero?" *China Information* 27, no. 2 (2013): 197–221, https://doi.org/10.1177/0920203X13482244.

[107] Eiji Oyamada, "Combating Corruption in Rwanda: Lessons for Policy Makers," *Asian Education and Development Studies* 6, no. 3 (July 10, 2017): 252. Office of the Ombudsman, "Annual Report July 2013–June 2014," 2014. www.minijust.gov.rw/file admin/user_upload/Minijust/Publications/Reports/MOJ_reports/Annual_Report_2013-2014.pdf

[108] Marie Chêne, "What Makes New Zealand, Denmark, Finland, Sweden and Others 'Cleaner' than Most Countries?," 2011, www.transparency.org/en/blog/what-makes-new-zealand-denmark-finland-sweden-and-others-cleaner-than-most-countries; Global Integrity, "Global Integrity Report 2009," 2009, cited in Eiji Oyamada, "Combating Corruption in Rwanda: Lessons for Policy Makers," *Asian Education and Development Studies* 6, no. 3 (July 10, 2017): 252, www.globalintegrity.org/wp-content/uploads/201 9/01/GIRNotebook2009_Rwanda.pdf.

of police and ordinary citizens in extrajudicial killings of hundreds of people. In the second month of his presidency, Duterte publicly announced the names of over 150 people he accused of engaging in drug-related corruption and gave them 24 hours to turn themselves in or risk being targets of a "hunt."[109]

Level of Centralization

Another important dimension that distinguishes different government approaches to retributive justice is the level of centralization or concentration in the administration of retributive justice. Is the pursuit of retributive justice initiated and controlled by the central government and national leaders? Or do subnational authorities have de facto discretion over how and whether they implement retributive justice? Consolidated democracies typically rely on a combination of the rule of law, law enforcement agencies, an independent judiciary, and a criminal justice system to ensure that government officials who abuse their offices are punished in a way that upholds society's values. Rule of law and an independent judiciary are both highly institutionalized and highly centralized state approaches to retributive justice common in consolidated democracies. States can also have highly institutionalized and centralized approaches to retributive justice without a strong rule of law, particularly if there is rule *by* law. Examples include supreme audit institutions with national jurisdictions, such as Brazil's Federal Court of Accounts or Argentina's National Auditor-General.

Ad hoc campaigns can also have a high degree of centralization in the sense that national leaders authorize the beginning and end of the campaign, and control the modes through which it is pursued, though the campaign is not governed by formal institutions or a regularized form of governance. In Duterte's current anti-crime and anti-corruption campaign, it remains to be seen how much top-down control he exerts over local authorities and whether he can switch off the violence at will. Given, however, that it is the president who authorizes amnesty for local actors engaging in extrajudicial punishments, it may prove to be quite centralized.[110]

---

[109] Himanshu Goenka, "Philippine Drug War: President Duterte Launches Corruption Purge," *International Business Times*, August 8, 2016.

[110] Amanda Taub, "How Countries Like the Philippines Fall into Vigilante Violence," *The New York Times*, September 11, 2016.

On the other side of the spectrum are decentralized approaches to retributive justice initiated at the local level. In 2004, for example, successful prosecution of corrupt legislators in Padang set off a wave of local ad hoc anti-corruption campaigns across Indonesia.[111] When retributive justice is relatively uninstitutionalized, subnational authorities may have considerable discretion over whether they sanction corrupt and misbehaving officials. In China, under Mao, even mass mobilization campaigns initiated at the center often devolved into locally directed ad hoc movements. Understanding whether government strategies are authorized by central authorities or by local authorities is important for understanding how these strategies affect citizen support for government and political participation. Citizens read these strategies as signals of the intentions and capacity of the level of government that initiates them and thus credit or blame different levels accordingly.

Formal institutions for sanctioning corrupt officials and upholding retributive justice can also vary greatly at the subnational level. Federal systems, of course, formalize such subnational variation in institutional arrangements. In 2003, Brazil implemented an anti-corruption policy that allowed for random audits of municipal governments, though implementation of these audits varies regionally.[112] In the United States, state governments vary widely in how they structure their institutions for managing public corruption and how strong these institutions are. In Massachusetts, the state's Judicial Conduct Commission investigates corruption among state judges. However, the Commission also reports to these judges and lacks any enforcement power. In contrast, Alaska's Commission on Judicial Conduct is composed of three state judges, as well as three attorneys and three members of the public who are appointed by the governor and approved by the Legislature. The commission's staff are civil servants and insulated as state employees. Moreover, the commission can independently initiate complaints on its own with the state supreme court mandated to impose discipline as required.

Subnational variation in formal institutions for retributive justice can also result from uneven state capacity.[113] Parallels can be found in

---

[111] Jamie S. Davidson, "Politics-as-Usual on Trial: Regional Anti-Corruption Campaigns in Indonesia," *The Pacific Review* 20, no. 1 (March 15, 2007): 75–99.

[112] Jacob Jensen and Terry Anderson, "A Qualitative Comparison of Anti-Corruption Measures in Guatemala and Brazil," *Journal of Politics and Democratization* 1, no. 2 (2016): 1–20.

[113] Hillel David Soifer, *Authority over Distance: Explaining Variation in State Infrastructural Power in Latin America*, Harvard University, 2006.

historical case studies before the consolidation of modern states. In medieval Spain, the different regions governed by the Crown of Aragon – Aragon, Valencia, and Catalonia – took diverse approaches to administrative reform and retributive justice. Because each of these regions had highly dissimilar legal traditions and cultures, regional administrators were compelled to test their strategies for reform locally, while judging perceptions of jurisdiction and legitimacy among the subjects in their region.[114] Similarly, in nineteenth-century China, the imperial court responded to the widespread anger with abuses of power by local state agents expressed during the Boxer Rebellion by calling on provincial governors to offer a variety of reform proposals. As a result, efforts in Shanxi province looked to traditional Chinese models of reform and contrasted with the efforts by Yuan Shikai, the Governor-General of Zhili and later the first president of the Republican period, which were based on Japanese and Western models.[115]

Focusing on Formal Subnational Bureaucratic Institutions of Retributive Justice

This book focuses on formal subnational bureaucratic institutions of retributive justice for both theoretical and policy reasons. First, this book seeks to understand when citizens decide to support the regime, engage in governance, and take action through the formal institutions for citizen participation provided by the state, rather than taking to the streets and voicing opposition to authorities and their institutions. If we want to understand when citizens utilize formal institutions to achieve their objectives, it makes sense to examine whether they see government authorities also using formal institutions to achieve government objectives. Deploying formal strategies for retributive justice is an important way in which government authorities model their commitment to signal the effectiveness of formal rather than informal institutions.

This book thus builds on research investigating how people's perceptions about bureaucratic institutions affect their political attitudes and behavior more generally. Vigoda-Gadot, for example, observes that

---

[114] Marta VanLandingham, *Transforming the State: King, Court and Political Culture in the Realms of Aragon (1213–1387)*, vol. 43, Groupe de Boeck, 2002.

[115] Roger A. Thompson, "Photomultiplier Tube Assembly," *Google Patents*, February 26, 1985.

citizen perceptions of bureaucratic politics influences their attitudes about democracy and their trust in government overall:

> When citizens perceive the bureaucracy as insensitive, feel that it promotes the interests of powerful individuals or groups based on political considerations, and believe that it engages in unfair practices, public attitudes toward democracy may become more cynical. . . . More actively, these perceptions may lead to diminished belief in the value of citizens' involvement and political efficacy, negatively affecting citizens' willingness to participate in politics.[116]

Immoral behavior in the bureaucracy can also affect citizen support for the regime and levels of participation.[117]

From a policy perspective, understanding the impact of formal institutions for retributive justice enables us to make concrete recommendations about the kinds of formal institutions that states and bureaucracies ought to focus on strengthening. The impact of informal or uninstitutionalized strategies for upholding retributive justice such as ad hoc campaigns can be fleeting since they may be discretionary and lack the backing of explicit authorization. In contrast, bureaucratic performance contracts can be an effective formal tool for increasing the ability of higher levels to hold local officials accountable for fiscal governance and public goods provision; not surprisingly, this institution is becoming increasingly popular as a policy intervention recommended by the World Bank and other international agencies. Focusing on subnational variation in these bureaucratic institutions is also helpful from a policy perspective since it can be easier to implement subnational pilots or find officials at subnational levels who are willing to push reforms than it is at the national level.[118]

Examining formal institutions for retributive justice at the subnational rather than the national level also has important advantages. Theoretically, it contributes to a growing literature on the unevenness of state capacity. Existing theories of how state capacity varies subnationally

---

[116] E. Vigoda-Gadot, "Citizens' Perceptions of Politics and Ethics in Public Administration: A Five-Year National Study of Their Relationship to Satisfaction with Services, Trust in Governance, and Voice Orientations," *Journal of Public Administration Research and Theory* 17, no. 2 (June 7, 2006): 291.

[117] Louis C. Gawthrop, "Democracy, Bureaucracy, and Hypocrisy Redux: A Search for Sympathy and Compassion," *Public Administration Review*, 57, no. 3 (1997): 205–10.

[118] For example, Manion gives the example of a local innovation in Hainan: the response of Hainan provincial authorities to the personal approval by a former president of the Hainan Provincial Construction Bank of easy loans to enterprises in return for massive bribes. The provincial government replaced this system with a sequential process that distributes functions of local approval, processing, and investigation among three different agencies. Melanie Manion, *Corruption by Design*, Harvard University Press, 2009.

tend to focus on coercive resources, the projection of infrastructural power, and public goods provision across localities without looking explicitly at variation in top-down institutions of bureaucratic accountability and sanctioning. But even in localities where coercive capacity, infrastructural power, and public goods provision are similar, citizen satisfaction, trust, and compliance with government can differ significantly. Looking at variation in formal bureaucratic sanctioning of local officials helps to explain this variation in citizen–state relations.

A subnational focus also hones in on the fact that bureaucratic institutions at the local level are the ones that are often the most likely to have an impact on citizen political attitudes and behaviors, especially in developing contexts. Central government authorities often seem distant and impossible to access. It is local government and local officials with whom citizens interact on a day to day basis (or at all).[119] Grassroots officials are the ones who directly enforce regulations. They may collect taxes on behalf of higher levels. Perhaps most important to the everyday lives of citizens, grassroots officials allocate and distribute the resources from the state that are critical to ordinary people. As Kruks-Wisner notes how villagers in India make claims on state resources, "Village-level officials are the first port of call for the vast majority, while contact with higher-level officials and politicians remains more limited."[120] In many places, local government is the face of the state.[121]

Finally, examining subnational variation has all the advantages for analytical inquiry that researchers typically acknowledge – the ability to hold constant features of the macropolitical context such as regime type, historical legacies, and political culture while isolating the impact of our main variable of interest, local bureaucratic institutions of retributive justice.

CONCLUSION

To be clear, this book is not about whether retributive justice concerns and punishment of corrupt officials *should* take priority over individual

---

[119] Michael Lipsky, "Street-Level Bureaucracy: An Introduction," in *The Policy Process: A Reader,* edited by Michael Hill, Harvester Wheatsheaf, 1993, 381–85.

[120] Gabrielle K. Kruks-Wisner, "Claiming the State: Citizen-State Relations and Service Delivery in Rural India," Massachusetts Institute of Technology, 2013, https://dspace.mit.edu/handle/1721.1/83760.

[121] Bernardo Zacka, *When the State Meets the Street: Public Service and Moral Agency,* Harvard University Press, 2017.

rights, or what the highest priorities of a mass public and political community ought to be. Instead, what this book argues is that retributive justice and the enforcement of penalties against wrongdoers within the state is *empirically* important to ordinary citizens and plays a significant role in their evaluations of the government and their decisions to take political action.

For the many people who live outside of consolidated democracies, corruption and malfeasance of officials can be a more pressing concern to ordinary citizens than the violation of liberal rights. As Rose, Mischler, and Haerpfer comment, in Eastern Europe after the fall of communism, "corruption replaced repression as the main threat to the rule of law."[122] In Russia, Putin rose to power on a public consensus that "law and order" and "predictable relations with the state" were more important than "earlier calls for freedom and individualism."[123] His initiation of institutional and legislative anti-corruption measures is seen by many as an improvement over the legal and political confusion of the 1990s.[124] When government authorities fail to uphold retributive justice, "[p]eople feel abandoned by the formal legal system, and are left to manage their own psychological fears and uncertainties."[125] As Enke's research shows, even in developed contexts, the need for social order and retributive justice may increase for citizens who feel their society is becoming more complex and insecure.[126]

Even among scholars who see some of the international anti-corruption campaigns over the last two decades as fundamentally illiberal, there is

[122] Richard Rose, William Mishler, and Christian Haerpfer, *Democracy and Its Alternatives: Understanding Post-Communist Societies*, Johns Hopkins University Press, 1998.

[123] Vadim Volkov, *Violent Entrepreneurs: The Use of Force in the Making of Russian Capitalism*, Cornell University Press, 2016, cited in Diana Schmidt, "Anti-Corruption: What Do We Know? Research on Preventing Corruption in the Post-Communist World," *Political Studies Review* 5, no. 2 (May 30, 2007): 202–32.

[124] Christopher F. Dugan and Vladimir Lechtman, "The FCPA in Russia and Other Former Communist Countries," *The American Journal of International Law* 91, no. 2 (April 1997): 378; Svetlana P. Glinkina, "The Ominous Landscape of Russian Corruption," *Transitions* 5, no. 3 (1998): 16–23; Diana Schmidt, "Anti-Corruption: What Do We Know? Research on Preventing Corruption in the Post-Communist World," *Political Studies Review* 5, no. 2 (May 30, 2007): 202–32; Vadim Volkov, *Violent Entrepreneurs: The Use of Force in the Making of Russian Capitalism*, Cornell University Press, 2016.

[125] Tom Tyler, Robert Boeckmann, Heather Smith, and Yuen J. Huo, *Social Justice in Diverse Society*, Westview Press, 1997.

[126] Benjamin Enke, Moral values and voting. *Journal of Political Economy*, 128, no. 10, (2020): 3679–3729. https://doi.org/10.1086/708857

a consensus that the use of harsh sanctions against wrongdoers has been very popular with ordinary citizens.[127] For ordinary citizens in many places, preserving a minimal level of public order and social stability is a higher priority than ensuring individual rights – which makes sense since without a basic level of public order and political stability, it is impossible to create and consolidate institutions and a rule of law that guarantees those rights. Ensuring retributive justice is almost a necessary prerequisite to ensuring distributive and procedural justice.

We need to recognize that robust institutions that promote retributive justice are an essential component of stable and legitimate political systems. Instead of sweeping fears about these primitive instincts under the rug, we need to engage in empirically informed discussions of how best to implement formal institutions for retributive justice based on reasoned deliberation rather than on emotional reactions.[128] When the US Supreme Court reinstated the death penalty in 1976, it acknowledged that "the instinct for retribution is part of the nature of man" but went on to discuss the importance of the community as a whole weighing in on what counts as fair retribution that benefits the community as a whole.[129] Some advocates of restorative justice argue that retributive and restorative justice are not necessarily that different or in conflict with one another when "retributivism responds to important moral concerns".[130] Similarly, recent debates among theorists argue that the principle of just deserts underpins not only retributive justice but also distributive justice.[131] People should receive the punishments as well as the benefits they deserve. This line of

---

[127] Paul M. Heywood and Staffan Andersson, "Anti-Corruption as a Risk to Democracy: On the Unintended Consequences of International Anti-Corruption Campaigns," in *Governments, NGOs and Anti-Corruption*, edited by Luís de Sousa, Peter Larmour, and Barry Hindess, Routledge, 2012, 33–50; Robert Klitgaard, *Controlling Corruption*, University of California Press, 1988.

[128] Geoffrey P. Goodwin and Dena M. Gromet, "Punishment," *Wiley Interdisciplinary Reviews: Cognitive Science* 5, no. 5 (September 2014): 562.

[129] *Gregg v. Georgia*, cited in Peter Liberman, "Retributive Support for International Punishment and Torture," *Journal of Conflict Resolution* 57, no. 2 (2013): 287.

[130] Lucy Allais, "Restorative Justice, Retributive Justice, and the South African Truth and Reconciliation Commission," *Philosophy & Public Affairs* 39, no. 4 (September 2011): footnote 73; see also Geoffrey P. Goodwin and Dena M. Gromet, "Punishment," *Wiley Interdisciplinary Reviews: Cognitive Science* 5, no. 5 (September 2014): 562.

[131] Dena M. Gromet, "Punishment," *Wiley Interdisciplinary Reviews: Cognitive Science* 5, no. 5 (September 2014): 562. Jeffrey Moriarty, "Against the Asymmetry of Desert," *Nous* 37, no. 3 (September 2003): 518–36; see also Samuel Scheffler, *Human Morality*, Oxford University Press on Demand, 1992; Samuel Scheffler, *Boundaries and Allegiances: Problems of Justice and Responsibility in Liberal Thought*, Oxford University Press on Demand, 2002.

thought is borne out by recent empirical research in political economy on the relationship between individual perceptions of deservingness and preferences for redistribution.[132]

In sum, if we are to devise careful institutional arrangements to uphold retributive justice while also protecting individual rights, we need to have an accurate, empirical understanding of how retributive justice concerns shape citizen and state behavior. In the following chapters, we take a closer look at how government authorities signal their commitment to retributive justice and how these signals affect citizen evaluations of government and their willingness to engage in governance.

[132] Charlotte Cavaillé and Kris-Stella Trump, "The Two Facets of Social Policy Preferences," *The Journal of Politics* 77, no. 1 (January 2015): 146–60.

3

Retributive Justice and State Production of Moral Order

Anti-corruption initiatives in China date back more than a thousand years. Does this mean that China has performed well at controlling corruption, or badly? The answer is more nuanced. Controlling corruption has not been the sole – perhaps not even the primary – purpose of China's anti-corruption initiatives. Government authorities since the imperial period have consistently and strategically promoted a political culture that constructs corruption as a persistent public problem and portrays themselves as crusaders against this evil. The narrative promoted by the government is that corruption is chronic due to the inevitable bad apples that make their way into government, usually at the local levels. As a result, society needs government authorities to find these bad apples and toss them out. By helping to persuade the public that it needs government provision of retributive justice, and creating a sense that government authorities at the top are allied with the public against bad local officials, anti-corruption initiatives have been central to the longevity of the Chinese state apparatus.

This strategy of constructing a public problem in order to earn credit for combatting it is by no means unique to China. Barrington Moore observes the same kind of approach taken by the Catholic Church in early modern Europe. Reflecting on the Church's "expropriation of guilt," Moore notes that Church authorities "help[ed] to create the sense of guilt and then provid[ed] the bureaucratic mechanisms for alleviating it. As an economist might put the point, the Catholic Church managed to create much of the demand and most of the supply."[1]

---

[1] Barrington Moore Jr., *Injustice: The Social Bases of Obedience and Revolt*, Routledge, 2016.

When retributive justice is central to the government's legitimation strategy (which could very well be always), authorities need to be able to answer the questions: "Who are the bad guys?" Who are the potential sources of disorder, instability, and contamination of society? In the case of China, the bad guys have often been defined as the corrupt individuals within the bureaucracy, while government authorities are the heroes who do battle with these villains to uphold order and prevent moral rot. In other places and at other times, the bad guys in a government's legitimation strategy might be criminals, illegal immigrants, drug traffickers and addicts, terrorists – or all of these.

Authorities, in other words, can strategically define immoral behavior and challenges to the social order and make them salient to the public so that retributive justice becomes a core public good that the state provides to its citizens. In this chapter, we see how two long-term strategies have enabled Chinese authorities playing the long game to establish a durable, lasting state. The first is the institutionalization of strategies for retributive justice and the punishment of corruption. The second is the systematic inculcation of a political culture that makes retributive justice central, not only to state legitimacy but also to the role that citizens/subjects expect to play in the political system. Democratic theory defines political participation as actions that citizens take to voice their interests. But by focusing on the importance of anti-corruption and retributive justice, authoritarian regimes like China can redirect citizen action by promoting a different definition of political participation. Popular or "democratic" participation is not voting or voicing input into the policymaking process. Instead, it is conceptualized as participation in governance and accountability – citizen monitoring and sanctioning state agents for misbehavior and malfeasance.

STATE BUILDING AND THE PRODUCTION OF MORAL ORDER IN COMPARATIVE PERSPECTIVE

Retributive justice is a core public good that the state provides, and the production of retributive justice and moral order is essential to state building. Before this chapter delves into the specifics of how Chinese authorities have used retributive justice to construct a durable state, it is useful to place China into comparative perspective and look briefly at the role that retributive justice and the production of moral order have played in European state building.

Similar to rulers in China who sought to implement their "mandate from heaven," monarchs in early modern Europe were seen by subjects and defined themselves as servants of God and thus explicitly responsible for upholding a moral order. To ensure their own salvation and the salvation of their subjects, monarchs and their agents were required to produce moral order by disseminating and enforcing the rules of God. The very terms "corrupt" and "corruption," as Genaux notes, were in fact biblical words that were "meant to express man's mortality in front of God's eternity and incorruption."[2]

To govern with justice was to uphold God's rules. Deviation from these rules, and the failure to punish such deviance, was said to be "corruption" because it led to the separation of the monarch's people from God. Political corruption, in the Christian tradition, was thus a failure by the political authorities to prevent the moral decay of the body politic:

The laws by which the whole community abides represent legitimate order and generate the hope of attaining, in spite of man's original corruption, salvation, redemption, eternity, and incorruption. ... [T]he kings are responsible for the totality of the human disorders. In other words, they have to answer for the dreadful progression of corruption, the latter being inevitable because of man's sinful nature.[3]

In this thinking, God made rulers responsible for producing a moral order for their people and held them to account when they failed to enforce this order by implementing retributive justice and punishing violators:

The sixth chapter of the Book of Solomon contains the crucial passage when the kings are put in front of their duty of justice directly under God's gaze and where the wisdom of their deeds in terms of incorruption is defined. According to this fragment the first duty of justice consists for the kings in remaining pious. They have to preserve and guarantee the general respect of God's Law, that is, of His word and of the cult dedicated to Him; the kings must punish idolatry, defined as the fact of becoming estranged from God and of preferring someone or something else to Him.[4]

State building in early modern Europe thus went beyond the creation of the institutions for resource extraction and coercive power on which political scientists have traditionally focused. As historians and sociologists have pointed out, such processes also required the development of institutions for *moral control*.[5] Corrigan and Sayer, for example, describe

[2] Maryvonne Génaux, "Social Sciences and the Evolving Concept of Corruption," *Crime, Law and Social Change* 42, no. 1 (August 2004): 15.

[3] Ibid., 20.   [4] Ibid., 20.

[5] Norbert Elias, *The Civilizing Process*, translated by Edmund Jephcott, vol. 1, Blackwell, 1978.

the formation of the English state as an extended process of "collective moral regulation" by the bourgeoisie. They highlight the ways in which the English state promoted activities, routines, and rituals to create and enforce how individuals understand their identities and relationships.[6] During the medieval period, the objective of this moral regulation was to restrict alternative social visions and religious doctrines. Punishment of wrongdoers was an essential component of this regulation. Ritualized public executions of heretics by burning were often carried out by civil authorities, not just the Church,[7] as heresy was defined broadly as any doctrine that challenged authority.[8]

The enclosure movement of the eighteenth century provides an illustration of how the English state subsequently constructed a moral order based on property rights and implemented the retributive justice needed to uphold it. As the capitalist gentry took advantage of their political power to transform public commons into private property, Corrigan and Sayer argue that property rights became the secular equivalent of religion.[9] In enshrining these as "rights" in addition to law, the gentry defined property rights as the basis of a moral order, thereby rendering the violation of property rights as not just a legal infraction but fundamentally immoral. Retributive justice in the form of severe punishment for violators was thus justifiable. By 1740, the theft of property worth just 1 shilling was punishable by death. What had been customary rights to use of common lands was now criminalized, enabling the gentry to use the full force of the state to execute and imprison those who violated the tenets of this new religion.

The main institutions for enforcing this new moral order were the *assizes* or county courts at the grassroots. These courts were the only point of contact for most people with the central state, and the "awesome centerpiece of the *assizes* was the ritual surrounding pronouncement of the death sentence."[10] Combined with the Crown's access to the pulpit as an instrument for state propaganda,[11] harsh punishment of those who

[6] Philip Corrigan and Derek Sayer, *The Great Arch: English State Formation as Cultural Revolution*, Blackwell, 1985.
[7] Ibid.
[8] Margaret E. Aston, "Lollardy and Sedition 1381–1431," *Past & Present* 17 (1960): 1–44, cited in Philip Corrigan and Derek Sayer, ibid.
[9] Philip Corrigan and Derek Sayer, *The Great Arch: English State Formation as Cultural Revolution*, Blackwell, 1985.
[10] Ibid.
[11] Louis B. Wright, *Religion and Empire: The Alliance between Piety and Commerce in English Expansion, 1558–1625*, 1943, University of North Carolina Press, cited in Philip Corrigan and Derek Sayer, ibid.

violated the moral order based on property rights through these local governance rituals constituted the exposure of most ordinary people to the English state during this period.

In short, retributive justice and the use of punishment to uphold a moral order were central for state builders in England seeking to persuade the public to subscribe to what Abrams calls the idea of the state, a construction "attributing unity, morality, and independence to the disunited, amoral, and dependent workings of the practice of government."[12] State building requires getting the public to see the practices and institutions of the state as coherent, morally motivated, and legitimate. While the institutions that rulers seek to build – armies, prisons, tax bureaus – are backed by a credible threat of coercive force, states cannot rely on the constant use of coercion. They must, as Levi points out, elicit a high degree of voluntary compliance.[13] And, as Abrams notes, "it is their association with the idea of the state that silences protest, excuses force and convinces almost all of us that the fate of the victims is just and necessary."

RETRIBUTIVE JUSTICE AND STATE BUILDING IN IMPERIAL CHINA: THE STRATEGIC PRODUCTION OF MORAL ORDER

While anti-corruption campaigns have been a key feature of the Chinese regime's governance strategies in the post-1978 reform period, retributive justice concerns are a deeply embedded element of state institutions and political culture that long predates current-day anti-corruption initiatives. In many ways, the two-millennia history of the Chinese state is a history of how authorities have responded to – and often strategically promoted – the public's concerns about moral order and retributive justice.

While the production and enforcement of a moral order through retributive justice is perhaps a common element of all long-standing states, it has been particularly salient in the case of China. Nascent states in Western Europe faced urgent pressures of war and interstate competition, as well as needing to be seen as a moral agent. In contrast, the main challenge facing state builders in China was expanding its bureaucratic control over territories and populations with less political and military sophistication. The imperial state needed to secure voluntary compliance

---

[12] Philip Abrams, "Notes on the Difficulty of Studying the State," *The Anthropology of the State: A Reader* 1 (2006): 75–77, 79, 81.
[13] Margaret Levi, *Of Rule and Revenue*, vol. 13, University of California Press, 1989.

with public security measures from a growing population of agricultural producers under constantly changing economic conditions, fiscal needs, and levels of social and ethnic diversity.

Routine governance, not war, was thus the problem. The solution was the development of a cultural and symbolic order that would enable its bureaucracy to expand its reach across the continent and govern an increasingly heterogeneous population. The Chinese state portrayed itself as the creator and enforcer of a value system that provided social order and meaning to the everyday lives of ordinary people. As Leonard and Watt note, "[f]or the Qing, the term 'state' conveys both less and more than the Western referent. While its bureaucratic functions, centering narrowly on tax collection and security, were more limited than those of modern governments, its overarching moral-cosmic functions far exceeded those of the secular state in the West."[14] In contrast to European states, which sought to mobilize coercive resources for military defense against external threats, Chinese rulers used coercion primarily for combatting enemies and criminals within their own states and societies.

As in the Judeo-Christian political culture in Europe, rulers in China were explicitly responsible for upholding morality in themselves and in society. If they failed to do so, violating their "mandate from Heaven" (*tianming*, 天命), they were seen to be subject to divine retribution in the form of meteorological events and natural disasters – literally "disasters from Heaven" or *tianzai* (天災) – such as droughts, floods, and earthquakes.[15] As Elvin notes, "Rainfall and sunshine were thought to be seasonal or unseasonal, appropriate or excessive, according to whether human behavior was moral or immoral."[16] The impact of one's behavior varied according to one's position in the social order. Immorality by an individual commoner counted for the least, while the actions of bureaucrats were more important, and the emperor's behavior was definitive.[17]

---

[14] Jane Kate Leonard and John Robertson Watt (Eds.), "Introduction," in *To Achieve Security and Wealth: The Qing Imperial State and the Economy, 1644–1911*, 2, Cornell University East Asia Program, 1992.

[15] Hanna B. Krebs, *Responsibility, Legitimacy, Morality: Chinese Humanitarianism in Historical Perspective*, Humanitarian Policy Group, Overseas Development Institute, 2014.

[16] M. Elvin, "Who Was Responsible for the Weather? Moral Meteorology in Late Imperial China," *Osiris*, 13, no. 1 (1998): 213, https://www.journals.uchicago.edu/doi/abs/10.1086/649286?journalCode=osiris

[17] M. Lewis, *Sanctioned Violence in Early China*, State University of New York Press, 1990, 138; M. Elvin, "Who Was Responsible for the Weather? Moral Meteorology in Late Imperial China," *Osiris*, 13, no. 1 (1998): 213.

The concept of the "heavenly mandate" also legitimated the public's right to rebel.[18] An emperor who was himself immoral, or unable to prevent immorality in the state and society, no longer had the right to rule. When this was the case, ordinary people were justified in protesting, and throughout Chinese history, such popular rebellions brought down numerous dynasties.

Thus, as with rulers in Western Europe, we see imperial authorities in China putting forward an idea of the state as a moral authority responsible for upholding an order rooted in natural law, albeit one defined by Confucian orthodoxy and ancient ideas of cosmic justice rather than by the Judeo-Christian tradition. And even more so than in Europe, where responsibility for moral order was divided between the church and the state, the Chinese state had sole responsibility for upholding this order. Confucianism was directly attached to the state, becoming the official state ideology during the Western Han dynasty (156–87 BC), and it never resided in an institution of its own.[19]

In sum, governance in China equaled moral rectification, and government authorities were explicitly responsible for the correction of immoral behavior.[20] It is not surprising that the historical record in China testifies to the importance of retributive justice and the production of moral order in the state's public rhetoric, governance initiatives, and bureaucratic institutions. In the rest of this section, we examine how imperial authorities promoted this idea of the state through three main strategies: initiatives for moral education of the public, moral codes of conduct for its officials, and punishment of poorly performing officials through institutions of retributive justice.

The Moral State as a Promoter of Moral Subjects

The imperial state's initiatives for moral rectification targeted both the mass public as well as its own bureaucratic agents. These initiatives included public education programs and curricula – community meetings where local officials gave lectures to ordinary people on guidelines for

---

[18] S. Lei and Y. Tong, *Social Protest in Contemporary China, 2003–2010: Transitional Pains and Regime Legitimacy*, Routledge, 2014.

[19] Ibid., 30–31.

[20] Chi-yun Chen, "Orthodoxy as a Mode of Statecraft: The Ancient Concept of Cheng," in *Orthodoxy in Late Imperial China*, edited by Liu Kwang-ching, University of California Press, 1990, 27–52, cited in Patricia M. Thornton, *Disciplining the State: Virtue, Violence, and State-Making in Modern China*, vol. 283, Harvard University Council on East Asian, 2007.

proper behavior at home as well as in society. For the public, the importance of moral order was thus an explicit priority promoted through public education by imperial authorities, rather than an implicit assumption known only to experts and elites who were educated in legal codes.[21]

County magistrates, the lowest level of formal government during the seventeenth and eighteenth centuries, were responsible for public moral education, in addition to tax collection, public works, and settling legal disputes. To regulate public morality, county magistrates were in charge of scheduling regular public lectures, organizing rituals to pay homage to local deities, and disciplining wrongdoers, both within government and in society.[22]

In the countryside, these activities were organized through the village compact system. Mandated in 1670, village compact meetings convened villagers for elaborate ceremonies at which an official lecturer read and explained each of the injunctions in the Sacred Edict, which contained sixteen maxims on proper behavior in all domains of life. At the meeting were also publicly posted lists or registers – "ledgers of merit and demerit" – of villagers who had performed virtuous and immoral acts. Such lists were posted in public places known as "exposition pavilions" alongside imperial edicts, and evil deeds would remain in the pavilions until wrongdoers had made amends.[23] Citing a Qing dynasty handbook for county magistrates, Javed notes that the imperial government motivated these initiatives explicitly in terms of their importance for maintaining social stability and ensuring the obedience of the public in a variety of ways, from refraining from criminal behavior to paying taxes.[24]

---

[21] Philip C. C. Huang, *Civil Justice in China: Representation and Practice in the Qing*, Stanford University Press, 1996.

[22] Robert J. Antony, "Subcounty Officials, the State, and Local Communities in Guangdong Province, 1644–1860," *Cornell East Asia Series* 114 (2002): 27–60, cited in Robert J. Antony and Jane Kate Leonard, "Dragons, Tigers, and Dogs: An Introduction," *Cornell East Asia Series* 114 (2002): 1–26; Philip C. C. Huang, *Code, Custom, and Legal Practice in China: The Qing and the Republic Compared*, Stanford University Press, 2001; Melissa Macauley, *Social Power and Legal Culture: Litigation Masters in Late Imperial China (Law, Society, and Culture in China)*, Stanford University Press, 1998; Bradly Reed, *Talons and Teeth: County Clerks and Runners in the Qing Dynasty*, Stanford University Press, 2000; Patricia M. Thornton, *Disciplining the State: Virtue, Violence, and State-Making in Modern China*, vol. 283, Harvard University Council on East Asian, 2007.

[23] Cynthia Joanne Brokaw, *The Ledgers of Merit and Demerit: Social Change and Moral Order in Late Imperial China*, vol. 1180, Princeton University Press, 2014.

[24] Jeffrey A. Javed, *Righteous Revolutionaries: Morality, Mobilization, and Violence in the Making of the Chinese State (Manuscript Draft)*, forthcoming.

There is also evidence that ordinary villagers were empowered to take an active role in upholding the imperial regime's moral order by monitoring local corruption and malfeasance. Drawing on a unique set of surveys conducted by the Japanese in North China from 1940 to 1942, Huang finds that out of forty-one lawsuits filed by villagers in three villages, five involved villagers suing local officials in court. In three of the cases, villagers were even able to get village and township officials removed, which suggested that the formal court system, at least sometimes, supported and legitimated popular participation in holding misbehaving officials accountable.[25]

The Moral State as a Promoter of Moral Officials

Imperial authorities also promoted the idea of the state as producer of moral order through the creation of formal codes for the moral conduct of bureaucrats and punishment of malfeasance. By the eighteenth century, *The Compendium of Magisterial Service*, a comprehensive handbook for county magistrates, had been drafted and started with the exhortation that "the key to good local government lay in the magistrate's 'personal self' (*shen*)."[26] This observation, Huang notes, drew on the Confucian classic, *The Great Learning (Daxue)*, which defined the Confucian scholar-official as an individual who pursues learning in order to "cultivate the self morally in order to bring order to the family, thus to government the state, and thus to bring peace to the empire." Benevolent government (*renzhi*) was literally government of men with moral character (*renzhi*).[27] Questions on these moral principles were a core part of the examination given to aspiring scholar-bureaucrats.

This ideal of the moral official was also expressed in *The Great Learning* through the concept of "parent-officials" (*fumuguan*), or officials who love the people as parents love their children. Such expectations did not arise from social embeddedness. County magistrates were rotated across localities so they lacked personal or community ties to their constituents. Instead, these moral responsibilities, conceptualized as strongly as familial obligations, were promoted through *state* initiatives directed toward both bureaucrats and the public. Official Qing documents often referred to county magistrates as "those who love the people" (*qinmin zhi*

[25] Philip C. C. Huang, *Civil Justice in China: Representation and Practice in the Qing*, Stanford University Press, 1996.
[26] Ibid.   [27] Ibid.

guan). Huang observes that the word *qin* means both parental love, as in the terms for father (*fuqin*) and mother (*muqin*), as well as "close to" as in *qinjin*. County magistrates were thus not only officials who loved the people, but also those closest to the people. As the face of the state, it was thus particularly important that they "be moral men who were benevolent and kindly toward their subjects."

Conceptualizing local officials as parent figures encouraged ordinary people to react emotionally to their behavior. By defining officials as parent figures who teach their people what is right and what is wrong because they love them infused an affective component to how ordinary people evaluated – and were encouraged by higher authorities to evaluate – local officials. An official who failed to do right by his people – who puts his own interests above those of the public, who embezzles public funds, or engages in predatory extraction – was seen to be as repugnant and unnatural as a parent who did not love his children.

The Moral State as a Punisher of Immoral Officials

An essential component of the state's depiction of itself as the producer of moral order was its continuous battle against immorality. Coercive power was important to state building in China not only – or even primarily – in terms of military resources for defense against external threats but also for combatting enemies and criminals among the state's own agents. This battle enabled imperial authorities to portray themselves as the protagonist in a fight against moral wrongdoing and decay. The narrative of the morally superior bureaucratic principal rooting out immoral bad apples among local state agents was repeated all the way down throughout the government to the grassroots levels. Huang notes that even county magistrates at the lowest level of the formal bureaucracy "portrayed themselves as moral gentlemen who had to battle constantly the moral depravity of the staff on which they relied for day-to-day operations."[28] Javed cites a Qing-dynasty county magistrate handbook drawing on the Rites of Zhou from more than 2,000 years ago (1046–256 BC) exhorting county officials to "signalize the good, separate the bad." By rooting out and punishing of evil, county officials could thus establish "the influence and reputation of their virtue."[29]

---

[28] Ibid.
[29] Jeffrey A. Javed, *Righteous Revolutionaries: Morality, Mobilization, and Violence in the Early Years of the People's Republic of China (Manuscript Draft)*, forthcoming.

In addition to promoting a political culture stressing the state's role in the creation of moral order, imperial authorities also developed bureaucratic institutions for retributive justice to enforce moral order. The prioritization of retributive justice is evident in the considerable effort invested into creating elaborate bureaucratic and legal codes on corruption and malfeasance. As far back as the eighth and ninth centuries, imperial authorities recognized the importance of criminalizing political corruption. Tang imperial law defined corruption as illicit official behavior crossing the boundary between the "public" (*gong*) and the "private" (*si*).[30] As Huang observes, this approach reinforced the image of the imperial state as benevolent and parental, helped it to maintain its absolute authority, and kept the political system from developing in the direction of liberal-democratic civil rights.[31]

Rather than leaving it only to social norms and ordinary citizens to pressure officials to live up to ideals, or creating independent courts to administer punishment through the rule of law, imperial authorities made the performance evaluation system the backbone of their bureaucratic approach to retributive justice. In this system, which was established during the time of the Yongzheng emperor during the seventeenth century and still exists in a version today, officials were assigned performance targets as well as deadlines for meeting those targets by their superiors at the next higher level of government. Annual reviews were conducted, and promotions and punishments were implemented accordingly. At the local level, county magistrates had performance targets to meet for tax collection and social order. The county magistrate's superior officer at the prefectural level set deadlines for the completion of tax collection and the resolution of serious crimes. Failure to meet these targets and deadlines could result in the recording of a demerit, a fine, a demotion, or dismissal from office.[32]

In addition to an annual examination of results (*kaocheng*), every three years there was a "great reckoning" (*daji*). During each "great reckoning," prefectural officials would prepare a personnel report for each county official and submit it to the provincial treasurer and provincial judge for review and comment. The governors and governor-generals of

[30] Patricia M. Thornton, *Disciplining the State: Virtue, Violence, and State-Making in Modern China*, vol. 283, Harvard University Council on East Asian, 2007.
[31] Philip C. C. Huang, *Civil Justice in China: Representation and Practice in the Qing*, Stanford University Press, 1996.
[32] Ibid.

each province would also review the administrative accomplishments and behavior of the forty or fifty county magistrates in their province and then submit them to the Board of Civil Office in Beijing for review. The Board office in Beijing then sorted the performance reports for all county magistrates in the country into three categories: outstanding, satisfactory, and unsatisfactory. Outstanding magistrates were rewarded with audience with the emperor and often a promotion. Satisfactory magistrates were retained.[33] Unsatisfactory magistrates were investigated and punished on the basis of the findings.

As we would expect based on a retributive justice model, punishment for poor performance was meted out not simply for deterring future misbehavior but in accordance with the severity of the moral violation. Bureaucratic investigations, for example, invested substantial time in assessing the reasons for the wrongdoing. If authorities had simply been using punishment to deter future wrongdoing, such efforts to assess the intentions of the suspect would have been unnecessary. Authorities not only devoted substantial time to determining the intentions of the wrongdoer but also adjusted the severity of the punishment in accordance with the results of their investigations in accordance with the retributive justice principle of "just deserts." Punishment was more severe for local officials when authorities determined they had committed administrative violations deliberately in pursuit of private interest than for officials who seemed to have committed the same violations out of neglect or incompetence. Authorities also prioritized punishment of wrongdoers over rehabilitation, consistent with a retributive justice model of punishment.

The state's prioritization of retributive justice is also evident in the amount of effort it invested into distinguishing gradations of moral violations and specifying punishments according to these nuances. Administrative codes as far back as the seventh and eighth centuries distinguished clearly between poor performance by government officials that violated moral values and performance problems that did not. Moral violations – referred to as crimes of "private interest" (*sizui*) – were defined as transgressions committed "owing to [the pursuit of] private interests, or if the act were intentional in nature, and not due to an administrative oversight." Administrative violations, however, were

---

[33] Satisfactory magistrates were generally retained and continued to have their conduct evaluated in "four-column registers" which listed individual ratings for "integrity" (*caoshou*), "administrative performance" (*zhengshi*), "talent" (*caijiu*), and age/physical fitness (*nianli*). Philip C. C. Huang, ibid.

ones that were committed unintentionally and where "the official's private interests were not involved." As a result, following a retributive justice principle of just deserts, administrative violations were classified as lighter violations (*gongzui*) with lighter penalties.[34]

Similar practices were continued by the Qing imperial government. Authorities invested time and effort into examining the reasons for violations of administrative rules. The administrative code categorized "unsatisfactory" performance by local officials into two different categories: problems due to lack of capacity and problems with moral character. During the Qing period, poor performance resulting from lack of capacity or lack of oversight was defined as issues related to old age (*nianlao*), infirmity (*youji*), instability (*fuzao*), lack of ability (*caili buji*), and nonfeasance of duty (*piruan wuwei*). Poor performance resulting from defects in moral character included issues resulting from avarice (*tan*), cruelty (*ku*), and impropriety (*bujin*).[35] If poor performance was determined to result from immoral intentions, these violations were then classified as criminal errors. Examples of such criminal errors included "corruption" (*tanwu*), defined as when the "official in question or his subordinates or family members intentionally withheld grain or money from the public coffers," and "depravity" (*tanlie*), defined as when officials "misused their authority to obtain resources forcefully or violated social norms."[36]

Bureaucratic discipline in China, therefore, was not simply about catching officials who were breaking administrative rules, a task that is relatively straightforward. Instead, investigations of wrongdoing were largely about *why* officials violated the rules. Consistent with a retributive justice model of punishment, higher-level bureaucratic principals made costly efforts to ascertain the reasons for these violations and

---

[34] *Da Qing Luli Huitong Xinzuan*, Wenhai chubanshe, 1966, cited in Patricia M. Thornton, *Disciplining the State: Virtue, Violence, and State-Making in Modern China*, vol. 283, Harvard University Council on East Asian, 2007.

[35] Those who violated administrative rules set by the Board of Civil Office had their cases reviewed and classified under one of eight legal categories (*bafa*) for which an official could be impeached. Patricia M. Thornton, *Disciplining the State: Virtue, Violence, and State-Making in Modern China*, vol. 283, Harvard University Council on East Asian, 2007.

[36] "Other charges stemming from the deliberate committing of crimes include the appropriation of embezzlement of resources from the public (*tanzang*), extortion (*lesuo*), and bribery (*shouhui*)." Patricia M. Thornton, *Disciplining the State: Virtue, Violence, and State-Making in Modern China*, vol. 283, Harvard University Council on East Asian, 2007.

to identify the particular individuals who would be assigned legal as well as moral responsibility for them.

Punishment of misbehavior among local state agents was public, severe, and connected to the seriousness of the moral violation, which showed the public that central authorities and higher-level bureaucratic principals were essential as champions of society's moral order. Retributive justice was clearly a higher priority than procedural justice. Suspects of moral violations were presumed guilty rather than innocent. Officials who were investigated for the moral crimes of avarice and cruelty and who were found innocent were dismissed and barred from future public office simply for being suspect.[37] Even local officials found guilty of wrongdoing due to relatively less serious moral violations were impeached and publicly dismissed in disgrace.[38] To make up for missing public funds, an individual's assets – and the assets of his family members – could be confiscated. In extreme cases, family members were even sold into servitude to make up the debt.[39]

Strategic Production of Corruption and Malfeasance

Imperial authorities promoted this narrative of a moral state waging war against its immoral agents as a deliberate strategy for shifting the blame for poor performance on to the shoulders of local officials. Local officials were set up to fail in a number of ways. First were the central government's unfunded mandates for local governments. Local governments were responsible for a wide range of infrastructural, military, and public goods provision expenses; yet they received very little fiscal support from the center. County officials who failed to achieve mandated targets on their performance contracts or who tried to shift public funds around creatively in order to complete these tasks were thus vulnerable to charges of illegally shifting funds (*nuoyong*); intentionally withholding money from public coffers, or "corruption" (*tanwu*); misusing their authority to obtain resources, or "depravity" (*tanlie*); or the embezzlement of

---

[37] Patricia M. Thornton, *Disciplining the State: Virtue, Violence, and State-Making in Modern China*, vol. 283, Harvard University Council on East Asian, 2007.

[38] Thomas A. Metzger, *The Internal Organization of Ch'ing Bureaucracy: Legal, Normative, and Communication Aspects*, vol. 7, Harvard University Press, 1973.

[39] Feng Erkang, *Yongzheng zhuan* (Biography of Yongzheng), Renmin chubanshe, 1985, 143–44, 147, cited in Patricia M. Thornton, *Disciplining the State: Virtue, Violence, and State-Making in Modern China*, vol. 283, Harvard University Council on East Asian, 2007.

resources from the public (*tanzang*).[40] Even underperformance due to lack of resources or capacity put local officials at risk for accusations of moral failings.

Second were administrative and legal codes that made local officials accountable not only for their own wrongdoing but also for the wrong-doing of everyone reporting to them, as well as the wrongdoing of all their predecessors in their position, even when they had no knowledge of these violations. Together, these two conditions made it nearly impossible for local officials *not* to be guilty of what the law defined as moral violations. Thornton finds that embezzlement among magistrates only played a clear role in one-fifth of the cases submitted for investigation by the Grand Secretariat during the Yongzheng period. Most cases were actually about mishandling of public funds that had "either been transferred to incoming magistrates by their predecessors, or were due to public works projects or military needs assigned by the center that could not be funded through very small central transfers."[41] Cases of tax arrears, or the failure of local governments to deliver their quota of tax payments to the center, were almost always categorized as criminal violations associated with political corruption (*tanwu, tanlie,* or *tanzang*). Thus, rather than fault ordinary people for failing to comply with the central government's demands for taxes, the center instead placed the blame for underpayment of central taxes on local officials and redefined the problem in terms of the moral failures of local officials.[42]

Third, the discretion given to local agents of the state also worked against them. By categorizing civil matters as "minor," the center deliberately avoided elaborating and standardizing the legal code to give local magistrates acting as representatives of the emperor leeway over interpretation. This strategy enabled higher-level principals to assign responsibility for interpretations resulting in bad outcomes to local agents and to blame them for "moral failures" when the public was unhappy with the outcome.[43]

Pressures on local officials were in fact so high that many people nominated for local offices did not want them and tried to decline them. Though not part of the formal bureaucracy, the *xiangbao* was

[40] Patricia M. Thornton, *Disciplining the State: Virtue, Violence, and State-Making in Modern China*, vol. 283, Harvard University Council on East Asian, 2007.
[41] Ibid.   [42] Ibid.
[43] Philip C. C. Huang, *Civil Justice in China: Representation and Practice in the Qing*, Stanford University Press, 1996.

a subcounty quasi-official for the local magistrate, overseeing the governance of several villages, and the lowest level agent of the state during the
Qing period. This post, Huang notes, "was often seen as a thankless
burden, to be avoided if at all possible." His examination of records in
Baodi county finds many cases of "nominated *xiangbao* seeking to avoid
the proffered appointment."[44] The same phenomenon persisted into the
Republican period. Based on his examination of documents from 120
cases of the appointment and removal of village heads in Shunyi county
near Beijing, Huang dryly comments, "The proportion of men who sought
to decline the 'honor' of being village head exceeds the proportion who
declined the *xiangbao* position in Baodi."[45]

RETRIBUTIVE JUSTICE, REVOLUTIONARY MOBILIZATION, AND LEGITIMATING THE MAOIST STATE

Mao and the Chinese Communist Party redefined the particular behaviors exemplifying virtue and morality. But the new party-state continued
to portray itself as a producer of moral order and to promote what
Lucian Pye once called the "enthusiasm for singling out enemies" in
Chinese political culture.[46] And it continued to use similar strategies
for doing so – moral indoctrination of both the public and its cadres, and
the use of retributive justice and punishment to enforce the new moral
order. As had been the case in the imperial period, the Maoist state
deployed its coercive resources not against external but internal enemies,
allying itself with the public against corrupt local officials. When class
proved to be an insufficiently salient identity for political mobilization,
the new communist authorities returned to the "popular tropes of good
and evil officials" that had been promoted by authorities during the
imperial period.[47] Corrupt local officials continued to be the bad guys,
now an impediment to revolutionary progress. In setting the stage for the

[44] Ibid.
[45] Philip C. C. Huang, *The Peasant Economy and Social Change in North China*, Stanford
University Press, 1985. For the Qing period, Thornton's research into the heavy-handed
investigation of local government failures to deliver taxes to the central government also
suggests that there was a "steady attrition of experienced personnel in the lowest ranks
of officialdom." Patricia M. Thornton, *Disciplining the State: Virtue, Violence, and
State-Making in Modern China*, vol. 283, Harvard University Council on East Asian,
2007.
[46] Lucian W. Pye, *The Spirit of Chinese Politics*, 2nd ed., Harvard University Press, 1992, 67.
[47] Jeffrey A. Javed, *Righteous Revolutionaries: Morality, Mobilization, and Violence in the
Early Years of the People's Republic of China (Manuscript Draft)*, forthcoming.

Cultural Revolution, for example, Mao pinpointed morally bankrupt local officials as the enemy that the party still needed to battle: "In our state at present approximately one-third of the power is in the hands of the enemy or of the enemy's sympathizers. We have been going for fifteen years and we now control two-thirds of the realm. At present you can buy a [party] branch secretary for a few packs of cigarettes, not to mention marrying his daughter."[48]

The Maoist State as a Punisher of Immoral Officials

The CCP's first anti-corruption initiatives date as far back as the civil war in the 1930s when it governed only parts of two provinces in China as the Chinese Soviet Republic.[49] Agencies for bureaucratic discipline established after 1949 in the People's Republic of China (PRC) had their institutional roots in this earlier period and were modeled after the Soviet system. The Worker-Peasant Supervisory Commission was established during the Chinese Soviet Republic period, in large part to prevent the corruption and bureaucratism that had delegitimized the Republican state, and became the Central Supervision Commission one month after the CCP came to power in 1949. Given a higher status than central government ministries, the Central Supervision Commission was empowered to review the actions of government agencies and agents and to investigate accusations from ordinary citizens of malfeasance and wrongdoing. Local commissions reporting to this central commission were created at each level of government from the province down to the county.[50]

Implementation of the CCP's cadre evaluation system also began in the early years of the PRC. Starting in 1954, each county's organization department was made responsible for regular personnel evaluations for all county and subcounty employees. Until the Cultural Revolution halted institutionalization on all fronts in the late 1960s, the cadre evaluation system involved an annual assessment (*jianding*) of each cadre's performance. Each cadre first prepared a self-assessment, which he or she then

---

[48] Frederick C. Teiwes, *Politics and Purges in China: Rectification and the Decline of Party Norms, 1950–1965*," 537, ME Sharpe (1979), cited by Patricia M. Thornton, *Disciplining the State: Virtue, Violence, and State-Making in Modern China*, vol. 283, Harvard University Council on East Asian, 2007.

[49] Xiaobo Lü, *Cadres and Corruption: The Organizational Involution of the Chinese Communist Party*, Stanford University Press, 2000.

[50] Ibid.

discussed in a group meeting with colleagues. One person then summarized the group's opinions of the cadre's performance and submitted it up to the county party branch, which would add their own comments and then file it in the cadre's dossier.[51]

The new party-state took the institutionalization of bureaucratic discipline and punishment seriously. Cadres for the organization department, which was in charge of top-down oversight of bureaucrats, were often younger, better educated, and recent recruits to the Party. The county organization department in charge of annual grassroots cadre evaluations worked closely with and was often situated in offices next to the county supervision committee, which investigated cases of wrongdoing and imposed punishments.[52] State supervisory institutions, however, were never autonomous from the CCP.[53]

Promoting Moral Citizens and Officials by Mobilizing Participation in Retributive Justice

As had imperial authorities, the new Maoist state also prioritized the importance of moral education for both the public and for its own new officials. As Strauss comments: "[A] vertically integrated unitary state of education and moral indoctrination for the untutored population was presumed to be part of the answer to most questions."[54] But while the imperial state had pursued top-down moral education delivered by elites to the masses and top-down sanctioning of lower-level agents by higher-level authorities, the Maoist state shifted to an approach of moral "learning by doing": ordinary citizens and the party-state's new cadres would receive their education in the CCP's new moral order by directly participating in its enforcement.

Mass Participation in Monitoring Local Officials. During the Soviet Republic period, the CCP experimented with different ways of involving ordinary citizens in monitoring local officials. One type of monitoring

---

[51] Patricia M. Thornton, *Disciplining the State: Virtue, Violence, and State-Making in Modern China*, vol. 283, Harvard University Council on East Asian, 2007.

[52] Ibid.

[53] Xiaobo Lü, *Cadres and Corruption: The Organizational Involution of the Chinese Communist Party*, Stanford University Press, 2000.

[54] Julia Strauss, "Morality, Coercion and State Building by Campaign in the Early PRC: Regime Consolidation and After, 1949–1956," *The China Quarterly*, no. 188 (December 21, 2006): 896.

institution was called "Shock Teams."[55] Three or four people on a Shock Team would visit government agencies, sometimes pretending to ask for assistance, and then report on the responsiveness of officials in these agencies. Another type of institution was a system of "worker and peasant reporters" who were embedded in local government offices and acted as informants to report corruption to supervisors at various levels.[56]

Even in a relatively centralized and top-down campaign like the Three-Anti Campaign – initiated in 1952 to combat "corruption, squandering, and bureaucratism" – the role of ordinary people was expanded. As a centralized campaign, higher level authorities coordinated campaign tactics and sought to construct formal institutions to implement the campaign. An Austerity Inspection Commission, for example, was formed at each level to coordinate campaign efforts across the party disciplinary inspection commissions, the administrative supervision commissions, the procuratorate, and the courts.[57] But despite this top-down approach, even the Three-Anti Campaign enlarged the space for ordinary people to participate in the reporting of corruption and malfeasance.[58] Lu estimates that more than 90 percent of the cases of graft and embezzlement investigated during the Three-Anti Campaign arose from the reports of ordinary people.[59]

Mass Participation in Retributive Justice and "the Expropriation of Moral Outrage." Participation in the monitoring of local officials had been allowed and somewhat encouraged even during the imperial period, but the imperial state did not have formal channels incorporating popular participation in the punishing of officials. For the first time in China's history, Mao authorized ordinary citizens and newly minted grassroots cadres to sanction officials for poor performance and malfeasance. Rather than relying on lectures to passive audiences, the CCP under Mao trained citizens and new cadres in the new moral order by mobilizing them to take action and personally punish those deemed immoral enemies of the revolution. By 1959, Mao had turned away from formal institutions for

---

[55] Shock teams engaged in what development practitioners now call social audits or "mystery shopper" evaluations.

[56] Xiaobo Lü, *Cadres and Corruption: The Organizational Involution of the Chinese Communist Party*, Stanford University Press, 2000.

[57] Ibid.

[58] Patricia M. Thornton, *Disciplining the State: Virtue, Violence, and State-Making in Modern China*, vol. 283, Harvard University Asia Center, 2007.

[59] Xiaobo Lü, *Cadres and Corruption: The Organizational Involution of the Chinese Communist Party*, Stanford University Press, 2000.

retributive justice to focus solely the use of mass campaigns to promote his revolutionary moral order. During the Great Leap Forward, the state supervisory apparatus was abolished, and virtually no bureaucratic institutions for control or discipline operated between 1959 and 1979.[60]

Under Mao, the CCP clearly sought to do what Barrington Moore calls "the expropriation of moral outrage." Maoist campaigns carefully staged "struggle sessions" at the local level. Visiting teams of officials from higher levels would select victims, frame and publicize their personal grievances as violations against the public and class struggle,[61] and organize spectators to join in deliberations and sentencing of the wrongdoers. In this way, the state took private matters and turned them into public fodder for political mobilization and legitimation of the new party-state. As Strauss notes, the CCP's objective was to leverage "the emotional affect and moral outrage of its citizens at polar ends of society – from poor peasant to privileged intellectual."[62]

One example of this approach was the ad hoc people's tribunal allowed by the CCP immediately after taking power. According to the Organic Regulations of the People's Regulations promulgated in 1950, these impromptu local courts had the power to arrest, try, and sentence criminals, political enemies, and corrupt officials on the spot, including to death.[63] Such extrajudicial trials and executions were framed by the new regime as "revolutionary justice" but sometimes differed little from state-sanctioned vigilantism. Thornton discusses one example from a 1951 Tianjin newspaper report that illustrates the tendency toward extremes of trial by mob:

The Beijing Municipal People's Government held a huge public meeting for the accusation of counterrevolutionaries in on May 20, 1951. Speaking before the aroused crowd, Lou Ruiqing, Minister of Public Security, "suggested" that some 220 criminals be sentenced to death. He was followed by Mayor Peng Zhen, who

---

[60] Ibid.
[61] Ann Anagnost, *National Past-Times: Narrative, Representation, and Power in Modern China*, Duke University Press, 1997.
[62] Julia Strauss, "Morality, Coercion and State Building by Campaign in the Early PRC: Regime Consolidation and After, 1949–1956," *The China Quarterly*, no. 188 (December 21, 2006): 904; see also Jeffrey A. Javed, *Righteous Revolutionaries: Morality, Mobilization, and Violence in the Early Years of the People's Republic of China (Manuscript Draft)*, forthcoming.
[63] Alice Tay, "Law in Communist China: Part One," *Sydney Law Review* 6, no. 2 (1968): 153–172, cited in Patricia M. Thornton, *Disciplining the State: Virtue, Violence, and State-Making in Modern China*, vol. 283, Harvard University Council on East Asian, 2007.

wound up the drama by saying: "What shall we do with such a group of beasts as these vicious despots, bandits, traitors, and special agents?" "Shoot them!" the audience shouted. "Right, they should be shot," the mayor replied. "Following this meeting we shall hand over the cases to the military court of the Municipal Military Control Commission for conviction. Tomorrow, conviction; the next day, execution." The crowd responded with wild applause and loud cheers.[64]

Struggle sessions and mass accusation meetings organized for land reform and the Campaign to Suppress Counterrevolutionaries also effectively expropriated personal grievances for regime consolidation. The people who were chosen to "speak bitterness" during these public meetings were specially chosen for the degree to which they would be likely to engage the emotions of the crowd – the very old, the very young, and women.[65] As Strauss notes, the public accusation meeting was "quite literally, a show put on by the new state, replete with staging, props, stock characters, rough working scripts, dramatic peaks, and a good round of final applause." When sufficient landlords could not be produced, local officials under the old regime filled in for them. These "state-managed spectacles," organized in every urban area and in most villages, were not the "formalized, bureaucratic affairs of woodenly delivered show trials of the Soviet Union." Instead, they were "deliberately used as a heuristic device to engage the emotions of the public, whip up hatred against designated class enemies and mobilize the masses into positive support for the regime."[66]

Such strategies served to define and enforce the communist moral order by drawing lines between the virtuous and the evil, or what Javed calls "moral boundary work." These strategies were likely informed by Mao's observations of peasant repertoires of contentious action against local landlords and officials discussed in his 1927 Hunan report.[67] Angry peasants in the rural uprisings of the early twentieth century, for example, would denounce local tyrants and corrupt officials by calling for their names to be put on registers similar to the ones listing virtuous and

---

[64] Patricia M. Thornton, *Disciplining the State: Virtue, Violence, and State-Making in Modern China*, vol. 283, Harvard University Council on East Asian, 2007.

[65] Julia Strauss, "Morality, Coercion and State Building by Campaign in the Early PRC: Regime Consolidation and After, 1949–1956," *The China Quarterly*, no. 188 (December 21, 2006): 908.

[66] Ibid., 906.

[67] Jeffrey A. Javed, *Righteous Revolutionaries: Morality, Mobilization, and Violence in the Early Years of the People's Republic of China (Manuscript Draft)*, forthcoming.

immoral individuals that the imperial state had implemented in village compact meetings.

Struggle sessions, as well as Communist propaganda techniques, also drew on the narratives, theatricality, and emotional charge of traditional folk operas, a common form of popular entertainment during the imperial period. Communist propaganda troupes performed "land reform operas" around the countryside, which appropriated the music, costuming, and narratives used by traditional operas to dramatize the struggle between good and evil officials, as well as the "benevolent center and the abusive localities."[68] As Hung notes, traditional operas had been "saturated with stories about the plight of commoners under evil officials, miserable subjects appealing to benevolent and parent-like higher authorities, and how the bad officials were penalized and avenged in the end."[69] The CCP simply took the place of the emperor and his court as the hero in these stories.

Punishments organized for the climaxes of struggle sessions, moreover, followed the "just deserts" principle of retributive justice, rather than resulting in a completely ad hoc manner from mob violence. This violence was not indiscriminate. Instead, the CCP clearly meted out different degrees of punishment to different kinds of wrongdoers during struggle sessions, promising leniency to those who confessed and agreed to follow the CCP, while executing only those perceived to be the most egregious transgressors. Citing a 1950 *People's Daily* editorial by the bureau head of the East China government, Javed notes that local governments in Anhui and Jiangsu released similar statements:

The struggle against the landlord class adopted a policy of differential treatment. Regarding landlords and local bullies guilty of great crimes, the government should actively arrest them and bring them to justice. This not only facilitates mobilizing the masses, it also can avoid the occurrence of random beatings and killings. Regarding unlawful landlords who sabotage land reform, they should be punished according to the Regulations on the Punishment of Unlawful Landlords – [officials] should widely use the People's Courts along with mass movements to resolutely suppress them. Regarding regular landlords who have committed wrongdoings, [officials] should mobilize the masses to carry out face-to-face 'reasoning struggles'. Regarding landlords who obey the law and bow their heads before the masses, they should be treated with magnanimity.[70]

---

[68] Ibid.

[69] Ho-fung Hung, *Protest with Chinese Characteristics: Demonstrations, Riots, and Petitions in the Mid-Qing Dynasty*, Columbia University Press, 2013, cited in Jeffrey A. Javed, ibid.

[70] Rao Shushi, "Summary of Experiences with Classic Land Reform Experiments in East China," *People's Daily*, December 20, 1950.

In a particularly graphic illustration of punishment according to the just principle of "an eye for an eye," peasants in Guangdong province "went so far as to use ritualized cannibalism to punish targets, mimicking the cruel local magistrate's practice of forcing family members, often father-son and brother-brother pairs, to kill and eat parts of the victim while he still lived."[71]

Also consistent with a model of retributive justice was the participation of third-party observers in the punishment of wrongdoers rather than just the immediate victims. Although struggle sessions started with individual victims stating their grievances against landlords and officials, the explicit objective of the struggle session was to redefine these wrongdoers as enemies of the general public. Organizers aimed to persuade everyone in attendance to think of themselves as the "aggrieved" and to take out their aggression on the wrongdoer. At times, this spontaneous violence could get out of hand, and official regulations were implemented to prohibit "reckless beatings and killings." A directive on land reform mass mobilization encouraged this violence: "When some peasants in the course of struggle are agitated by righteous indignation and spontaneously attack landlords, we do not right then and there pour cold water [on them], which would hurt the masses' mood."

Cadre Participation in Retributive Justice. The CCP also indoctrinated new party members and consolidated their control over their local state agents by mobilizing the participation of grassroots cadres in the implementation of retributive justice against their corrupt colleagues, some of whom were holdovers from the old regime. As did imperial authorities, the CCP promoted the battle of good rulers against evil officials and counterrevolutionaries at every level down to the grass roots. As Lu notes, during the CCP's 1951 Three-Anti Campaign against corruption, squandering, and bureaucratism, newly minted local cadres of the CCP were encouraged by higher-level officials to speak out and expose their corrupt superiors "without fear of repercussions." Such power could be exhilarating for new converts to the party. According to a retired official interviewed by Lu, "many cadres, particularly young, new cadres, felt that no other political parties would have let lower-rank staff openly chastise

---

[71] Lucien Bianco, "Peasant Movements," *The Cambridge History of China* 13, no. 2 (1986): 311–12, cited by Jeffrey A. Javed, *Righteous Revolutionaries: Morality, Mobilization, and Violence in the Early Years of the People's Republic of China (Manuscript Draft)*, forthcoming; see also Fernando Galbiati, *P'eng P'ai and the Hai-Lu-Feng Soviet*, Stanford University Press, 1985.

(*douzheng*) their superiors."[72] Such opportunities illustrated the PRC's "extraordinary efforts to mobilize the patriotic and moral commitments of basic-level cadres of poor peasant background (many of whom were not Party members at all)."[73]

Mobilizing the participation of cadres in struggle sessions and mass campaigns also helped to consolidate the party's control over its agents in that it forced officials to demonstrate their loyalties to the party by implementing harsh punishments against their colleagues and in some cases, friends. Initially, as Strauss notes, there was significant foot-dragging in the implementation of the 1950 campaign against counter-revolutionaries as many local officials felt that their colleagues from the previous regime simply needed intensive reeducation, denying that their own offices harbored counterrevolutionaries and opposing the necessity of shooting people. After, however, Luo Ruiqing, the minister of public security, publicly reprimanded most of the major cities in the south in 1951, city and local governments were forced to implement harsh punishments, including execution. This initiative, as Strauss notes, "stiffen[ed] the resolve and [overcame] the natural scruples of provincial and sub-provincial cadres, while expanding the directly coercive institutions of the state."[74]

DEGENERATION OF RETRIBUTIVE JUSTICE DURING THE CULTURAL REVOLUTION

After initial successes with regime consolidation in the early 1950s, the CCP embarked their most ambitious campaign yet in 1958 with the Great Leap Forward. The resulting famine and crisis of legitimacy, however, marked, as Shih observes, "nothing less than the demise of the CCP party-state as moral agent."[75] Anxious to shore up citizen confidence in their

---

[72] Xiaobo Lü, *Cadres and Corruption: The Organizational Involution of the Chinese Communist Party*, Stanford University Press, 2000.

[73] Julia Strauss, "Morality, Coercion and State Building by Campaign in the Early PRC: Regime Consolidation and After, 1949–1956," *The China Quarterly*, no. 188 (December 21, 2006): 903.

[74] Ibid., 904; see also Julia C. Strauss, "Paternalist Terror: The Campaign to Suppress Counterrevolutionaries and Regime Consolidation in the People's Republic of China, 1950–1953," *Comparative Studies in Society and History* 44, no. 1 (2002): 80–105.

[75] In the Great Leap Forward, "the Chinese moral regime reached its climax," and its huge failure signaled "nothing less than the demise of the CCP party-state as a moral agent." Chih-Yu Shih, "The Decline of a Moral Regime," *Comparative Political Studies* 27, no. 2 (July 1994): 272–301; Patricia M. Thornton, *Disciplining the State: Virtue, Violence, and*

ability to govern and renew the idea of the party-state as champions of a revolutionary moral order, the CCP subsequently embarked on a series of campaigns through the 1960s mobilizing citizens to attack their "true enemies" – corrupt and immoral local officials. During the Anti-Rightist Campaign, the Socialist Education Campaign (also known as the Four Cleanups), and ultimately, the Cultural Revolution, Mao mobilized the masses to attack party-state officials who "had become bureaucratic and corrupt."[76] Large numbers of officials were found guilty during these initiatives. Lu estimates that 3 percent of the 410,000 people who were investigated during the Five Anti Campaign started in March 1963 were found guilty and that in some places, as many as 7.6 percent were found to be involved in "stealing state assets."[77] Citizens who participated actively in these campaigns were rewarded with party membership. In the later stages of the Socialist Education Campaign, Lu reports that 940,000 new members were admitted to the Party in 1965, and 3.23 million in 1966, most of whom had been activists in the campaign.[78]

But such widespread mass mobilization to participate in retributive justice outside of formal institutions made it too easy for people to pursue personal vendettas and political advantage. Such campaigns created an incentive to engage proactively in accusing and punishing others to demonstrate one's "redness" and moral righteousness. Punishment and violence evolved into tools for obtaining personalistic benefits and political power, rather than as a way of upholding retributive justice and moral order. As punishment became capricious rather than principled, the party-state lost its moral authority.

Although mass campaigns during the Socialist Education Movement and the Cultural Revolution temporarily shored up support in the CCP, the party-state's claim to upholding retributive justice ultimately weakened during this period. With Mao locating immorality in the basic institutions of government, defining transgressions broadly, and enabling punishment without trial by judicial authorities or even investigations, local officials who had been trying to do their job became alienated and all too often unfairly persecuted. Public trust in the CCP's authority and institutions declined precipitously.

State-Making in Modern China, vol. 283, Harvard University Council on East Asian, 2007.
[76] Xiaobo Lü, *Cadres and Corruption: The Organizational Involution of the Chinese Communist Party*, Stanford University Press, 2000.
[77] Ibid.   [78] Ibid.

REINSTITUTIONALIZATION AND RETRIBUTIVE JUSTICE IN THE POST-MAO PERIOD

The chaos of the Cultural Revolution resulted in a breakdown of state institutions and legitimacy. During this period, Lu observes that "organizational constraints on individual cadres were ... the weakest in CCP history." He argues that immediately after the Cultural Revolution, corruption increased dramatically as fiscal resources began flowing through the system before the restoration of formal bureaucratic institutions of supervision and discipline.[79]

Rebuilding Bureaucratic Institutions of Supervision and Discipline

Seeking to reestablish order, government authorities in the post-Mao period turned back to the reinstatement of formal, institutionalized mechanisms for supervising and disciplining officials. This change in strategy eliminated the direct role of citizens in the punishment of corruption and malfeasance. Starting in 1977, discipline inspection committees (DICs) were reinstituted within the Party committees that existed at each level from the township up to the central government. Each level of government from the county upward also established a supervision bureau that was responsible for disciplining employees in government agencies.[80] Institutions such as party disciplinary commissions, government supervision bureaus, fiscal auditing agencies, anti-corruption bureaus, and public procuratorates were reinstated.[81] Staffing and resources to disciplinary institutions increased dramatically. Cai estimates that in Guangdong province, for example, the number of disciplinary agencies at the county level and higher increased by 2.6 times and the number of employees by 1.5 times.[82]

The primary mechanism implemented for top-down control of local officials was the cadre responsibility system (*gangwei zerenzhi*). Originally promoted by Liu Shaoqi in the 1960s as the administrative guarantee system (*baogan zhidu*), the cadre responsibility system was resurrected in 1979 after

---

[79] Ibid.

[80] Yongshun Cai, *State and Agents in China: Disciplining Government Officials*, Stanford University Press, 2014.

[81] Xiaobo Lü, *Cadres and Corruption: The Organizational Involution of the Chinese Communist Party*, Stanford University Press, 2000.

[82] Yongshun Cai, *State and Agents in China: Disciplining Government Officials*, Stanford University Press, 2014.

the start of reforms.[83] Resurrecting the long-standing Chinese institutions of performance contracts, a series of central directives between 1986 and 1989 mandated an annual performance evaluation for local officials.[84] In 1988, the first countywide implementation of performance contracts between township leaders and county governments took place in Henan province.[85]

A robust body of scholarship has suggested that the cadre evaluation system of the reform period has been an effective instrument used by higher-level authorities to discipline lower-level agents, especially at the lowest levels of the township and village. In the cadre evaluation system, cadres in the Party and government are assigned performance targets. Targets fall into three categories: soft, hard, and priority targets with "veto power." Soft targets are the lowest priority and refer to performance in domains such as cultural and social development. Hard targets typically involve economic development and public finance, such as a specific income per capita growth rate for the year or tax revenues to be submitted above. Priority targets "with veto power" usually involve the highest priorities of the central government as well as high priorities for specific localities. Although all targets are tied to the calculation of cadre salaries and bonuses, when cadres fail to achieve priority targets, their performance on all other targets is irrelevant and they are subject to removal from office.

In addition to veto targets, performance contracts also have "hard targets" and "soft targets." Hard targets are easily quantifiable targets that also have a major impact on prospects for bonuses and, for officials at the township level and higher, for promotion. Ong (2012) reports that in addition to salary penalties, higher-level principals also have other ways of sanctioning lower-level agents who fail to achieve hard targets. Counties, for example, sometimes rank all the townships in their county, from best to worst, in terms of their performance on hard targets. These rankings are not only circulated by the county government to all the townships, but in county meetings, township

---

[83] Lily L. Tsai, *Accountability without Democracy: Solidary Groups and Public Goods Provision in Rural China*, Cambridge University Press, 2007.

[84] Yasheng Huang, "Administrative Monitoring in China," *The China Quarterly* 143 (September 12, 1995): 830–31.

[85] Ministry of Organization, "Notice Regarding Implementation of the Annual Job Evaluation System for Leading Cadres of Local Party and Government Organs (Guanyu Shixing Defang Dangzeng Lingdao Ganbu Niandu Gongzuo Kaohe Zhidu de Tongzhi)," 1988, as cited in Richard J. Latham, "The Implications of Rural Reforms for Grass-Roots Cadres," in *The Political Economy of Reform in Post-Mao China*, edited by Elizabeth J. Perry and Christine Wong, 1985, Harvard University Asia Center, Harvard Contemporary China Series vol. 2, 169; Tony Saich, *The Blind Man and the Elephant: Analysing the Local State in China*, Routledge, 2009.

leaders are also seated according to their respective ranking to reinforce the importance of meeting the targets.[86,87]

Studies of the cadre evaluation system in China have shown that these bureaucratic sanctioning institutions have "teeth." A local official, quoted by Cai, notes, "Given the various 'one-item' veto responsibilities, we wish we could keep one eye open even when we sleep. We are anxious all the time, fearing that we will be required to take responsibility." Another county Party secretary comments, "Like scared birds, we are on high alert, worrying about production safety, sudden events, mass petitions, and other large-scale incidents that will result in punishment."[88]

Anti-Corruption Campaigns in the Post-Mao Period

During the 1980s, the CCP under Deng Xiaoping focused primarily on fostering economic growth and rebuilding institutions. During the Deng period, anti-corruption campaigns ceased to be a way of disciplining government officials. Despite the reestablishment of institutional mechanisms for bureaucratic supervision, however, corruption continued to plague the regime. Local disciplinary commissions often lacked autonomy from local officials who often intervened in corruption investigations and engaged in "local corruption protectionism."[89]

In 1989, things came to a head. Although the Tiananmen protests are often seen as pro-democracy demonstrations, corruption was a central concern for student protestors. The Chinese dissident Leng Wenbao, for example, noted that the demonstrations were in fact "primarily a protest against corruption."[90] Such concerns about the failure of the state to punish corruption and uphold retributive justice were the ones that resonated the most with urban residents.[91]

---

[86] Lynette H. Ong, *Prosper or Perish: Credit and Fiscal Systems in Rural China*, Cornell University Press, 2012.

[87] Lily L. Tsai, *Accountability without Democracy: Solidary Groups and Public Goods Provision in Rural China*, Cambridge University Press, 2007; see also Bill K. P. Chou, "Implementing the Reform of Performance Appraisal in China's Civil Service," *China Information* 19, no. 1 (March 22, 2005): 47–49.

[88] Yongshun Cai, *State and Agents in China: Disciplining Government Officials*, Stanford University Press, 2014.

[89] Xiaobo Lü, *Cadres and Corruption: The Organizational Involution of the Chinese Communist Party*, Stanford University Press, 2000.

[90] Carolyn L. Hsu, "Political Narratives and the Production of Legitimacy: The Case of Corruption in Post-Mao China," *Qualitative Sociology* 24, no. 1 (2001): 25–54.

[91] Craig J. Calhoun, *Neither Gods Nor Emperors: Students and the Struggle for Democracy in China*, University of California Press, 1997, 249.

Government authorities were quick to respond by invoking themselves as upholders of retributive justice in their public statements about the demonstration. Within weeks of the protests, the state media highlighted anti-corruption efforts in response to the "anger of the people." As Hsu notes, "the Party was still the main character, but instead of portraying itself as the victim, now it was the avenger working on behalf of its citizens." This change in rhetoric depicted the party-state as a moral champion, ready to respond to citizen concerns by punishing wrongdoers among its agents.[92]

Concrete actions backed these rhetorical responses. Manion argues that the subsequent 1989 anti-corruption campaign, with its strategy of widespread investigations and punishments, succeeded in pushing back corruption rates below a tipping point beyond which corruption would have overwhelmed the regime's enforcement resources.[93] Compared to the period between 1978 and 1986, when no provincial or central officials were investigated for corruption, seventy-eight provincial and central government officials were prosecuted between 1992 and 1997, including one member of the Politburo. These prosecutions also had teeth. In a study of 2,500 cases of corruption investigations of individual officials reported by the Procuratorial Daily from 1993 to 2010, Cai finds that 2,430 of these cases reported on the punishment meted out to convicted officials. Most were given prison sentences, but 2.9 percent were executed, and 14 percent were given either suspended death sentences or life in prison. By comparison, 0.5 percent of murder convictions in the United States result in the death sentence.

Such punishments again accorded with the principles of retributive justice, at least for the sample of cases reported by the government to the public. Disciplinary actions were portrayed as following the retributivist principle of just deserts, which dictates that punishment ought to be heavier when moral violations are more severe. Cai finds for a sample of 133 cases compiled for the period 1990–2005 that government officials who failed to fulfill their responsibilities but did not pursue personal gains received less severe punishments than those who benefited privately, holding other factors constant. Officials who were less directly responsible

---

[92] Carolyn L. Hsu, "Political Narratives and the Production of Legitimacy: The Case of Corruption in Post-Mao China," *Qualitative Sociology* 24, no. 1 (2001): 44.

[93] Melanie Manion, *Corruption by Design*, Harvard University Press, 2009, cited in Andrew Wedeman, "Anticorruption Campaigns and the Intensification of Corruption in China," *Journal of Contemporary China* 14, no. 42 (February 2005): 93–116.

for an event also experienced lighter punishments than those who were directly responsible.[94]

Although ordinary citizens no longer have the opportunity to participate directly in the punishment of corruption and malfeasance, the current-day government continues to make punishment of corruption severe and highly visible in order to alleviate the retributive justice concerns of the public. While it is unclear, as Wedeman argues, that such punishment successfully deters misbehavior, the "sound and fury" of these anti-corruption initiatives may still play an important role in signaling the intentions of government authorities to uphold a moral order.[95]

CONCLUSION

Throughout Chinese history, government authorities have promoted an idea of the state as the producer of moral order and the punisher of first resort. Chinese political culture has long viewed the state in the way Durkheim views it, as "above all, supremely, the organ of moral discipline."[96]

This view is not unique to China. As James Madison famously remarked in *The Federalist Papers*, "If men were angels, no government would be necessary." One of the primary functions of government, regardless of regime type and context, is to regulate the behavior of its agents and its citizens so that state and society operate predictably according to established values and normative principles, even when individuals may be tempted to do otherwise.

This chapter illustrates the central role of retributive justice strategies for sustaining a moral order and for signaling to the public that the state is doing its job. Even when – perhaps, especially when – the punishment of corruption and wrongdoing has tipped over into violent spectacle, these strategies have been surprisingly popular. E. P. Thompson has observed the same of eighteenth-century England where elites maintained public order and "the ritual of public execution was a necessary concomitant of a system of social discipline where a great deal depended upon theatre."[97]

[94] Yongshun Cai, *State and Agents in China: Disciplining Government Officials*, Stanford University Press, 2014.
[95] Andrew Wedeman, "Anticorruption Campaigns and the Intensification of Corruption in China," *Journal of Contemporary China* 14, no. 42 (February 2005): 94.
[96] Emile Durkheim, "The Division of Labour in Society," *Free Press* (first published 1893), 1964.
[97] Edward P. Thompson, "Patrician Society, Plebeian Culture," *Journal of Social History* 7, no. 4 (1974): 390.

One thing that is noteworthy about the Chinese case and other authoritarian contexts is the way in which authorities define citizen participation not as action taken to influence the selection of officials or the representation of societal interests, as participation is conceptualized in democratic theory, but as citizen action taken to monitor and/or sanction officials for misbehavior and malfeasance. The mass mobilization campaigns of the Maoist period gave new meaning to the idea of "rule by the people," the literal translation of "democracy" in Chinese. These campaigns conceptualized popular participation in politics, not as citizens voicing their interests in a policymaking process but as citizens participating in the identification and punishment of corruption and wrongdoing. To many in China, "rule by the people" does not connote representation but instead participation in governance and retributive justice.

As development interventions by international actors focus increasingly on encouraging citizen participation in monitoring and sanctioning to hold officials accountable, the case of China may be particularly relevant for understanding the trajectory of political development and state-building in developing contexts today. This may be ironic, given that many international actors hope to promote democracy alongside development; yet they fail to realize that participation to hold governments accountable is not the same as – and perhaps often substitutes for – participation to voice one's policy preferences and interests.

State builders in the developing world may also have – or at least think they have – more in common with the case of China for another reason. In contrast to nascent states in Western Europe, which faced urgent pressures of war and interstate competition as well as the need to forge national identities based on moral principles, Chinese state builders saw their main challenge as creating a cultural and social order that would enable its bureaucracy to expand its territorial reach and govern its increasingly heterogeneous population. It is perhaps not surprising that government authorities in developing countries where ethnic diversity is an issue and the state struggles to project its infrastructural power into the periphery find China a compelling model.

4

Evaluating the Impact of Retributive Justice on Citizen Evaluations of Government Authorities in Rural China

In the previous chapter, we examined the strategies that the Chinese state has employed at various points in history to address – and sometimes benefit from – citizen concerns about retributive justice. This chapter shows how retributive justice concerns shape citizen attitudes and behavior toward government authorities in China.

We begin with three narratives that ordinary people in rural China frequently use to explain what they expect from government authorities and how they make decisions about whether to participate in local governance and politics. These narratives emerged from open-ended qualitative interviews with randomly sampled households conducted in three different regions of rural China. This initial phase of the research was conducted in 2010–11 and helped to generate the hypotheses about retributive justice concerns in this study, even before Xi Jinping's current anti-corruption campaign heightened the political salience of retributive justice. Although the narratives related in the chapter will be familiar to many, I draw on them here to concretize the ways in which ordinary people speak about their desire for government authorities to uphold retributive justice and their concerns about engaging or cooperating with authorities who fail to do so.

The second part of the chapter provides experimental evidence for the hypothesis that citizen concerns about retributive justice play a role in their evaluations of government authorities and in their political behavior. If citizens care about retributive justice and the use of punishment to uphold moral order, then we should expect to see the following empirical relationships. First, we should expect punishment of corruption to increase citizen support of government authorities – even in the absence of evidence that levels of actual corruption have decreased. Second, we should see that anti-corruption punishment does not only increase citizen evaluations of government competence but it also signals to citizens that authorities share their moral commitments.

Through a series of experiments embedded in original, in-person field surveys administered in two regions of China in 2016–17, we provide evidence for these observable implications of a model of retributive justice. We find that citizens prefer government authorities who punish corruption and malfeasance, and we find that anti-corruption punishment carries as much or more weight than welfare provision or institutions for citizen participation, suggesting that retributive justice concerns can be just as important as concerns about distributive and procedural justice (and perhaps more so). Two of these experiments also utilize an innovative approach to mediation analysis with multiple mediators to examine the mechanisms through which top-down punishment affects citizen evaluations to provide additional evidence for a retributive justice theory. Consistent with this theory, these analyses suggest that government leaders who punish lower levels for corruption affect citizen preferences by increasing positive citizen evaluations of their moral character as well as their competence. In addition, we find that even for government authorities who do not, or cannot, succeed in other areas that are often believed to be main drivers of public support – economic growth, welfare provision, and institutions for democratic participation – citizen support for authorities who punish corruption remains the same – good news for authoritarian officials who hope to stay in power during economic downturns or avoid political reforms.

WHAT DO CITIZENS EXPECT OF THEIR GOVERNMENT
AUTHORITIES? HYPOTHESIS GENERATION AND QUALITATIVE
RESEARCH IN THREE COMMUNITIES

To develop an initial understanding of how ordinary people saw the government and how they evaluated government officials, I conducted open-ended, in-depth interviews together with Chinese research assistants in 2010–11 with thirty households randomly sampled from villages in three different regions. We interviewed each household one to three times. The purpose of this qualitative research was to understand the terms citizens themselves used to describe their views of government authorities and to generate hypotheses about how citizens form their evaluations of these authorities and make their decisions about participating in local governance and politics.

Designing this phase of the research took into account several objectives. First, I wanted to ensure that I heard views from a range of households. These interviews were not designed to generate data from a representative sample of a larger population, but I did want to include a range of perspectives on local governance and citizen–government relations. This consideration shaped the way in which both communities and respondents were sampled. Given the enormous variation in economic development, political institutions, and social structures across China, I wanted to make sure that we heard from individuals from different regions. At the same time, China spans a very large geographical area, and transportation in rural areas can be challenging. We were limited by time and resources in the number of different regions to which we could travel in order to conduct repeated in-depth interviews.

To meet all these considerations, I decided to work in three provinces with very different economic, social, and geographical characteristics – Shaanxi, Fujian, and the provincial-level jurisdiction of Beijing.[1] Within each of these provincial-level units, I worked with research assistants to select a municipality that would be willing to host researchers. Within each municipality, we then randomly selected a rural township and village within that township to conduct our qualitative research. Within each village, we employed a random walk procedure to select ten households for our sample.

Second, I wanted to hear how ordinary people spoke about local government and local officials while presuming as little as possible about what aspects of local government behavior and performance were most important to them, or even about whether they saw local government as relevant to their lives at all. As a result, the interview protocol was left as open and general as possible. Conversations lasted between 20 minutes and 3 hours. We informed respondents that they could conclude the conversation whenever they wanted, and we ended the interview when they seemed to lose interest or become impatient. The questions used to guide our conversations simply consisted of the following questions:

[1] The provincial-level jurisdiction of Beijing covers a territory approximately equal to the state of Connecticut. Urban Beijing is of course highly developed, but rural Beijing is relatively poor, with per capita consumption almost identical to the national average. According to the Beijing Statistical Yearbook 2016, the monthly average per capita consumption of rural Beijing residents was 1,318 yuan (195 USD), very close to the national average of 1,309 yuan (194 USD).

- What are the biggest difficulties that you and other villagers face in everyday life?
- Do you or others ever ask village or township officials for help with these difficulties?
- Do you or others ever interact with village or township officials for any other reasons?
- How do village and township officials react to approaches from ordinary people?
- Do village and township officials ever approach ordinary people?
- What kinds of interactions and relationships do ordinary people and local officials have?

To build trust and maximize the open-endedness of our conversations, we also attempted to visit households two or three times over a period of three years. During follow-up visits, we asked the questions we may not have had time for on a previous visit, and we inquired about changes in their everyday lives since our last visit. For households that we were unable to reach during follow-up visits, we again used a random walk procedure to draw replacement households for additional interviewing.

These conversations helped me generate hypotheses specifically about the commonly held and socially shared criteria that ordinary people use to discuss and justify their evaluations of government officials in conversations with each other. But they reveal little about the psychological traits or beliefs that might influence individual evaluations of government. Even when a degree of trust and familiarity is built through repeated visits, when outsiders come into a rural community, the conversation almost certainly constitutes what James Scott calls a public transcript, or the socially and politically acceptable ways in which ordinary people feel comfortable talking publicly about power and those in power (as opposed to hidden transcripts where individuals might develop critiques of power relationships and privately question their domination by the powerful). In Chapter 3, we saw how the Chinese state has for centuries promoted retributive justice concerns and the state's role in upholding the moral and social order through institutions for retributive justice.

We see through the interviews discussed in this chapter that the state's public discourse around retributive justice is reflected in popular narratives told by ordinary people. It is likely, however, that public transcripts have an effect on the ways in which people think and behave. By reflecting and sustaining cultural and social norms about government behavior and public discussion of government behavior, these narratives may influence individual beliefs about government, as well as generate the common knowledge that affects the decisions of individuals to take political action and coordinate with others. Understanding and analyzing elements of these narratives might thus help us understand important components of how people evaluate government authorities and how they decide when to participate in governance and cooperate with government requests. These criteria may to some extent be promoted by the rulers themselves, but they may also have their own causal impact on the behavior of individuals.

Finally, it is worth noting that I conducted this stage of the research without knowledge of the literature on retributive justice. Therefore, one shortcoming is that the interview protocol lacked detailed questions that would have allowed me to examine views on retributive justice with greater nuance. The advantage, however, is that I had no prior beliefs about the importance of retributive justice that would have inadvertently influenced the responses of our interviewees, the behavior of the research assistants who conducted some of the interviews, or our interpretations of the interview data.

To summarize, the aim of this qualitative research was to understand the socially acceptable criteria that ordinary citizens use in public discussions with each other to evaluate local governance and what they expect from local government officials. The qualitative interviews do not tell us how common particular criteria may be among ordinary people in rural China, or what types of people tend to have particular criteria. Nor do they tell us about the psychological traits of individuals that might influence citizen evaluations. Instead, what the following narratives suggest is that retributive justice concerns and institutions of top-down punishment may play a significant role in how citizens say they judge government authorities and their performance.

FINDINGS FROM THE QUALITATIVE RESEARCH: POPULAR NARRATIVES ABOUT LOCAL GOVERNANCE

This section describes three narratives that respondents repeatedly used in order to illustrate their views of how government authorities behave as well as how they ought to behave. These narratives were striking not because they were the only ways in which respondents described their expectations of local government and local officials but because they suggested that citizens had criteria for government authorities that were not addressed by existing political science theories and that I had not initially considered – specifically, citizens saw effective top-down supervision and punishment of lower-level misbehavior as a core criterion for government performance and a type of public good that the government was expected to provide. Moreover, top-down supervision was desirable not just for instrumental reasons such as preventing their hard-won income from going to bribes and predation. People also wanted top-down punishment because they believed that government authorities had a moral responsibility to identify and weed out officials with poor moral character, that punishment of such bad apples was critical for social order, and that failure to punish wrongdoers was a signal of whether higher authorities themselves had moral character – all core tenets of a retributive justice model of governance.

Narrative 1: "All crows are black." Citizen Disengagement and the Absence of Retributive Justice

When we asked villagers about the problems that they faced in their daily lives, they could easily have given any number of responses. They could have raised the problem of fluctuating crop prices, their unstable incomes, and the lack of nonagricultural employment opportunities in their communities. They could have pointed to the open sewers and dirty roads in their communities. They could have gotten angry about being left out of the frantic pace of development in China's booming cities with skyscrapers getting thrown up left and right. They could also have expressed uncertainty and fear about the government's repressiveness and a desire to have more say in the decisions of government authorities.

All of these issues came up at least once in our interviews. Respondents, however, rarely stopped to elaborate on the details of these problems. Instead, they proceeded to focus on how these problems, at their root, were due to corruption and bad officials. In many cases, their immediate answer to our question was simply that the biggest problem in their everyday lives was government corruption.

Mrs. Chen, a woman in her fifties who lives in Broken House Village, about 100 km northwest of central urban Beijing, was one of the respondents who saw government corruption as the main problem in her daily life.[2] When we asked what difficulties her family faces, Mrs. Chen immediately started talking about how no one in her family was able to get the

---

[2] Interviews with Mrs. Chen (pseudonym), household no. 23, Broken House Village, Beijing Municipality, July 4, 2009 and July 22, 2010. Note: All names of interviewees and villages have been anonymized. Household numbers refer to interview codes rather than addresses.

village's officials to employ them as street sweepers for the village. Opportunities for nonagricultural income are rare in Broken House, especially for middle-aged and illiterate villagers like Mrs. Chen. Jobs like street sweepers that the village authorities provide are thus extremely valuable.

In Broken House, however, village officials give these jobs out to their friends rather than to the people who most need the extra income. When we asked her why she thought this was happening, Mrs. Chen immediately attributed the problem to collusion between the village officials and the levels of government immediately above them – township, county, and less frequently, municipality or prefecture. Instead of monitoring and punishing the village officials who were violating regulations by allocating benefits to their friends rather than to the poor, the higher levels of local government were in on the scheme: "Village-level officials, township-level officials, county-level officials – they all have regulations they are supposed to follow in their work that tell them what procedures they are supposed to follow." According to Mrs. Chen, the reason that villagers were unable to benefit from public investment in welfare benefits and public goods provision was because local officials at multiple levels were working together to embezzle public funds: "But when we hear that they have funding for something, we never see it used for anything."

When villagers spoke about local government corruption, they often attributed these problems to the moral failings of the individuals in office. Respondents tended to make what psychologists call dispositional attribution rather than situational ones, explaining poor governance and the lack of bureaucratic discipline as problems of individual character or personal disposition rather than a result of structural problems created by the political system. As one villager in Shaanxi put it: "It's just like the saying, all crows are black. Immorality [among officials] is really boundless now. Whoever has money has the final say."[3] When people see corruption among village officials going unpunished, they often express beliefs that township officials were "in on it" and that both township and village officials were "bad types" who had no intrinsic motivations for working in the public interest.

On the one hand, this approach to blaming authorities makes sense because individuals generally want to avoid being seen as critical of the central government or the regime's leadership. At the same time, however,

[3] Interview with Mrs. Wang (pseudonym), household no. 2, Li Family Forest Village, Shaanxi Province, July 23, 2010.

the fact that both the state and society allow public discourse about corruption to focus on the moral failings of officials implies that it is politically and socially acceptable to voice the belief that the regime should take responsibility for punishing and weeding out these individuals when possible – in other words, for upholding retributive justice.

Our interviewees often passed moral judgment not only on the village officials who engaged in corruption but also the township authorities who failed to punish them. Villagers also frequently explained their reluctance to ask authorities for help and engage in political action by pointing to both immoral officials at the grass roots as well as the immoral officials above who fail to punish them. Mrs. Xiao, for example, was another of our respondents in Beijing's Broken House Village. A young mother who works in a local sweater factory, she gave birth to her second child, a daughter, which violated the government's birth planning regulations. Village officials required Mrs. Xiao's family to pay a 20,000 yuan fine, but she reports that another villager who had an " above quota" child was only charged a 10,000 yuan fine because her brother was a village official. When we asked whether she reported the discrepancy to anyone, Mrs. Xiao replied: "If you go to the township to register a complaint (*xinfang*), [the officials] are all in cahoots with one another (*yi huo de*). When you go the complaint office (*xinfang ju*), even before you have left the office, the officials have called your village's officials and told them you are visiting. Then they run you out of their office."[4] Once an individual returns to his or her village after attempting to complain about village officials at the township government, he or she is then subject to possible harassment and discrimination.

Respondents in other villages expressed similar sentiments linking corruption, the lack of bureaucratic discipline, and citizen disengagement. People in Shaanxi's Li Family Forest Village reported that money had mysteriously disappeared from government payments for land that was appropriated from them. No one, however, bothered to report the missing money because of the generally shared belief that their voices do not count, that there is no point in taking action. As one person noted, "Report what? To whom? The village officials and township officials have the same interests. That's the reality."[5] Or, as Mr. Zhu, the owner

---

[4] Interview with Mrs. Xiao (pseudonym), household no. 30, Broken House Village, Beijing Municipality, June 13, 2009. Also interviewed on June 18, 2009.
[5] Interview with Mr. Chang (pseudonym), household no. 3, Li Family Forest Village, Shaanxi Province, July 23, 2010.

of a plumbing equipment business in Fujian's Grass Temple Village, commented: "Officials always protect each other (*guan guan xiang hu*). Who's ever heard of an official accusing another official of wrongdoing? Everyone complies with officials. No one will fight against an official. . . . It doesn't matter if it is the officials in the township or the officials in the village. They are all officials, and they all protect each other."[6] Since ordinary people felt like they faced bad officials at multiple levels united against them, they generally choose to disengage.

In sum, respondents repeatedly told a narrative of immoral officials united against citizens who, as a result, rationally chose to disengage from interacting with the political system. Government corruption was the top problem, not just for the general public but also for the day-to-day tasks that ordinary people needed to get done for their families and their livelihoods. Moreover, individuals did not attribute this corruption as a function of the "system" but as a result of the poor moral character of the individuals in office, an argument that has been encouraged by centuries of rhetoric and education from the Chinese state.

Narrative 2: The Ideal of Judge Bao and the "pure official" as Punisher

Many of our respondents reported disengagement, but they also discussed the conditions under which they would take action. To explain, many brought up the well-known figure of Judge Bao, a Song Dynasty government official in the eleventh century. "For almost a thousand years now," the historian Wilt Idema observes, "Judge Bao (*Bao gong*) has served as the preeminent embodiment of justice in China."[7]

But what type of justice does the ideal of Judge Bao exemplify? Judge Bao is not a Robin Hood figure who redistributes wealth from the rich to the poor. Nor is he a champion of procedural justice and democracy like Thomas Paine who campaigns for ordinary people to have a role in governing themselves. More than any other conception of justice, Judge Bao embodies retributive justice. He represents the state as the punisher of first resort. As Idema notes, he "sees to it that the criminal, irrespective of his position and connections, will be punished. It is especially this latter

---

[6] Interview with Mr. Zhu (pseudonym), household no. 14, Grass Temple Village, Fujian Province, June 21, 2009. See also Lianjiang Li, "Support for Anti-Corruption Campaigns in Rural China," *Journal of Contemporary China* 10, no. 29 (November 2, 2001): 577.
[7] Wilt L. Idema, *Judge Bao and the Rule of Law: Eight Ballad-Stories from the Period 1250–1450*, World Scientific, 2010, ix.

quality that has endeared Judge Bao to Chinese audiences for centuries."[8] As the exemplar of the "pure official" (*qingguan*), Judge Bao punishes criminals, even when it is the family of the emperor himself who abuse their position to extort money from farmers.[9] Interestingly, Judge Bao is frequently portrayed as relishing the pain that he inflicts on criminals – especially high-ranking officials who have abused "their privileged positions in order to give free rein to their lust and greed. In fact, descriptions of the various forms of punishment that Judge Bao uses are so prominent and described with such detail for the enjoyment of readers that Idema nicknames one author of these texts, the 'Master of Judicial Torture.'"[10]

Celebrated for centuries in literature and rural folk operas, and the subject of a popular series airing on television during this phase of research, respondents we interviewed repeatedly used Judge Bao as a convenient shorthand explanation of what they looked for in government officials. One such respondent was Mrs. Liang, a woman in her fifties whom we interviewed in Fujian's Grass Temple Village.[11] Mrs. Liang and her husband work hard to support not only themselves but also their unmarried adult son living at home and Mrs. Liang's elderly mother-in-law. They are too old to grow turf grass as a cash crop as many of their neighbors do. Instead, their livelihood comes from a variety of sources – growing vegetables to sell at a local market, running a small corner store out of the front of their house, and renting rooms in their house to migrants from the interior who have moved to the area in search of employment.

When we asked Mrs. Liang what her family found most difficult on a daily basis, her response was, "Not enough money." This answer surprised us. Her household did not seem particularly poor. Yes, they hustled to ensure a steady income, and their house was not newly renovated. But their house was large and typical of middle-income families in the village. To understand her definition of what it meant to have enough money, we asked whether there were others in her neighborhood who did

---

[8] Ibid.; see also Wilt L. Idema, "Judge Bao Selling Rice in Chenzhou," in *Judge Bao and the Rule of Law: Eight Ballad-Stories from the Period 1250–1450*, 31–66, World Scientific, 2010.

[9] Ibid.

[10] Wilt L. Idema, *Judge Bao and the Rule of Law: Eight Ballad-Stories from the Period 1250–1450*, World Scientific, 2010, xxxii–xxxiii; see also Perry Link, *The Uses of Literature: Life in the Socialist Chinese Literary System*, Princeton University Press, 2000.

[11] Interview with Mrs. Liang (pseudonym), household no. 21, Grass Temple Village, Fujian Province, June 23, 2009.

have enough money. Her response: "The people in those really tall houses over there, that you see with so many floors – those are the people with money. They even have cars to drive to work. You should go interview *them*."

"Those people" turned out to be the village officials. We had started our conversation by asking Mrs. Liang to tell us about their everyday problems. The first problem that Mrs. Liang chose to raise was the privilege enjoyed by village officials, which she attributed to corruption and embezzlement.

We asked what, in Mrs. Liang's opinion, would a better state of affairs look like? Her response: "Nowadays, where are you going to find a Judge Bao (*Bao Qingtian*)?" According to Mrs. Liang, the solution to getting rid of corruption among village officials was to make sure that their supervisors at the township and county levels had the moral fiber to investigate and punish them. Instead, higher-level local authorities with the strong moral compass of Judge Bao were virtually nonexistent. Without officials like Judge Bao, she lamented, "[a]ll officials at all levels just protect each other. That's how society is nowadays. It's useless to take action."

To illustrate this point, she elaborated on the issue of the unusually large houses belonging to village officials. Grass Temple is not far from the city of Xiamen. Land prices are rapidly increasing. Expanding one's house can be an important source of both rental income as well as compensation from the government if village land and buildings are expropriated for commercial development. As a result, ordinary villagers are rarely able to get permission to expand their houses because local governments want to minimize the amount of government if land is expropriated. Village officials, however, are able to expand their houses at will, without supervision, much less punishment, from above: "You can see their tall houses – not one applied for and received permission for their construction. ... So what if it is unfair? What recourse do you have?"

Once again, the lack of morally upstanding officials in the township as well as the village government meant that the rational thing to do, it seemed to Mrs. Liang, was nothing. Complaining or engaging with government authorities was pointless. Officials would only help those who were willing and able to bribe them: "Nowadays, the government only helps the rich. We are not rich so they do not help us, they don't care enough to help us get loans." She concluded by recommending to my student research assistant sarcastically: "When you grow up, you should become an official too. You will have lots of money if you go and become an official. If you have power, you will have money."

Mr. Liang, her husband, expressed similar sentiments.[12] In his view, if there were higher-level local authorities who were willing to punish village officials for malfeasance, ordinary people would be willing to go to them and engage in local governance: "If there was a Bao Qingtian, every citizen would listen to him and work with him." The problem is that officials who have moral character like Judge Bao are nowhere to be found. "If you become a member of the Party, you should work in the public interest. But where can you find an official who works in the public interest? They work in the interest of filling their own pockets." The lack of clean officials at higher levels, Mr. Liang believes, is what perpetuates corruption at lower levels: "When there is money at the top, there is always money to be had at the bottom." In Mr. Liang's view, there need to be higher-level officials who refrain from malfeasance and who are willing to discipline misbehavior at lower levels.

Without upstanding officials at higher levels and effective top-down supervision, citizens like Mr. Liang feel there is no point in taking action. "Villagers are trapped. There's nothing they can do. They don't have any capabilities. They are at the bottom of the hierarchy. If it doesn't directly affect our interests, we don't bother to do anything." Without officials like Judge Bao, ordinary people fear retribution from authorities for making complaints. As Mr. Liang noted ominously, "The bad guys always lurk in the shadows, whereas the good guys who report on the bad guys stand in the light. So it's easy to see the good guys and find them."

Citizens like Mr. Liang find it much easier to take action and ask higher levels for assistance when they see higher-level officials who are willing to call out corruption and punish misbehavior because such actions signal officials who seem to care about the public interest. In the Judge Bao stories, punishment by government authorities is important because it maintains the social order and upholds society's core values. Idema notes of the pure officials in the Judge Bao stories:

In their efforts to maintain the proper social order and to eliminate all crime, these pure officials ... do away with thieves and murderers, lecherous monks and adulterous wives, corrupt officials who disregard the law .... Elites and commoners in both traditional and modern China viewed these pure officials as the staunch defenders of the highest spiritual and social values of Chinese culture.[13]

[12] Interview with Mr. Liang (pseudonym), household no. 21, Grass Temple Village, Fujian Province, June 26, 2009.
[13] Wilt L. Idema, *Judge Bao and the Rule of Law: Eight Ballad-Stories from the Period 1250–1450*, World Scientific, 2010, x.

Like others, Mr. Liang noted that if there were a Judge Bao in office, "villagers would certainly take action." Respondents like Mr. and Mrs. Liang believe that government authorities have a responsibility to act in public interest. They express beliefs that higher levels should be holding lower levels accountable for their performance and that citizens should be able to complain about poor performance and malfeasance by lower-level officials. As Mr. Liang noted, "All officials, whether they are at higher levels or lower levels, should be supervised and evaluated."

In Judge Bao's stories too, retributive justice is not just important, it trumps other principles of justice. There are only passing mentions of citizen concerns about distributive justice – and even these are often connected to retributive justice (e.g., Judge Bao's rulings on cases of government officials stealing grain intended for famine relief). Procedural justice concerns are almost entirely absent. Judge Bao is praised for his honesty and pursuit of the public good, but his efforts do not go toward upholding fair procedures or citizen participation in decision making. There is no due process where the accused are innocent until tried. In fact, the opposite is true. Suspects can be locked up for any period of time. Confession is required to resolve a case, but Judge Bao has no compunction about using trickery and extreme torture to extract a confession.[14] Criminals have fundamentally wicked natures. Because they are, by definition, unredeemable, there is no need for Judge Bao to follow procedures that ensure their individual rights. The fact that Judge Bao seems to relish inflicting pain and punishment on criminals is presented as completely consistent with his reputation for justice.[15]

Narrative 3: "Our lives would be so much better if there were still struggle meetings." Nostalgia for Maoist Retributive Justice

That there is any nostalgia for the Maoist period at all can be surprising, given the widespread disorder and violence that resulted from its mass mobilization campaigns. Maoist initiatives such as the land reform movement, the Socialist Education Movement, and the Cultural Revolution led to widespread fear and persecution, and in the case of the Great Leap Forward, to terrible famine.

---

[14] Ibid., xxxiii.

[15] As the elder brother of Empress Cao warns his mother, "He loves to sentence the emperor's kin and relatives." Wilt L. Idema, ibid., xxxiii–xxxiv.

Yet, as others have reported, citizens frequently voice enthusiasm and approval of these campaigns – even older individuals who personally suffered their destructive aspects. In Ching Kwan Lee's study of labor protest in urban China, she interviews one factory worker who says: "Everyone here says this: our lives would be so much better if there were still struggle meetings and political campaigns."[16] On the one hand, such statements could be people viewing Maoist practices "through rose-colored lenses," as O'Brien and Li have argued.[17] On the other hand, the tremendous costs inflicted by Maoist campaigns make nostalgia for these campaigns a powerful rhetorical device for villagers who want to communicate how much weight ordinary people place on the problem of corruption and their expectation that government authorities should be the primary punishers of this corruption.[18]

Take the case of one farmer we interviewed in Shaanxi's Li Family Forest Village, Mr. Zhou.[19] In some ways, Mr. Zhou, who was in his seventies, had little reason to view the Maoist era favorably. From 1968 to 1972, Mr. Zhou was a young man in his twenties with a stable and prized job in the No. 71 factory. When the Cultural Revolution started, he lost this job and was sent back to his village with hundreds of other workers. For a few years, he taught in the local school, but in 1978 he was asked to step down to make way for more qualified teachers. Since then, Mr. Zhou and his wife have relied on farming a plot of about one-third of an acre, which provides them with food for subsistence and some vegetables to sell at the periodic market.

As with many of our interviews, we started out by asking Mr. Zhou to tell us about some of his personal history and his family. Upon hearing that his two adult sons also live in the village with their families instead of having migrated elsewhere for employment, we asked whether they also farm. This question led to Mr. Zhou telling us about one of the biggest challenges facing their family – that neither his newest daughter-in-law nor his three grandsons have been allocated farm land by the village's

[16] Ching Kwan Lee, "From the Specter of Mao to the Spirit of the Law: Labor Insurgency in China," *Theory and Society* 31, no. 2 (2002): 213.

[17] Kevin J. O'Brien and Lianjiang Li, "Campaign Nostalgia in the Chinese Countryside," *Asian Survey* 39, no. 3 (May 1999): 384.

[18] Elizabeth J. Perry, "From Mass Campaigns to Managed Campaigns: 'Constructing a New Socialist Countryside,'" in *Mao's Invisible Hand: The Political Foundations of Adaptive Governance in China*, edited by Sebastian Heilmann and Elizabeth J. Perry, 31, Harvard University Asia Center, 2011.

[19] Interviews with Mr. Zhou (pseudonym), household no. 9, Li Family Forest Village, Shaanxi Province, July 24, 2010 and July 27, 2010.

officials. Land allocation is a highly contentious issue within villages, especially ones like Li Family Forest, which is located in a mountainous area where farming plots vary widely in their access to water. Land is owned by the village as a whole, and village officials oversee its distribution. Although major redistribution of land within the village is only allowed every thirty years by law, village small groups – or subcommunities – are allowed to make small adjustments within the subcommunity when the size of one's family changes due to marriage or childbirth. In Mr. Zhou's small group, however, the head of the small group has been reluctant to call a village meeting to discuss readjustments within the small group.

It was at this point in the conversation that Mr. Zhou began to express dissatisfaction with the village's officials and nostalgia for the Maoist period. In his view, the village head and the small group head "only care about money and only run in the direction of where there is money. You can't pin them down [and get them to respond to you] unless you have money to give them." During the Maoist period, there was also corruption and malfeasance – but the difference was that higher-level officials responded. "Officials back then would strike hard (*qiang xi*). If someone reported a problem, the officials would address it right away."

To illustrate the contrast in bureaucratic discipline between now and in the Maoist period, Mr. Zhou brought up recent issues with the previous village head. This village official had sold timber from the village's public land worth hundreds of thousands of yuan. But word had gotten out that only 20,000 yuan showed up in the village's accounts. The village head was eventually prosecuted, but Mr. Zhou argues that Maoist-era bureaucratic control and discipline were so effective that such corruption would never have happened in the first place. Glancing at me and my research assistants, and estimating our ages, Mr. Zhou continued, "You don't even know about the Socialist Education Movement. In the time of Mao Zedong, you couldn't even get one cent [embezzled] through all the scrutiny of the village accountants and custodians."

As with the villagers who referenced the Judge Bao stories, Mr. Zhou praised the severe punishments imposed on wrongdoers during the Maoist period:

You never experienced the Cultural Revolution and the Four Clean-Ups Movement. In those times, if you dared to cut a single piece of wood [from the village's public forest], you would be put into prison. There was someone from the village who cut one small tree down. He was criticized fiercely and made to stand all day in the public square holding up the log on his shoulders.

Other scholars have also observed strong citizen approval for the harsh punishment of corruption. Lianjiang Li, for example, notes that in his interviews conducted in the late 1990s, "quite a few respondents suggested the most effective way of handling corruption was to launch a 'strike hard' (*yan da*) campaign to impose swift and severe punishment on corrupt officials. Typical suggestions included 'throw them in jail!', 'kill them all!', and even 'skin them alive!'"[20]

For Mr. Zhou, top-down imposition of harsh punishments during the Maoist period signaled that higher levels had a clear sense of right and wrong. Morality undergirded the regime's actions in a way that no longer seems true in the uncertainties of the reform period. Mr. Zhou remembers things as more black and white in Mao's time: "Things then were very simple." In contrast, "nowadays, people are more complicated and flexible."

This flexibility is not a good thing in Mr. Zhou's view. Corruption and the lack of oversight from higher levels, according to him, result from moral failings rather than the wrong incentive systems. He likens corruption to gambling in the sense that both are symptoms of an underlying moral malaise in society: "Things can't go on this way, with the government not putting an end to the common practices of corruption and gambling." Mr. Zhou sees both these behaviors as ways in which the wicked take resources from innocent victims: "There was a woman who was so focused on playing *mahjong* that she wasn't watching her daughter, who was playing in the street and got hit by a car and died. Gambling is an abomination. It's another form of stealing."

The ways in which Mr. Zhou compares local governance in his village with local governance during the Maoist period are consistent with what we would expect given a retributive justice theory of citizen engagement. Mr. Zhou first voices nostalgia for the Maoist period of his own accord when he starts discussing corruption and venality among the grassroots officials in his locality. As he recalls it, the Maoist period was a time when higher levels upheld moral values, in large part by carrying out retributive justice on those who engaged in immoral behaviors like corruption and gambling. In contrast, today's officials are immersed in corruption. Although implementation of oversight and good governance is possible in the sense that the government has the capacity to implement oversight of lower-level officials, corruption, like gambling, is addictive in an all-

---

[20] Lianjiang Li, "Support for Anti-Corruption Campaigns in Rural China," *Journal of Contemporary China* 10, no. 29 (November 2, 2001): 577.

encompassing way and has sapped the will of higher-level authorities to act in morally upstanding way and carry out their responsibilities to the public.

Without higher-level authorities who are willing to punish the wicked, Mr. Zhou fears that the moral order of society will collapse. "The overall direction of the government is good, but corruption and gambling destroy the fabric of society. Some people regard these activities as their jobs and make a living out of it. People are nowhere as good as they were during the Maoist period."

Narratives of nostalgia for Maoist-era anti-corruption campaigns and their extreme punishments also illustrate how retributive justice concerns often take precedence over procedural justice for Chinese villagers. Despite being too young to remember the Maoist period personally, Mr. Deng, a father of two young children in his forties in Broken House Village, expressed his strong approval of the way in which corrupt officials were dealt with during that time as a way of expressing how much more important punishment of corruption is compared to the rule of law:

If the law is not flexible – well, for example, take corruption. It's very simple. Take the officials in our village. In Mao's era, if you embezzled hundreds of thousands of yuan like they do, you would have been put in prison for ten years. Or, if you embezzled half a million yuan, you would have been imprisoned for life. And they would have confiscated all your assets.[21]

The fact that higher-level authorities follow the law more closely than they did in the Maoist period is unfortunate in Mr. Deng's eyes: "But according to the present laws, it is not legal to punish officials in this way."

As with respondents who see Judge Bao as an exemplar of good governance, Mr. Deng does not care whether higher-level authorities follow due process when it comes to corruption and malfeasance among local officials. Mr. Deng explains:

Officials who truly want to help ordinary citizens are all flexible about implementing the law as long as they stick to broad principles. If you ask me to choose, I will always vote for the official who thinks of the law as flexible. If you do everything according to the law, you can't get anything done – it will suffocate you.

For villagers like Mr. Deng, procedural justice and the rule of law are secondary to the importance of upholding retributive justice and the punishment of wrongdoers.

---

[21] Interview with Mr. Deng (pseudonym), household no. 29, Broken House Village, Beijing Municipality, June 11, 2009.

SUMMARY OF HYPOTHESES GENERATED FROM QUALITATIVE RESEARCH

What do these three narratives suggest about the criteria that citizens in authoritarian regimes use to form their preferences for government authorities? To begin with, the people we interviewed saw government corruption and punishment of corruption not just as general public problems but as salient challenges that they faced in their everyday lives. Anti-corruption punishment was not just something distant that belonged to politicians and leaders at the top, but it was something they thought about on a daily basis – even when there was no active anti-corruption campaign going on at the time. Punishment of corruption, or the lack thereof, was an important criterion that they used to evaluate government authorities. In fact, many reported that punishment of corruption sometimes took priority over other concerns for welfare provision, distributive justice, democratic reforms, and procedural justice.

They also expressed a belief – one that had been promoted by the state itself – that government authorities had a moral obligation to punish corruption. Consistent with the retributive justice model posited in Chapter 2, effective top-down punishment was seen not just as a signal of state capacity but also as an indication that higher levels had moral character and a clear sense of right and wrong. Lack of punishment, on the other hand, was seen as a signal that immoral individuals are in power. When government authorities lacked morality, it was rational for them to disengage, but if higher levels signaled moral character through punishment and retributive justice, they were more willing to go to government authorities with their problems and to cooperate with government initiatives.

We now turn to an empirical evaluation of these observable implications (which the next chapter continues). We start with the following specific hypotheses. First, we should expect that citizens will prefer higher-level government authorities who punish wrongdoing among lower-level officials (Hypothesis 1). In comparison to other criteria that have been shown to be important for citizen support – economic performance, welfare provision, and democratic reforms – we might expect punishment and retributive justice to be as important as these other concerns. Second, we should find that citizens not only prefer these authorities because they view them as more competent but also because they evaluate the moral character of these authorities more highly (Hypothesis 2).

HYPOTHESIS TESTING

To test these hypotheses, I conducted a series of three empirical studies in 2016–17 together with Minh Trinh and Shiyao Liu: (1) Study 1, an in-person field survey of nearly 400 respondents in rural Fujian administered in July 2016; (2) Study 2, an in-person field survey of over 900 respondents from rural areas outside of municipal Beijing administered in January 2017; and (3) Study 3, an online survey of 1,150 respondents, primarily from urban areas, administered December 2016–January 2017.[22]

Study 1 provides an initial assessment of whether top-down punishment of corruption plays any part in citizen evaluations of authorities (Hypothesis 1) through a conjoint experiment that asks the respondent to choose between two hypothetical candidates for the role of township leader. By randomly varying whether these hypothetical candidates pursue strategies consistent with retributive justice, procedural justice, distributive justice, and economic growth, we are able to show not only that top-down punishment matters in citizen preferences for different types of leaders but also that it matters at least as much or even more than some of the other actions. We assume that in order for public support for anti-corruption punishment to exist at the aggregate level, at the individual level citizens must have strong and stable preferences for local officials who punish subordinates for corruption.

Building on these initial results, Study 2 investigates the mechanisms through which top-down punishment affects citizen evaluations. The literature posits two main mechanisms through which anti-corruption punishment might lead to increased citizen support. The first is through improving competence evaluations. Citizens may see authorities who punish corruption as more competent at their jobs, more capable of ensuring their subordinates implement policies correctly, and, as Chapter 2 notes, better at deterring future corruption. Punishment of lower-level corruption can increase citizen beliefs about the ability and reliability of higher-level officials, which may increase their support of these officials.

The second mechanism is by improving moral character evaluations. A model of retributive justice posits that punishment of corruption also tells citizens about the moral commitments and benevolent intentions of

---

[22] Parts of this section are also discussed in the following: Lily L. Tsai, Minh D. Trinh, and Shiyao Liu, "What Makes Anticorruption Punishment Popular? Individual-level Evidence from China," *Journal of Politics*. Accepted for publication on December 11, 2020. https://www.journals.uchicago.edu/toc/jop/current.

those in office. When citizens see their authorities punishing corruption and crime, it can strengthen their belief that authorities care about right and wrong. Anti-corruption punishment may thus increase citizen support even if citizens have no evidence that these initiatives actually reduce the incidence of corruption. Sampson (2005), for example, observes that arrests and indictments for corruption in postcommunist Romania sent signals to the public that "morality is being safeguarded."[23] Similarly, scholars of the Soviet Union have argued that the real purpose of anti-corruption initiatives was to boost public support and not to improve government performance (Holmes 1993, 204).[24] When Tyler and Degoey disaggregate survey data on citizen trust in institutions, and distinguish between citizen beliefs in the benevolence of authorities and citizen beliefs in the competence of authorities, they find that benevolence shapes citizen willingness to accept the decisions of authorities. They conclude that citizens are more concerned about the moral character of those in power than their practical ability to solve problems.[25]

Study 2 thus implements a second in-person field survey and conjoint experiment that integrates an innovative causal mediation analysis in order to evaluate moral character assessments as a mediator of the effects of top-down punishment on citizen preferences. This survey both replicates the findings from the first survey and shows that top-down punishment leads citizens to prefer an official through improving citizen evaluations of his moral character in addition to his competence (Hypothesis 2).

Study 3 replicates the findings from Study 2's rural population and assesses its external validity for an urban online population. Finally, as an auxiliary check, in Studies 2 and 3, we also examine the impact of top-down punishment on moral character evaluations as a separate outcome variable, as well as looking at moral character evaluations as a mediator.

---

[23] Steven Sampson, 2005, "Integrity Warriors: Global Morality and the Anti-Corruption Movement in the Balkans," in *Corruption: Anthropological Perspectives*, edited by Dieter Haller and Cris Shore, Pluto Press: 103–30.

[24] Leslie Holmes, *The End of Communist Power: Anti-Corruption Campaigns and Legitimation Crisis. Europe and the International Order*, New York, NY: Oxford University Press, 1993.

[25] Tom R. Tyler, "Trust and Democratic Governance," in *Trust and Governance*, edited by Valerie Braithwaite and Margaret Levi, vol. 1, 285, New York: Russell Sage Foundation, 1998; Tom R. Tyler, "Procedural Justice, Legitimacy, and the Effective Rule of Law," *Crime and Justice* 30 (January 2003): 283–357; Tom R. Tyler and Peter Degoey, "Trust in Organizational Authorities: The Influence of Motive Attributions on Willingness to Accept Decisions," in *Trust in Organizations: Frontiers of Theory and Research*, edited by Roderick M. Kramer and Tom R. Tyler, 16–38, Thousand Oaks, CA: Sage, 1996.

STUDY 1: EVALUATING THE IMPACT OF RETRIBUTIVE JUSTICE
WITH CONJOINT ANALYSIS

Study 1 embeds a conjoint experiment in a field survey to test the first hypothesis: Citizens will prefer higher-level authorities who punish wrong-doing among lower-level officials (Hypothesis 1). We seek to find out how the preference for punishment of corruption stacks up relative to other considerations known to drive public support in authoritarian regimes, in particular the concerns over economic growth, social welfare, and channels for political participation. Conjoint experiments enable us to assess the importance of each of these attributes by presenting respondents with profiles of hypothetical government officials with randomly assigned characteristics and then asking respondents to choose which profile they prefer. This random assignment of characteristics enables us to identify the causal influence of each characteristic on an individual's choice or preference of official.[26]

Data

Study 1 was conducted through an in-person survey in 2016. In this study, we surveyed 392 individuals selected through a multistage sampling process from two counties in different prefectures in Fujian province.[27] These counties were selected to vary in economic development, geography, and social structure. Our selection of field sites was also constrained to places where our Chinese academic collaborator had social networks and could obtain research access. One county was hard to reach due to the mountainous terrain – 80 km from the provincial capital but accessible only with a 2-hour drive. The other was relatively far from the provincial capital but close to the coastal city of Putian.[28] The resulting sample is

---

[26] Jens Hainmueller, Daniel J. Hopkins, and Teppei Yamamoto, "Causal Inference in Conjoint Analysis: Understanding Multidimensional Choices via Stated Preference Experiments," *Political Analysis* 22, no. 1 (2013): 1–30; R. Duncan Luce and John W. Tukey, "Simultaneous Conjoint Measurement: A New Type of Fundamental Measurement," *Journal of Mathematical Psychology* 1, no. 1 (January 1964): 1–27.

[27] This survey was conducted in collaboration with Professor Yingying Wen of China Youth University of Political Studies.

[28] In each county, we randomly sampled one township, and then within each township, we used stratified random sampling based on quartiles of average household income to select twelve villages. Because one township consisted of only eight villages, we included all eight in our sample. Finally, within each village, we used a random walk protocol to select about twenty respondents each, making sure that no two respondents come from the same households. As part of the random walk protocol, two enumerators were assigned to each village, with one starting the random walk from the village center and the other from

TABLE 4.1 *Demographics, Fujian 2016*

	Fujian 2016	Census 2016
Age >= 40	0.44	0.46
Female	0.45	0.49
Education >= High school	0.44	0.26
Per capita consumption (monthly, CNY)	986	1,075.90
N	392	N/A

Sources: Fujian Statistical Yearbook 2017.

roughly similar in terms of socioeconomic characteristics to the census data for Fujian (see Table 4.1).[29]

Research Design

Because we wanted to evaluate the impact of anti-corruption punishment on citizen preferences for local officials, and to understand how much this strategy for public support matters compared to other types of strategies, this study utilized a technique that is designed to achieve these goals in a less conspicuous manner than direct or leading questions on a survey. Conjoint experiments present respondents with a choice of two profiles, in this case, of two hypothetical officials. Each hypothetical official's profile is made up of a combination of different attributes. This technique is well suited to our purposes because it allows us to assess whether the

---

the village border. The number of respondents per village fluctuated due to practical reasons, for example, some villages were less accessible, but within each village the random walk procedure ensured that the respondents who were selected into the sample did not differ in important ways to those who were not. For example, sampled respondents may live closer to main roads than those who did, but we do not believe the difference to be significant.

[29] Our sample is roughly similar in terms of socioeconomic characteristics to the census data for Fujian. In our survey, the self-reported average per capita monthly consumption is 986 yuan (roughly 146 USD). The rural average per capita consumption in 2015 as reported by Fujian Statistical Yearbook 2016 was 997 yuan (roughly 147 USD). Our sample is 45 percent female, compared to 49 percent in the Fujian 2015 census. In our data, 23 percent of respondents have no formal education or only primary school education, 31 percent of junior school level, 23 percent of high school level, and 23 percent of above high school levels. In comparison, the census data show 37 percent of the population have no formal education or only primary school education, 39 percent of the population of junior school level, 15 percent of high school education, and 10 percent of above high school education. The self-reported average age is 37.20 years.

respondent cares about a particular attribute when choosing between two different profiles, and how much each attribute matters relative to the other attributes.

One important advantage of this technique is that respondents are not asked to reveal information that might make them feel uncomfortable. If, for example, the respondent lives in a township where the township leader does a poor job promoting economic growth, the respondent may not want to tell the researcher that the most important criterion in his evaluation of township authorities is economic performance. In conjoint tasks, respondents are asked only to choose a candidate that represents a bundle of attributes but not to explain their choices. It is thus difficult to know a respondent's priorities just by looking at which candidate they prefer. Because an individual's preferences are harder to infer, they are more likely to respond truthfully.

Another important advantage for the researcher is that aggregate preferences for each of the conjoint attributes can be recovered in the form of average marginal causal effects (AMCEs).[30] The effects are causal because both candidates' attributes are randomized and are thus independent. The conjoint experiment presents each person with profiles of two hypothetical candidates for the role of township leader. Each profile provides information about the candidate on four attributes (Table 4.2). Each attribute is presented as a statement about an achievement that the candidate has or has not accomplished ("positive" or "negative"), and each attribute corresponds to one of the factors that scholars argue are essential to shaping citizen evaluations of government.

In order to ensure that respondents found this exercise naturalistic and easy to comprehend, we piloted this survey extensively. In response to feedback from these pilots, we revised the phrasing of the attributes to improve comprehension to fit for the context, but no one felt that these attributes were unimportant in shaping their opinions, nor did anyone suggest that we should substitute in other attributes that were more important.

Few people in our pilot research criticized the artificiality of the exercise (though complaints about other aspects of the survey, such as its duration, were freely offered). Asking villagers to express their preference for different township leaders did not surprise them. Despite the lack of national-level

---

[30] Jens Hainmueller, Daniel J. Hopkins, and Teppei Yamamoto, "Causal Inference in Conjoint Analysis: Understanding Multidimensional Choices via Stated Preference Experiments," *Political Analysis* 22, no. 1 (2013): 1–30.

TABLE 4.2 *Conjoint attributes and statements used to explain the attributes to respondents*

Attribute	Statement
Punishment (*Retributive justice*)	The township leader punishes/does not punish village officials who misuse public funds
Election (*Procedural justice*)	The township leader guarantees/does not guarantee that village elections are fair
Welfare [*dibao*] (*Distributive justice*)	The township leader ensures/does not ensure that minimum income subsidies (*dibao*) have been given to those in need
Growth (*Economic performance*)	The township leader keeps/does not keep economic growth in the township above national average (7 percent)

elections in China, ordinary citizens are often polled by authorities about their opinions of different local officials and candidates for the local office.

In our conjoint experiment, we individually randomized each attribute of each candidate to be either "positive" or "negative," resulting in 256 possible pairs of candidates. We randomized the profiles on tablet computers carried by enumerators, but our presentation of the profiles involved several innovative components designed to ensure that our rural respondents fully understood the experiment (following Meyer and Rosenzweig).[31] One innovation involved representing the attributes using cartoons and two-character abbreviations of the attribute to ease comprehension and increase engagement (see Figure 4.1). A second was presenting the profiles on a laminated conjoint table and changing the attribute levels on the table manually so that enumerators could show respondents that the choice of profiles in each conjoint round was different from the previous one.[32] A picture of the enumeration process can be found in Figure 4.2.

---

[31] Alexander Meyer and Leah R. Rosenzweig, "Conjoint Analysis Tools for Developing Country Contexts," Working paper, 2016. https://polmeth.org/files/polmeth/files/tpm_v23_n2.pdf#page=2

[32] We randomized the profiles using a software run on tablets carried by enumerators, but to ensure that respondents fully understand the experiment, we had enumerators present the profiles to respondents by vertically affixing four laminated labels onto a laminated conjoint table with Velcro tapes to represent the two attributes. The laminated labels have a two-word description next to a cartoon illustrating each attribute. While placing the labels onto the conjoint table, enumerators verbally explained to the respondents the

FIGURE 4.1 Conjoint with four main attributes.

After explaining the randomized profiles of hypothetical township leaders, enumerators then asked each respondent to choose which of the two candidates they would prefer to serve as their township official, and to rate each candidate on a scale from 1 to 10. The probability that respondents are asked to choose between a candidate who is good on every attribute and a candidate who is bad on every attribute is low. Most choices are between candidates who are a mix of both positive and negative attributes. As a result, when choosing between two candidates,

meaning of each attribute following predefined scripts. Afterward, they put down for each candidate a tick or a cross next to the label to indicate whether the attribute is positive or negative for the candidate. They also asked questions to verify that the respondents understood the board correctly as we intended.

FIGURE 4.2 Enumeration in field, Beijing 2016.

the respondent typically has to prioritize some attributes over others based on their relative preferences for these attributes. In this experiment, we asked each respondent to repeat the conjoint experiment six times. We also randomized the order of attributes by respondent, as suggested by Hainmueller et al., to avoid a scenario where respondents focus more on the attributes that are shown on the upper side of the board.[33]

Results

Results from Study 1 confirm the hypothesis that citizens prefer higher-level authorities who punish wrongdoing among lower-level officials (Hypothesis 1), which is what we would expect if they value retributive

---

[33] Jens Hainmueller, Daniel J. Hopkins, and Teppei Yamamoto, "Causal Inference in Conjoint Analysis: Understanding Multidimensional Choices via Stated Preference Experiments," *Political Analysis* 22, no. 1 (2013): 1–30.

justice. As Figure 4.3 shows, respondents indeed support candidates who carry out top-down punishment of village officials for malfeasance. Holding everything else constant, respondents prefer candidates who supervise and punish village officials to those who do not. As evident in the top-most estimate, respondents value township party secretaries with a track record of punishing corrupt village officials; these township officials are roughly 20 percent more likely to be preferred by respondents, holding everything else constant.

Moreover, this effect of punishment of corruption is just as large as that of the implementation of free and fair village elections. It is smaller than the preference for economic performance or for welfare provision, which is not surprising given the long-standing emphasis on performance-based support for the regime.

We also find that punishment provides government authorities with an independent source of public support. In other words, citizens still prefer township officials who can punish even when they do not (or cannot) deliver other desirable outcomes. Specifically, for each of the three other attributes – Growth, Welfare, and Election – we estimate two AMCEs of Punishment, one using only profiles with a positive value for that attribute and one using only profiles with a negative value, and then plot them onto Figure 4.4 as triangles and dots, respectively. The results are nearly identical across

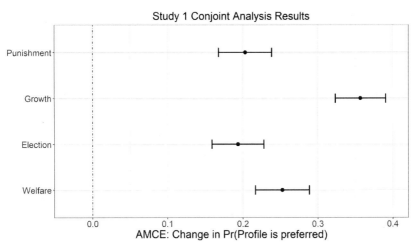

FIGURE 4.3 AMCEs of "punishment" and other conjoint attributes on respondent's choice of township party secretary, Fujian 2016. Ninety-five percent confidence intervals calculated using standard errors clustered at respondent level.

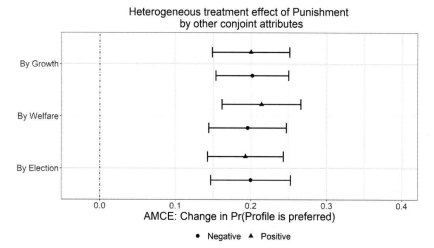

FIGURE 4.4 AMCEs of punishment conditioning on other attributes, Fujian 2016. Ninety-five percent confidence intervals calculated using standard errors clustered at respondent level.

different values of each attribute. Regarding Growth, the top two data points in Figure 4.4 show that our respondents express as much support for punishment by township officials who succeed in promoting growth as they do for punishment by township officials who fail to do so. Similarly, there is no difference in the conditional AMCEs of Punishment across values of Welfare and Election. This suggests that citizens' preference for top-down punishment is neither moderated by nor substituted for their record in other policy areas – politicians who fail in these areas can still gain an equal amount of support by punishing their wrongdoing subordinates. In other words, as a source of public support, top-down punishment is independent from economic growth, welfare provision, and promotion of formal participation.

STUDY 2: INVESTIGATING MORAL CHARACTER EVALUATIONS AS AN OUTCOME AND WITH MEDIATION ANALYSIS

Study 2 both replicates Study 1's test of the first hypothesis and tests the second hypothesis: Moral character evaluations mediate the effect of top-down punishment of corruption and malfeasance on citizen preferences for these officials (Hypothesis 2). A model of retributive justice posits that citizens prefer township officials who punish not only because they view these officials as more competent – more able to catch wrong-doers and deter wrongdoing – but also because they view these officials as morally good. If this is indeed true, public support for anti-corruption punishment arises not only because punishment may instrumentally improve government performance but also because they signal the author-ities' commitment to moral values and moral order.

Data

Study 2 was conducted through another in-person field survey, this time administered in rural counties of Beijing municipality, in 2017. Again, in collaboration with a Chinese academic, we surveyed 892 individuals selected through a multistage sampling process from two rural counties within Beijing, which encompasses not only urban Beijing but also a provincial-level jurisdiction spanning a territory slightly larger than the state of Connecticut.[34]

The counties were again selected to vary in economic and social condi-tions, subject to where our Chinese academic collaborator had social networks and could obtain research access. One county, located in a mountainous area north of Beijing, was a 2-hour drive and 120 km from the city center. The second county was on the border with the less developed province of Hebei, 75 km from downtown Beijing.[35] While urban Beijing is highly developed, rural Beijing is relatively poor with per capita consumption in rural Beijing almost identical to the national average.[36]

Research Design

Study 2 builds on the initial findings from Study 1, which showed that top-down punishment of corruption and malfeasance has a positive effect on

---

[34] As Beijing Municipality is slightly larger than the state of Connecticut, our field sites were distant from urban areas. Within each township, we randomly sampled ten villages using stratified sampling based on quintiles of average household incomes (with the exception of one township for which total population was used instead of average household income due to data availability). Within each village we employed a random walk protocol similar to what we did in the Fujian study, targeting about twenty respondents from each village.

[35] One of the four townships in our sample was a Manchu autonomous township.

[36] According to the Beijing Statistical Yearbook 2016, the monthly average per capita consumption of urban Beijing residents was 3,054 yuan (451 USD), while rural Beijing residents consumed only 1,318 yuan (195 USD), very close to the national average monthly per capita consumption – 1,309 yuan (194 USD).

citizen evaluations of township authorities and provided the first piece of evidence for the importance of retributive justice concerns. Study 2 first replicates the findings from Study 1 with a different sample. A retributive justice model of citizen evaluations of government, however, also implies that top-down punishment signals to citizens that higher-level authorities are not just competent but also have moral character. Study 2 thus also seeks to investigate how citizens interpret top-down punishment of corruption by higher-level authorities. One possibility is that citizens do not take top-down punishment as signaling anything about higher levels. Citizens simply want misbehaving officials to be punished, and they make no inferences about the moral character or institutional capacity of higher-level authorities.[37] Another possibility is that citizens see punishment as a purely instrumental way of deterring future malfeasance and improving government performance. When they see higher levels punishing misbehavior, they simply see such punishment as an indication that the government has sufficient resources and capacity to be effective.

The third possibility, which is consistent with a retributive justice argument, is that citizens care about punishment not only because they would like to deter future misbehavior but also because they believe that the government has a normative obligation to uphold society's basic values and moral order by punishing state agents who fail to respect them. Thus, the retributive justice model would predict that citizens who see higher levels punishing corruption and malfeasance among lower levels will not only view higher-level authorities as more competent at catching wrongdoers and deterring future wrongdoing, but also as having better moral character and an intrinsic commitment to the public good.

To evaluate whether this third possibility is correct, Study 2 modifies the conjoint experiment in Study 1 to enable us to conduct mediation analysis. In this analysis, we seek to estimate the indirect effect of top-

---

[37] Alternatively, it may also be that respondents in a conjoint experiment do not evaluate any of the attributes at all according to their substantive content. Instead, inattentive respondents simply take a cognitive "shortcut" by reducing each attribute to a vague measure of "goodness," and then simply choose the candidate with a greater number of positive attributes. The design of the conjoint experiment helps to mitigate this problem considerably by presenting respondents with candidates who have the same number of positive attributes, but who differ in which attributes are positive. In this section, we also help to reject this interpretation of the findings by investigating people's preferences for the substantive ideas behind an attribute. To do so, we focus on whether the AMCEs for the top-down punishment attribute truly reflect citizen preferences for retributive justice and not just preferences for "another good thing."

down punishment ("Punishment") through two mediators: moral character evaluations ("Moral") and competence evaluations ("Competence"). Most features of the conjoint experiment remain the same. We presented respondents with the profiles of two candidates for the role of township leader, we explained and verified their understanding of the information, and then we asked them to choose between the two candidates and also to rate them numerically.[38]

To investigate how "Punishment" affects citizen preferences, Study 2 adds two attributes to the candidate profiles (see Figure 4.5). The two new attributes, "Moral" and "Competence," represent two potential mediators of "Punishment." They are introduced to respondents using the statements, "The township official is a selfless person," and "The township official is a competent person." These two attributes are not only of theoretical interest, but they also correspond to what pilot research showed to be the two most common ways that Chinese citizens interpret top-down punishment of corruption and malfeasance by township authorities. Providing respondents with explicit information about the candidates' moral character and competence through these conjoint attributes forces respondents to interpret the other attributes as conceptually distinct from moral character and competence.

"Moral" and "Competence" thus represent two pathways through which respondents may mentally process our information about the candidates' accomplishments in retributive justice before making their decision about which candidate they prefer. We are interested in knowing whether information about top-down punishment leads people to evaluate the candidate not only as competent but also as morally just. In other words, we evaluate whether the effect of "Punishment" on respondents' evaluation "flows through" both "Moral" and "Competence."

Causal Mediation Analysis Using the Serial Split Sample Design

To evaluate the indirect effect of "Punishment" through "Moral" and "Competence," we build on the parallel design approach proposed by Imai, Tingley, and Yamamoto (2013). Their parallel design approach is an experimental design that identifies the indirect effect of a treatment variable on an outcome through a mediator by using two randomized experiments conducted "in parallel." In a causal process, as described by Figure 4.6,

---

[38] In this experiment, we used a five-point scale instead after finding out that it is cognitively easier for respondents to understand.

FIGURE 4.5 Conjoint profiles with four main attributes and two mediators.

a treatment T (in our case, "Punishment") may have both a direct effect on an outcome Y (the respondent's choice of township leader) and an indirect effect through a mediator M ("Moral" or "Competence"). In the parallel design approach, the sample is split into two experiments, with the first experiment randomizing only the assignment of treatment and the second experiment randomizing both the assignments of treatment and mediator.

As shown in Figure 4.6, since the indirect effect of the treatment through the mediator is transmitted naturally to the outcome in the first experiment but is interrupted in the second experiment, it is possible – with a number of assumptions – to identify and estimate the indirect effect

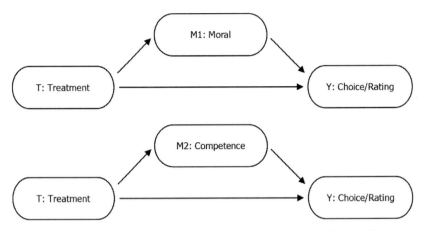

FIGURE 4.6 Diagram showing a causal process with independent mediators.

of T on Y through M as the difference between the average treatment effect in the first experiment and an average of the average treatment effects in the second experiment, where the second average is taken over different randomized values of the mediator:

$$\delta = [\mathbb{E}(Y_i|T_i = 1, D_i = 2) - \mathbb{E}(Y_i|T_i = 0, D_i = 2)]$$

$$-\sum_{m}[\mathbb{E}(Y_i|T_i = 1, M_i = m, D_i = 1) - \mathbb{E}(Y_i|T_i = 0, M_i = 1, D_i = 1)]\Pr(M_i = m)$$

where $D_i = 1$ if observation is obtained from the "first experiment" and $D_i = 2$ if it is obtained from the "second experiment"; M_i indicates the assigned value of the mediator, and T_i indicates the main treatment attribute of interest ("Punishment").

To estimate the indirect effect of "Punishment" through "Moral" and "Competence," we adopt an experimental design that closely follows Imai, Tingley, and Yamamoto's parallel design, which we refer to as mediation analysis with serial split sample or "serial design."[39] We present respondents with different versions of the conjoint experiment, with different rounds resembling the first and second experiments in the parallel design approach. Specifically, one conjoint round features only four of

---

[39] Kosuke Imai, Dustin Tingley, and Teppei Yamamoto, "Experimental Designs for Identifying Causal Mechanisms," *Journal of the Royal Statistical Society: Series A (Statistics in Society)* 176, no. 1 (January 2013): 5–51.

	"First experiment"	"Second experiment" for "Moral" as mediator	"Second experiment" for "Competence" as mediator
Presented	Growth	Growth	Growth
	Welfare	Welfare	Welfare
	Election	Election	Election
	Punishment	Punishment	Punishment
		Moral	Competence
Hidden	Moral	Competence	Moral
	Competence		

FIGURE 4.7 Example of a serial split sample design integrating mediation analysis and conjoint analysis to explore the indirect effect of either "moral" or "competence" as mediators.

the six attributes, with the mediator of interest hidden from the respondent so that they have to mentally impute a value for each candidate (see Figure 4.7). This round resembles the first experiment in Imai, Tingley, and Yamamoto's parallel design framework.[40] In another conjoint round, we present five attributes (the original four plus the mediator of interest), with all attribute values randomly assigned. This round resembles the second experiment in the parallel design framework.

Our design, however, differs from Imai, Tingley, and Yamamoto's parallel design in that our experimental setup is not "parallel": whereas Imai, Tingley, and Yamamoto proposed splitting the sample in two and running each experiment on a separate half, we expose each individual respondent to every version of the experiment.[41] In effect, we take as our unit of analysis respondent rounds instead of respondents, and split the sample within the same respondent. Our approach gives us more statistical power but also requires us to make an additional assumption of no

[40] Ibid.   [41] Ibid.

carry-over effect, that is, each respondent's experience in earlier rounds does not influence their thought processes in later rounds. In addition to the identification assumptions proposed in Imai, Tingley, and Yamamoto – the sequential ignorability assumption, consistency, and no interaction effects – our design also assumes no carry-over effects and no design effects.[42] A detailed discussion over these assumptions can be found in the chapter appendix.

In this design, the indirect effect through the mediator of interest is calculated as the difference between the AMCE of "Punishment" in the round where we randomly assign the value of the mediator attribute ("Moral" is positive) and reveal it to the respondent, and the AMCE of "Punishment" where we hide it and the respondent infers it mentally, averaged over the realized distribution of the hidden mediator. For each respondent, we include a "first experiment" round with the mediator of interest hidden from the respondent. We also include two "second experiment" rounds: one for each of the two mediators of interest, "Moral" and "Competence." We reuse the "first experiment" round to calculate the two indirect effects.

Causal Mediation Analysis with Serial Split Sample Design and Multiple Mediators

Our serial design, which allows for the estimation of indirect effects through one mediating variable, mirrors approaches implemented in recent studies by Acharya, Blackwell, and Sen and Huddleston and Weller.[43] This approach, however, may be problematic when we suspect that multiple mediators mediate the effect of the treatment on the outcome, as we do here. The reason is because when multiple mediators exist, it is entirely possible for the mediators to interact with each other. The indirect effect through one mediator may also flow through another.

In our case, we posit two mediators – "Moral" and "Competence." Our review of the literature, moreover, suggests that there has been no theoretical or empirical research on whether individuals form opinions about the moral character of others first, or their competence first, or

[42] Ibid.
[43] Avidit Acharya, Matthew Blackwell, and Maya Sen, "Analyzing Causal Mechanisms in Survey Experiments," *Political Analysis*, 26, no. 4, (2018): 357–78; R. Joseph Huddleston and Nicholas Weller, "Unintended Causal Pathways: Probing Experimental Mechanisms through Mediation Analysis," *SSRN Electronic Journal*, 2017, http://dx.doi.org/10.2139/ssrn.2964336.

whether they form opinions about these traits simultaneously. The problem is that if multiple mediators exist, and we do not know what theoretical and empirical relationships exist between them, then by only estimating the indirect effect of one of the mediators, our estimate of this indirect effect may be biased. For example, if individuals first form their evaluations of the competence of others, and these evaluations shape their evaluations of another's moral character, then, if we simply estimate the indirect effect of "Moral" without examining its relationship to "Competence," our estimated indirect effect of "Moral" also includes at least some of the indirect effect of "Competence" on our outcome of interest.

Figure 4.8 illustrates these problems by showing the different possible causal pathways leading from "Punishment" to citizen preferences for township leaders. The dashed line connecting M_1 and M_2 represents the potential interaction effect between the mediators, effect of which direction and magnitude we do not know.

This diagram shows that in order to evaluate the relationship(s) that may exist between two mediators, we need to be able to estimate the five quantities of interest that would constitute an "indirect effect":

(1) The *combined indirect effect* flowing through both "Moral" and "Competence," which accounts for the sum of any indirect effect flowing through each of the mediators, along with any interaction effect between them.

(2a) The *individual natural indirect effect of "Moral,"* or the indirect effect that flows through "Moral" when we allow "Competence" to vary naturally. This quantity of interest is what we calculate in the analysis above for the indirect effect of "Moral."

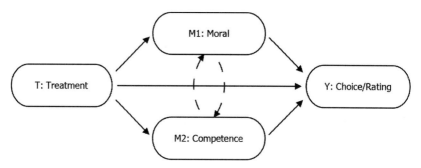

FIGURE 4.8 Diagram showing a causal process with two dependent mediators.

(2b) The *individual controlled indirect effect of* "*Moral*," or the indirect effect that flows through "Moral" when we hold "Competence" constant.

(3a) The *individual natural indirect effect of* "*Competence*," or the indirect effect that flows through "Competence" when we allow "Moral" to vary naturally. This quantity of interest is what we calculate in the analysis earlier for the indirect effect of "Competence."

(3b) The *individual controlled indirect effect through* "*Competence*," or the indirect effect that flows through "Competence" when we hold "Moral" constant.

Figure 4.8 provides a diagram showing the causal pathways identified by the five indirect effects that arise out of a causal process with two dependent mediators. The distinction between these five indirect effects is unimportant when only one mediator is considered relevant. It is also not needed when we believe only a single mediator out of several suspects actually matters, since estimates for the five indirect effects will be indistinguishable. Finally, when there are multiple mediators but there is no relationship or interaction between the mediators, that is, the mediators are activated independently, the two individual indirect effects will be identical and sum up to the combined indirect effect. In these three situations, the traditional mediation analysis with parallel design (e.g., Imai, Tingley, and Yamamoto 2013; Acharya, Blackwell, and Sen 2017) will suffice.

However, if there are interactions between multiple mediators, the conventional approach to mediation analysis will no longer be sufficient. In particular, if the respondents' imputations for one mediator are correlated with their imputation for the other mediator, there will be a difference between the individual natural and controlled indirect effects. In this situation, a direct adaptation of the parallel design approach allows for either the individual controlled indirect effects or the individual natural indirect effects to be estimated, but never both. In Acharya, Blackwell, and Sen, for example, both of the paper's studies consider treatment variables separately from mediators, meaning that the indirect effects that they estimate are equivalent to individual natural indirect effects.[44]

---

[44] Avidit Acharya, Matthew Blackwell, and Maya Sen, "Analyzing Causal Mechanisms in Survey Experiments," *Political Analysis*, 26, no. 4, (2018): 357–78.

It is important to clarify which indirect effects are being estimated. Looking only at the individual controlled indirect effects may underestimate the part of the effect flowing through both mediators. Looking only at the individual natural indirect effects leads to a problem similar to omitted variable bias. At the same time, the small magnitude of individual indirect effects may mean that only combined effects can be reliably detected; focusing on either indirect effects may lead to the incorrect conclusion that neither mediator has an indirect effect even when both of them combined do. As a result, the traditional parallel design when applied to multiple mediators may paint an incomplete or inaccurate picture of the causal relationship.

Our solution for this problem is to design our experimental setup in such a way that all five indirect effects can be identified and estimated. We achieve this by repeating our serial design to cover each of the indirect effects, but instead of having two experiment rounds for each indirect effect, wherever appropriate we use some experiment rounds as both a "first-experiment" round for one effect and a "second-experiment" round for another. This allows us to reduce the number of needed conjoint rounds to a total of six.

Figure 4.9 illustrates a set of six conjoint rounds that a respondent may experience, with each round labeled with the role(s) it plays in estimating our five quantities of interest. As shown, each respondent is presented with the same two candidates in all six rounds. In Rounds 2 through 6, we hide some attributes and shuffle the order of the remaining attributes.[45] In Rounds 3 and 4, we specifically hide either the Moral attribute or the Competence attribute, so that respondents mentally impute the values of these attributes for both profiles when they choose between the two candidates. In Round 6, we hide not one but both potential mediating attributes. Again, our serial design splits into "first experiment" and "second experiment" "respondent-rounds" for each respondent instead of across groups of individual respondents.

---

[45] In a pilot, we tested our conjoint experiment with a number of Chinese political scientists and could verify that they were not able to detect that the profiles were identical across rounds. Additionally, because our enumerators presented the conjoint attributes with labeled stickers and laminated conjoint table, they had to take off the stickers and clean the table after each round. This process made it even less likely that respondents would be able to notice that the profiles in successive rounds were identical but only presented in a different order.

Round 1	Round 2	Round 3	Round 4	Round 5	Round 6
"Second-experiment" for (1b) (2b) (3)	*Wash-out*	*"First experiment"* for (2b) "Second experiment" for (1a)	*"First experiment"* for (1b) "Second experiment" for (2a)	*Wash-out*	*"First experiment"* for (1a) (2a) (3)

Presented

Round 1	Round 2	Round 3	Round 4	Round 5	Round 6
Growth	Dibao	Growth	Growth	Election	Growth
Dibao	Election	Dibao	Dibao	Punishment	Dibao
Election	Punishment	Election	Election	Moral	Election
Punishment	Moral	Punishment	Punishment	Competence	Punishment
Moral	Competence	Moral	Competence		
Competence					

Hidden

Round 1	Round 2	Round 3	Round 4	Round 5	Round 6
	Growth	Competence	Moral	Growth	Moral
				Dibao	Competence

FIGURE 4.9 An example of the sequence of attributes being revealed to and hidden from a respondent according to the parallel design. The second row indicates how AMCEs calculated using data from each round are used to calculate different indirect effects.

As we note in the preceding section, our approach requires us to make an assumption of no carry-over effects, in that a respondent's experience in earlier rounds does not influence their thought processes in later rounds. We take several steps to make this assumption more plausible. First, we shuffle the order of attributes for each round. Second, as Figure 4.9 indicates, we also insert between experiment rounds two "wash-out" rounds (Rounds 2 and 5), in which we hide an attribute randomly chosen from "Punishment," "Election," "Growth," and "Welfare." These wash-out rounds make it more difficult to deduce that we are specifically interested in "Moral" and "Competence" when they are individually hidden in Rounds 3 and 4. Respondents observe that some attributes are dropped or hidden after Round 1 but no particular pattern is apparent to them.

In addition, we also need to make the assumption of no design effects, which requires that a respondent does not change his or her response in later rounds simply because these rounds are presented differently, for example, with fewer attributes. Although it is not possible to conclusively prove or disprove the validity of this assumption, our inclusion of "wash-out" rounds allows us to estimate the extent of this design effect under some stringent assumptions.

We can use this setup to identify and estimate the *combined indirect effect* through both mediators (3) when we use Round 6 as the "first experiment" and Round 1 as the "second experiment." The only difference between these two rounds is whether the effect is allowed to flow naturally through both of the mediators.

We can also use the setup illustrated in Figure 4.9 to identify the *individual natural indirect effects* (1a and 2a). With Round 6 as the "first experiment," Rounds 3 and 4 serve as the "second experiment" where the single mediator of interest (either "Moral" or "Competence") is given while the other mediator is allowed to vary naturally.

Finally, we can also use this setup to identify the *individual controlled indirect effect* by using Rounds 3 and 4 as the "first experiment" and Round 1 as the "second experiment." Rounds 3 and 4 assign the value of the other potential mediator so that the respondent only mentally infers the value of the mediator of interest.

For every quantity of interest, we employ the same estimation procedure as before:[46]

$$\delta = \text{AMCE when mediating attribute is hidden}$$

$$- \text{ AMCE when mediating attribute is revealed}$$

$$= [\mathbb{E}(Y_i|T_i = 1,\ D_i = 2) - \mathbb{E}(Y_i|T_i = 0,\ D_i = 2)]$$

$$-\sum_m [\mathbb{E}(Y_i|T_i = 1, M_i = m, D_i = 1) - \mathbb{E}(Y_i|T_i = 0, M_i = m, \\ D_i = 1)]\text{Pr}(M_i = m)$$

where $D_i = 1$ indicates a round in which the mediator is revealed to respondents (the "first experiment") and $D_i = 2$ indicates a round in which the mediator is hidden (the "second experiment"); M_i indicates the assigned value of the mediator, and T_i indicates the main treatment

---

[46] Kosuke Imai, Dustin Tingley, and Teppei Yamamoto, "Experimental Designs for Identifying Causal Mechanisms," *Journal of the Royal Statistical Society: Series A (Statistics in Society)* 176, no. 1 (January 2013): 5–51.

attribute of interest ("Punishment").[47] We use the same calculation for all five indirect effects, changing only the sample to estimate different indirect effects, such that each indirect effect is estimated using only data from the relevant "first experiment" and "second experiment" rounds as described earlier.

Results

First, the results from Study 2 conducted in rural Beijing replicate our finding in Study 1, which was conducted in the southern Chinese province of Fujian (Figure 4.10). These results again confirm Hypothesis 1 – that top-down punishment has a significant effect on citizen preferences and evaluations of township authorities. As Figure 4.10 shows, respondents value candidates who punish wrongdoing among lower-level officials. As with Study 1, the magnitude of the effect of top-down punishment is as important as the implementation of free and fair village elections in determining citizen preferences for township leaders.

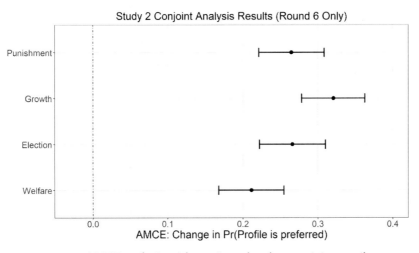

FIGURE 4.10 AMCEs of "punishment" and other conjoint attributes on respondents' choice of township secretary, Beijing 2017. Ninety-five percent confidence intervals calculated using standard errors clustered at respondent level.

---

[47] This indirect effect corresponds to what Acharya Blackwell and Sen call the Average Difference in Natural Mediator Effects (ADNME). Avidit Acharya, Matthew Blackwell, and Maya Sen, "Analyzing Causal Mechanisms in Survey Experiments," *Political Analysis*, 26, no. 4, (2018): 357–78.

Second, in Table 4.3, we present our estimates for all the five indirect effects of "Punishment" through the two mediators "Moral" and "Competence," using both the respondents' binary choice and their numeric ratings for the two profiles as the outcome measures. Note that we present p-values from randomization inference because indirect effects are almost by definition much smaller in magnitude compared to the total treatment effects, which introduce problems with statistical power even for sample sizes as large as ours. Using randomization inference to test the sharp null hypothesis of no individual treatment effect (Fisher's null) is less demanding in terms of power than standard inference, which tests the null hypothesis of no *average* treatment effect (Neyman's null).

Substantively, the main results in Table 4.3 are consistent with Hypothesis 2 that moral character evaluations mediate the effect of top-down punishment of corruption on citizen preferences for these officials. They show that top-down punishment influences citizen preferences through changing citizen evaluations both of moral character as well of competence. Specifically, we find that there is a statistically significant combined indirect effect of "Punishment" through "Moral" and "Competence." This combined indirect effect through both Moral and Competence is positive and statistically significant at the 0.05 level. Results are similar when we consider the AMCEs of "Punishment" on the respondents' numerical ratings for the candidates. Again, the combined indirect effect is found to be positive and statistically significant.

There is also suggestive evidence of individual indirect effects going through each mediator, but these are not statistically significant, likely because we are underpowered for this analysis. Among these results, the individual natural indirect effects are identical to those estimated in recent studies with causal mediation analysis using survey experiments.[48] The estimated effect through "Moral" in particular is found to be one-fifth of the total effect of "Punishment" when considering binary choice as the dependent variable, and one-sixth when considering numeric rating as the dependent variable.

Note that these effects are large enough that they would have been considered statistically significant under a less conservative level of 0.1.

---

[48] Avidit Acharya, Matthew Blackwell, and Maya Sen, "Analyzing Causal Mechanisms in Survey Experiments," *Political Analysis*, 26, no. 4, (2018): 357–78; R. Joseph Huddleston and Nicholas Weller, "Unintended Causal Pathways: Probing Experimental Mechanisms through Mediation Analysis," *SSRN Electronic Journal*, 2017.

TABLE 4.3 *Estimates of indirect effects of punishment through moral and/or competence on respondents' evaluation of township party secretary, Beijing 2017*

Dependent variable: Choice

	Combined indirect effect	Individual natural indirect effects		Individual controlled indirect effects	
		Moral as Mediator	Competence as Mediator	Moral as Mediator	Competence as Mediator
	(1)	(2a)	(3a)	(2b)	(3b)
Total effect	0.265	0.265	0.265	0.215	0.217
	(0.000)	(0.000)	(0.000)	(0.000)	(0.000)
Indirect effect	0.070	0.047	0.047	0.024	0.023
	(0.031)	(0.069)	(0.069)	(0.241)	(0.228)

Dependent variable: Rating

	Combined indirect effect	Individual natural indirect effects		Individual controlled indirect effects	
		Moral as Mediator	Competence as Mediator	Moral as Mediator	Competence as Mediator
	(1)	(2a)	(3a)	(2b)	(3b)
Total effect	1.218	1.218	1.218	0.773	1.008
	(0.000)	(0.000)	(0.000)	(0.000)	(0.000)
Indirect effect	0.508	0.206	0.457	0.051	0.303
	(0.001)	(0.077)	(0.001)	(0.376)	(0.023)

Randomization inference *p*-values in parentheses

The same cannot be said about the individual controlled indirect effects, which are both smaller and statistically indistinguishable from zero, a result that seems at odds with the positive and significant combined indirect effects. The large difference between the two types of indirect effects arise from a positive correlation between respondents' mental imputation for "Moral" and "Competence" – when not given information on both attributes, respondents in this experiment tend to believe that moral township leaders must also be competent.

STUDY 3: ASSESSING EXTERNAL VALIDITY FOR AN ONLINE URBAN POPULATION

Studies 1 and 2 provide survey experimental evidence that, consistent with a retributive justice model, citizens prefer government authorities that implement top-down punishment of misbehaving local officials (Hypothesis 1) *and* that top-down punishment influences citizen perceptions of the moral character of government authorities as well as their competence and capacity (Hypothesis 2).

But how do we know that these findings generalize beyond the rural population in our two field surveys? Study 3 addresses this question by conducting an identical version of Study 2 on an entirely different population.

Data

We commissioned Survey Sampling International (SSI) to implement a survey in December 2016 and January 2017 using a quota sampling strategy based on age and gender. Our sample consists of 1,152 opt-in respondents from a population that SSI had recruited and screened. Each participating respondent was paid a small amount of money upon completion of the survey. We set up quotas based on age and gender to ensure that the sample covered a distribution across these demographic characteristics.

Our aim in Study 3 was to find out whether the results from Studies 1 and 2 would hold for a population that differed dramatically from the rural respondents in the Fujian and Beijing field surveys and for a different mode of survey administration. In contrast to the field surveys, which were administered through in-person interviews, Study 3 was administered via an online survey.

The online study sample was indeed starkly different from our Fujian and Beijing samples. As evident in Table 4.4, the online sample was biased toward highly educated, relatively wealthy urban respondents.[49]

Results

Despite these dramatic differences in the demographics of respondents in Study 3, the results are strikingly similar to what we found in Studies 1 and 2. Findings from Study 3 again support our first hypothesis that top-down punishment has a positive effect on citizen preferences for leaders. As Figure 4.11 shows, the AMCE of "Punishment" is even larger than the AMCE for "Election" for this population.

The findings from Study 3 also replicate the findings from the mediation analyses in Study 2. Consistent with a retributive justice model, top-down punishment has a combined indirect effect through both "Moral" and "Competence" (Table 4.5). As with Study 2, this result holds regardless of whether we are looking at the respondents' binary choice outcome or their numeric ratings of the candidates. As with Study 2, the estimates for the different individual indirect effects suggest a possible indirect effect going through individual mediators, but again these results are not statistically significant.[50]

It is not surprising that the results from Studies 1 and 2 replicate for an urban population. Studies of urban China have also reported that retributive justice concerns are often expressed by urban workers and labor protesters, though these concerns are typically accompanied by

---

[49] In comparison, according to 2016 China Statistical Yearbook, in 2015, only 56 percent of the national population resided in urban areas. Levels of education were also much lower for the national population: 32 percent of the population received no formal education or only primary school education, 38 percent junior school, 16 percent high school, and 13 percent above high school education. The average monthly household expenditure in 2015 was 2,832 yuan (roughly 419 USD).

[50] Unlike Study 2, however, it is the individual controlled indirect effects, not the individual natural indirect effects, that are larger and approaching statistical significance. Although these results are more consistent with the positive and statistically significant estimates for the combined indirect effects, analysts who had chosen instead to focus on the individual natural indirect effects—in particular those who follow the traditional parallel design (Acharya, Blackwell, and Sen; Huddleston and Weller) – would have arrived at a very different conclusion. Avidit Acharya, Matthew Blackwell, and Maya Sen, "Analyzing Causal Mechanisms in Survey Experiments," *Political Analysis*, 26, no. 4, (2018): 357–78; R. Joseph Huddleston and Nicholas Weller, "Unintended Causal Pathways: Probing Experimental Mechanisms through Mediation Analysis," *SSRN Electronic Journal*, 2017.

TABLE 4.4 *Summary statistics for samples of the three studies*

	Fujian 2016	Beijing 2017	Online 2016
Age	38.54	46.99	41.91
	(se = 0.34; n = 340)	(se = 0.23; n = 888)	(se = 0.19; n = 1152)
Age >= 40	0.44	0.7	0.52
	(se = 0.04; n = 340)	(se = 0.03; n = 888)	(se = 0.02; n = 1152)
Female	0.45	0.52	0.48
	(se = 0.04; n = 344)	(se = 0.02; n = 889)	(se = 0.02; n = 1152)
Education >= High school	0.44	0.38	0.97
	(se = 0.04; n = 343)	(se = 0.02; n = 891)	(se = 0.03; n = 1152)
Party member	0.11	0.16	0.28
	(se = 0.02; n = 342)	(se = 0.01; n = 890)	(se = 0.02; n = 1109)
Household consumption	4211.86	3301.24	7420.65
	(se = 237.91; n = 312)	(se = 108.51; n = 880)	(se = 1029.31; n = 1107)
N	392	897	1152

demands for lost welfare benefits and appeals to distributive justice and a subsistence ethic.[51] Feng Chen's study of labor protests in Henan, for example, describes how workers were motivated to protest in part because of a desire for the government to prosecute their corrupt factory manager. In marching through the streets, they not only carried banners demanding unemployment benefits and welfare provision, but

---

[51] See, for example, Ching Kwan Lee, "The 'Revenge of History,'" *Ethnography* 1, no. 2 (December 24, 2000): 220; William Hurst and Kevin J. O'Brien, "China's Contentious Pensioners," *The China Quarterly* 170 (June 25, 2002): 345–60; see also Yongshun Cai, "The Resistance of Chinese Laid-off Workers in the Reform Period," *The China Quarterly* 170 (June 25, 2002): 327–44; Feng Chen, "Subsistence Crises, Managerial Corruption and Labour Protests in China," *The China Journal* 44 (July 2000): 41–63; Ching Kwan Lee, "From the Specter of Mao to the Spirit of the Law: Labor Insurgency in China," *Theory and Society* 31, no. 2 (2002): 204.

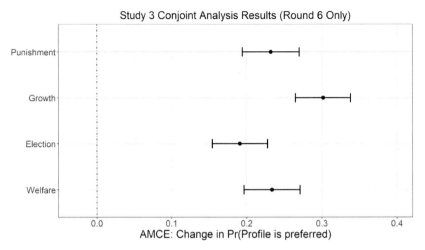

FIGURE 4.11 AMCEs of "punishment" and other conjoint attributes on respondents' choice of township party secretary, online 2016. Ninety-five percent confidence intervals calculated using standard errors clustered at respondent level.

also ones that said, "Severely Punish Z!"[52] Chen interprets these protests as "retributive action," defined by Charles Tilly as a long-standing form of food riot in which the crowd directly metes out punishment of an authority for embezzling from or profiteering from the food supply.[53]

Research by Ching Kwan Lee on worker protests also provides examples of workers who express beliefs in the importance of retributive justice. In one case, laid-off factory workers at a state-owned enterprise publicly humiliated their general manager for what they perceived as his corrupt behavior:

Disgruntled by management's extravagance in hard times, workers held the general manager hostage as he prepared for an official "inspection tour" in Thailand with his wife. They loaded Huang (the manager) into the back of a flatbed truck and forced him into the painful and demeaning "airplane position" bent at the waist, arms straight out at the sides. Then they marched 10 kilometers through the

---

[52] Feng Chen, "Subsistence Crises, Managerial Corruption and Labour Protests in China," *The China Journal* 44 (July 2000): 41–63.

[53] See Tilly on four types of food riots. Charles Tilly, "From Mobilization to Revolution," in *Collective Violence, Contentious Politics, and Social Change: A Charles Tilly Reader*, edited by Ernesto Castañeda and Cathy Lisa Schneider, 71–91, Routledge, 2017.

TABLE 4.5 *Estimates of indirect effects of punishment through moral and/or competence on respondents' evaluation of township party secretary, online 2016*

Dependent variable: Choice

	Combined indirect effect	Individual natural indirect effects		Individual controlled indirect effects	
		Moral as Mediator	Competence as Mediator	Moral as Mediator	Competence as Mediator
	(1)	(2a)	(3a)	(2b)	(3b)
Total effect	0.232	0.232	0.232	0.214	0.212
	(0.000)	(0.000)	(0.000)	(0.000)	(0.000)
Indirect effect	0.053	0.019	0.012	0.043	0.036
	(0.022)	(0.243)	(0.337)	(0.071)	(0.096)

Dependent variable: Rating

	Combined indirect effect	Individual natural indirect effects		Individual controlled indirect effects	
		Moral as Mediator	Competence as Mediator	Moral as Mediator	Competence as Mediator
	(1)	(2a)	(3a)	(2b)	(3b)
Total effect	0.946	0.946	0.946	0.894	0.803
	(0.000)	(0.000)	(0.000)	(0.000)	(0.000)
Indirect effect	0.324	0.105	0.057	0.259	0.215
	(0.013)	(0.220)	(0.346)	(0.039)	(0.052)

Randomization inference *p*-values in parentheses.

rain to the downtown and paraded him through the street . . . just like the Cultural Revolution.[54]

Nostalgia for the harsh punishments of corruption during the Maoist period is again evident among citizens in urban China. Lee, for example, reports a factory worker musing, "People always say these cadres would have been criticized and executed many times over now for the amount of their grafts."[55] Consistent with a retributive justice theory, in these cases, punishment of corrupt officials is important to protesters, independent of whether they are able to get the government to meet their demands for welfare benefits.

Moral Character Evaluations as an Outcome: Findings from Studies 2 and 3

What happens when we look at moral character evaluations as a separate outcome? In addition to examining moral character evaluations as a mediator of the effect of top-down punishment on citizen preferences for township authorities, we also asked a separate question after the conjoint tasks, asking respondents to provide rating scores of each hypothetical township official's moral character. As we can see in Figure 4.12, the results are again consistent with a retributive justice theory. Top-down supervision and punishment have a positive effect on respondent ratings of the moral character of township officials that is as large or larger than economic performance, the implementation of elections, or the provision of social welfare.

SUMMARY OF RESULTS FROM CONJOINT ANALYSIS

In sum, findings from these studies provide substantial evidence for the importance of retributive justice concerns in the formation of citizen evaluations of government authorities in authoritarian contexts. In addition to the citizen concerns with economic growth, procedural justice, and distributive justice that previous literature has highlighted, these

---

[54] *Far Eastern Economic Review*, June 26, 1997, cited in Ching Kwan Lee, "Pathways of Labour Insurgency," in *Chinese Society: Change, Conflict and Resistance*, edited by Elizabeth Perry and Mark Selden, 87–109, London: Routledge, 2003.

[55] Ching Kwan Lee, "From the Specter of Mao to the Spirit of the Law: Labor Insurgency in China," *Theory and Society* 31, no. 2 (2002): 213; see also, for example, Kevin J. O'Brien and Lianjiang Li, "Campaign Nostalgia in the Chinese Countryside," *Asian Survey* 39, no. 3 (May 1999): 384.

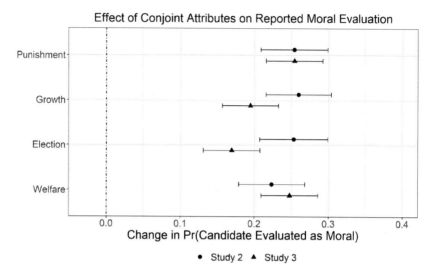

FIGURE 4.12 AMCEs of the four conjoint attributes on individual evaluation of township official's moral character. Ninety-five percent confidence intervals are shown using standard errors clustered at individual level. (See Appendix for table).

results strongly suggest that we need to pay more attention to the importance of retributive justice and the way in which citizens have a fundamental desire for top-down punishment of corruption and wrongdoing by higher-level authorities. Even when government authorities fail on other dimensions, they can still garner substantial approval and support from citizens when they show that they are willing to punish corruption and malfeasance. These results also highlight the importance of moral character in citizen evaluations of government authorities. Punishment and sanctioning of misbehaving officials may build trust and confidence in the intentions and moral character of higher-level authorities.

These survey experiments asked respondents to evaluate hypothetical government officials, but we should note that these experiments were conducted in 2016 and early 2017 at the beginning of Xi Jinping's anti-corruption campaign. During this period, Xi's campaign was generally viewed by the public as motivated by a genuine commitment to weeding out corrupt officials. Between 2013 and 2016, at the outset of the campaign, Xi made significant effort in demonstrating through speeches as well as investigations of high-ranking officials that officials in his own political faction were not exempt from the campaign.

It is thus not surprising that the findings from the conjoint experiments (as well as from our preliminary fieldwork and pilots of the survey) are consistent with the interpretation that ordinary villagers in rural China took the campaign at face value rather than seeing it as a way for Xi to get rid of his political enemies. If the campaign had been seen by respondents as a "tiger hunt" during our studies, conjoint profiles with top-down punishment of corruption would have little value for the provision of retributive justice and thus would have had little or no impact on their preferences for and moral character evaluations of higher-level officials. Instead, what we see is clear evidence that anti-corruption punishment plays a role in citizen evaluations of government authorities. As the research by Xi et al. shows, it was not until in the run-up to the nineteenth Party Congress in October 2017, after our experiments were conducted, that a "tiger hunt" aspect of the campaign emerged and officials with political connections to Xi Jinping became less likely to be investigated for corruption.[56]

CONCLUSION

We see from both the narratives told by ordinary people in qualitative interviews, as well as from survey experimental research, that citizens expect higher-level government authorities to uphold society's moral order and address citizen concerns about retributive justice by punishing corruption and misbehavior among lower-level government agents. As Li and O'Brien have observed, people "yearn for agents of higher levels appearing in their villages to clean things up."[57] Ordinary people do not view themselves as principals holding village officials accountable as their agents; instead, they view higher-level township authorities as the principals who are responsible for supervising and disciplining village officials. Consistent with a theory of retributive justice, citizens see higher-level authorities that discipline lower levels for misbehavior and poor performance as having better moral character. Additionally, citizens seem to prioritize retributive justice as much or more than procedural justice and distributive justice.

The next question is whether these findings apply in real-world settings. Individuals in authoritarian China demonstrate a concern for retributive justice in their evaluations of government authorities when presented with

---

[56] Tianyang Xi, Yang Yao, and Qian Zhang, "Dilemmas of Autocratic Governance: Theory and Evidence from the Anti-Corruption Campaign in China," 2018.

[57] Kevin J. O'Brien and Lianjiang Li, "Campaign Nostalgia in the Chinese Countryside," *Asian Survey* 39, no. 3 (May 1999): 377.

hypothetical top-down institutions of discipline and punishment and hypothetical officials. Do citizens evaluate their local officials as more moral when their locality's institutions of top-down discipline are stronger? Are citizens in these localities more likely to engage with the political system and comply with government regulations? In the next chapter, we draw on data from original surveys conducted both before and after the launch of the current anti-corruption campaign in China – as well as data from beyond China – to answer these questions.

Chapter 4 Appendix

TABLE 4A.1 *List of interviewed households*

Household number	Interviewee name (Pseudonym)	Place (Village pseudonym)	Date of first interview	Date of second interview	Date of third interview
1	Li	Li Family Forest Village, Shaanxi province	July 22, 2010	July 28, 2010	July 30, 2010
2	Wang	Li Family Forest Village, Shaanxi province	July 23, 2010	July 25, 2010	
3	Chang	Li Family Forest Village, Shaanxi province	July 23, 2010	July 26, 2010	
4	Liu	Li Family Forest Village, Shaanxi province	July 23, 2010		
5	Chen	Li Family Forest Village, Shaanxi province	July 23, 2010		
6	Yang	Li Family Forest Village, Shaanxi province	July 23, 2010	July 26, 2010	
7	Huang	Li Family Forest Village, Shaanxi province	July 24, 2010	July 27, 2010	
8	Zhao	Li Family Forest Village, Shaanxi province	July 24, 2010	July 29, 2010	
9	Zhou	Li Family Forest Village, Shaanxi province	July 24, 2010	July 27, 2010	
10	Wu	Li Family Forest Village, Shaanxi province	July 24, 2010	July 29, 2010	
11	Zeng	Li Family Forest Village, Shaanxi province	July 30, 2010		
12	Xu	Grass Temple Village, Fujian province	June 21, 2009	June 28, 2009	Aug 14, 2010

(continued)

TABLE 4A.1 *(continued)*

Household number	Interviewee name (Pseudonym)	Place (Village pseudonym)	Date of first interview	Date of second interview	Date of third interview
13	Sun	Grass Temple Village, Fujian province	June 21, 2009	June 27, 2009	Aug 13, 2010
14	Zhu	Grass Temple Village, Fujian province	June 21, 2009	June 27, 2009	
15	Ma	Grass Temple Village, Fujian province	June 22, 2009		
16	Hu	Grass Temple Village, Fujian province	June 22, 2009	June 26, 2009	Aug 14, 2010
17	Guo	Grass Temple Village, Fujian province	June 22, 2009	27 June, 2009	Aug 15, 2010
18	Lin	Grass Temple Village, Fujian province	June 22, 2009	27 June, 2009	Aug 14, 2010
19	He	Grass Temple Village, Fujian province	June 23, 2009	26 June, 2009	Aug 12, 2010
20	Gao	Grass Temple Village, Fujian province	June 23, 2009	Aug 14, 2010	
21	Liang	Grass Temple Village, Fujian province	June 23, 2009	26 June, 2009	Aug 12, 2010
22	Zheng	Broken House Village, Beijing provincial unit	June 8, 2009		
23	Chen	Broken House Village, Beijing provincial unit	June 13, 2009	July 4, 2009	July 22, 2010
24	Song	Broken House Village, Beijing provincial unit	June 8, 2009		
25	Xie	Broken House Village, Beijing provincial unit	June 11, 2009	June 13, 2009	

(continued)

TABLE 4A.1 *(continued)*

Household number	Interviewee name (Pseudonym)	Place (Village pseudonym)	Date of first interview	Date of second interview	Date of third interview
26	Tang	Broken House Village, Beijing provincial unit			
27	Han	Broken House Village, Beijing provincial unit	June 11, 2009		
28	Cao	Broken House Village, Beijing provincial unit	June 8, 2009	June 15, 2009	July 20, 2010
29	Deng	Broken House Village, Beijing provincial unit	June 11, 2009	June 18, 2009	July 20, 2010
30	Xiao	Broken House Village, Beijing provincial unit	June 13, 2009	June 18, 2009	
31	Feng	Broken House Village, Beijing provincial unit	June 11, 2009	June 17, 2009	

Note: All households were visited three times. Households that were interviewed less than three times either had no one at home or declined to be interviewed again.

TABLE 4A.2 *AMCEs on respondent ratings of the moral character of township party secretary in Beijing 2017 survey and online 2016 survey reported in Figure 4.12*

| | Dependent variable Binary evaluation of Moral Character | |
	Online 2016 survey	Beijing 2017 survey
	(1)	(2)
Supervision	0.254^{***}	0.254^{***}
	(0.019)	(0.023)
Growth	0.195^{***}	0.260^{***}
	(0.019)	(0.022)
Election	0.169^{***}	0.253^{***}
	(0.020)	(0.023)
Dibao	0.248^{***}	0.223^{***}
	(0.020)	(0.023)
Constant	0.072^{***}	0.005
	(0.016)	(0.017)
Observations	2,204	1,532
	R^2 0.190	0.242

Note: $^{*} p < 0.1; ^{**}p < 0.05; ^{***}p < 0.01$

5

Retributive Justice and Citizen Engagement in Rural China and Beyond

Not only does the importance of retributive justice arise of its own accord in unstructured conversations with ordinary people in reform-era China, but as the previous chapter shows, there is also evidence that these concerns about retributive justice play a significant role in their evaluations of and preferences for government authorities. Even when government authorities fail on other dimensions, they can still garner substantial approval and support from citizens when they show they are willing to punish corruption and malfeasance. Top-down punishment not only signals state capacity and competence to citizens but also builds trust and confidence in the intentions and moral character of higher-level authorities.

The question now is whether these findings apply to the real world. Individuals in authoritarian China demonstrate a concern for retributive justice in their evaluations of government authorities when presented with hypothetical top-down institutions of discipline and punishment and hypothetical officials. But how generalizable are these findings? Do we see similar patterns between real-world institutions and citizen evaluations of their actual officials? Do retributive justice and top-down institutions for discipline affect behavioral outcomes? And are retributive justice concerns unique to China, or are they salient in other contexts?

This chapter assesses the external validity of the findings presented in Chapter 4 through a range of empirical investigations drawing on original observational and experimental data. Retributive justice is consistently an important concern across different time periods, contexts, and populations. I start with an "easy test" – investigation of the salience of retributive justice concerns during the intensification of Xi Jinping's anti-corruption campaign using data from a 2017 survey I conducted in rural Beijing. Do citizens seem to have retributive justice concerns outside of an artificial survey experiment? Are these concerns correlated with behavioral outcomes? Given that the campaign likely rendered concerns about anti-corruption punishment and moral order highly salient, this investigation is of a "most likely" case for the model of retributive justice. As we would expect, these data show that citizens in localities with stronger top-down institutions for bureaucratic discipline also have more positive moral character evaluations of local authorities, higher levels of participation, and higher willingness to engage in voluntary compliance with government regulations.

What about a somewhat harder test? Were retributive justice concerns salient before Xi Jinping made anti-corruption the keystone of Chinese politics? To answer this question, I look back at the Wen Jiabao period. Drawing on data from a nationally representative survey I conducted in 2008,[1] I find that similar patterns also exist between top-down bureaucratic discipline and citizen engagement in rural China even when there is no ongoing anti-corruption campaign to heighten the salience or political desirability of retributive justice concerns. Though I cannot evaluate how changes over time might affect the degree of salience for retributive justice without panel data, the findings presented here suggest that retributive justice concerns do exist across different time periods.

This chapter also expands the investigation to look at an urban Chinese population. Based on another series of survey experiments conducted in 2016, we see that the implementation of top-down institutions for bureaucratic discipline can also have an impact on voluntary compliance with taxation among residents of urban China.

Finally, the chapter concludes with a discussion of the generalizability of a retributive justice model beyond China. Findings from a unique, cross-national survey experiment conducted in fifty countries in 2017 suggest that retributive justice institutions also have an impact on citizen willingness to comply with taxation around the world.

RETRIBUTIVE JUSTICE AND LOCAL GOVERNANCE IN RURAL CHINA

Before we turn to an empirical assessment of how important retributive justice concerns have been for citizen evaluations of government

---

[1] Xizang Province (Tibet), however, was excluded from the sampling due to logistical challenges.

authorities in current-day China, it helps to have some background context on how government authorities have sought to provide retributive justice since 1978. This section thus starts with an overview of how government's strategies for top-down discipline and anti-corruption have evolved during the post-Mao period.

Formal Bureaucratic Institutions for Top-Down Supervision: The Cadre Evaluation System

After the end of the Cultural Revolution in the late 1970s, government authorities sought to rebuild and reinstate top-down institutions for bureaucratic supervision and discipline. At the grassroots level, the primary institution for regulating the behavior of local officials in rural China became the cadre evaluation system.[2] Whiting shows that the performance targets for economic development set by the cadre evaluation system played a central role in the extraordinary rural development of the 1990s by encouraging the promotion of rural industry by township and village officials. Edin argues that the performance contracts of the cadre evaluation system have played a critical role in restraining cadres from corruption and rent-seeking in the creation of local industry.[3]

The cadre evaluation system, as we saw in Chapter 3, exists at all levels of the political system, but it has been especially salient at the grassroots level. Village officials are frequently punished through administrative institutions. Of the 1,122 cases of administrative discipline occurring between 1995 and 2010, collected by Cai, 67 percent of village party secretaries were removed from office and/or expelled permanently – compared to 51 percent of township party secretaries, and only 20–30 percent of city and county party secretaries.[4] High rates of discipline and punishment at the lowest levels are particularly important as citizen evaluations of the regime as a whole are influenced by the grassroots officials with whom ordinary citizens interact the most and see as the face of the state.

Performance contracts give local officials specific targets such as the provision of public goods or enforcement of birth quotas. These targets

[2] Yongshun Cai, *State and Agents in China: Disciplining Government Officials*, Stanford University Press, 2014.
[3] Maria Edin, "Why Do Chinese Local Cadres Promote Growth? Institutional Incentives and Constraints of Local Cadres," *Forum for Development Studies* 25, no. 1 (January 1998): 100.
[4] Yongshun Cai, *State and Agents in China: Disciplining Government Officials*, Stanford University Press, 2014, 75.

have different priority levels. Mandatory or veto targets (*yipiao fojue*, literally "targets with veto power") are the highest priority. If they are not met, higher level officials punish lower-level officials by docking their salaries or removing them from office. Townships vary in the way that they structure sanctions for not meeting veto targets. As one example, officials in a village might have basic wages of 1,000 yuan per month. They are then awarded points for good performance for a maximum score of 100 points. For each point, they receive another 20 yuan in salary bonuses with a possible maximum bonus of 2,000 yuan. If there is, however, even one birth over the village's quota, they receive only their basic salary of 1,000 yuan, regardless of how well they performed in other areas.[5]

In addition to what targets are set by the performance contracts, the cadre evaluation system also provides an institutionalized annual process for assessing the behavior of lower-level officials, auditing their accounts, and investigating irregularities. The annual review process that accompanies the system of performance contracts is often the first line of defense against corruption and malfeasance in village public administration and finance. Such reviews entail audits as well as opportunities for citizens to make their views and opinions known. When irregularities come to light, these may trigger more extensive investigations.

Localities, however, vary widely in how closely they supervise lower-level officials and punish malfeasance. Local authorities have significant discretion over how much bureaucratic discipline they want to exert, and when to punish individual wrongdoers. Wu and Zhu point out that "leader-directed Chinese-style anti-corruption" initiatives vary in strength across "different time periods and across localities under different central and local leaders."[6] Cai documents immense variation across localities in punishment of lower levels by middle-level principals, and notes that "[t]he operation of disciplinary institutions is under the influence of Party and government leaders at each level."[7] This regional variation is corroborated by data from our 2008 nationally representative

[5] Lily L. Tsai, *Accountability without Democracy: Solidary Groups and Public Goods Provision in Rural China*, Cambridge University Press, 2007. See also Lynette H. Ong, *Prosper or Perish: Credit and Fiscal Systems in Rural China*, Cornell University Press, 2012.

[6] Yiping Wu and Jiangnan Zhu, "Corruption, Anti-Corruption, and Inter-County Income Disparity in China," *The Social Science Journal* 48, no. 3 (September 2011): 435–48.

[7] Yongshun Cai, *State and Agents in China: Disciplining Government Officials*, Stanford University Press, 2014.

survey. Though economic development and public goods provision were the highest priority on 35 percent of performance contracts given by township officials to village authorities, only about half of these contracts were backed with punishment for poor performance.

Localities also vary in the targets that townships set for the village officials who report to them. Studies of the cadre responsibility system have shown that targets are typically set from above based on the priorities of higher levels. Ong finds that despite vast differences in income per capita, proximity to an urban center, economic structure, and natural resources, all the townships in her study, scattered across the three very different provinces of Zhejiang, Shandong, and Hebei, had hard targets for economic development that were almost identical.[8] Similarly, Oi et al. suggest that township oversight over villages is strongest in places where counties have increased oversight over townships rather than a function of what goes on in the villages within townships.[9]

Given the structure of public administration in China, the discretion exercised by township officials in how they supervise village authorities is not surprising. County officials have little ability to audit township officials directly. Instead, township government leaders are audited by their own township audit bureaus and discipline inspection commissions. Thus, when township authorities choose to discipline village officials for poor performance and malfeasance, they generally do so of their own volition. Because township governments in China have so much discretion over the design of performance contracts to supervise village officials and whether they enforce punishments for officials who fail to live up to their responsibilities, performance contracts with explicit penalties can signal the intentions of the individuals in office at the township level and whether they are "good types."[10]

[8] Lynette H. Ong, *Prosper or Perish: Credit and Fiscal Systems in Rural China*, Cornell University Press, 2012; see also Kevin J. O'Brien and Lianjiang Li, "Selective Policy Implementation in Rural China," *Comparative Politics* 31, no. 2 (January 1999): 167; see Thomas P. Bernstein and Lü Xiaobo, *Taxation without Representation in Contemporary Rural China*, vol. 37, Cambridge University Press, 2003.

[9] Jean C. Oi, Kim Singer Babiarz, Linxiu Zhang, Renfu Luo, and Scott Rozelle, "Shifting Fiscal Control to Limit Cadre Power in China's Townships and Villages," *The China Quarterly* 211 (September 8, 2012): 669.

[10] See Maria Edin, "Remaking the Communist Party-State: The Cadre Responsibility System at the Local Level in China," *China: An International Journal* 1, no. 1 (2003): 1–15; Maria Edin, "State Capacity and Local Agent Control in China: CCP Cadre Management from a Township Perspective," *The China Quarterly* 173 (March 20, 2003): 35–52. In contrast to Edin, Landry is more skeptical about the cadre responsibility system's ability to sanction officials. Pierre F. Landry, *Decentralized Authoritarianism in China: The*

The Changing Role of Citizen Participation in Retributive Justice

In contrast to the Maoist period, when citizens were encouraged to participate in punishment directly through struggle sessions and violence against malfeasant officials, government authorities deliberately situated these actions outside the boundary of conventional participation after the start of reforms in 1978. Formal channels for citizen monitoring of officials existed – citizens were allowed to register complaints and report cases of corruption and poor performance – but state-led popular sanctioning ceased. As Wedeman notes, anti-corruption initiatives in the reform period have called for "increased public involvement … wherein the 'masses' are asked to report corrupt cadres but not allowed to take an active or leading role, as was the case in a Maoist campaign."[11]

This redefinition of citizen participation as the monitoring of officials rather than both monitoring and sanctioning is consistent with what McCubbins and Schwartz have called a system of "fire-alarm accountability." Citizens monitor government officials for corruption and poor performance and alert higher-level authorities by "ringing the alarm" through complaint channels. Higher-level authorities are then the ones who respond, investigate, and impose punishment. Recent studies suggest that many of the corruption investigations now conducted by the government are initiated in response to citizen complaints. Hsu notes that in March 1998, the Party Central Commission for Discipline Inspection reported that 90 percent of corruption cases in China were reported by individual citizens.[12] Cai estimates that 60–80 percent of corruption cases investigated by legal departments were initially reported by the public through letters, visits, online reports, emails, and phone calls. In 2001, the Supreme Procuratorate reported that citizen complaints accounted for 70 percent of the corruption cases investigated.[13]

Though government authorities have circumscribed citizen participation in this way, the regime's encouragement of participation has not been

Communist Party's Control of Local Elites in the Post-Mao Era, Cambridge University Press, 2008.

[11] Andrew Wedeman, "Anticorruption Campaigns and the Intensification of Corruption in China," *Journal of Contemporary China* 14, no. 42 (February 2005): 93–116.

[12] Carolyn L. Hsu, "Political Narratives and the Production of Legitimacy: The Case of Corruption in Post-Mao China," *Qualitative Sociology* 24, no. 1 (2001): 46–47.

[13] Yongshun Cai, *State and Agents in China: Disciplining Government Officials*, Stanford University Press, 2014.

limited to rhetoric.[14] Many local governments have taken steps to implement new formal channels for citizens to provide information and make complaints about misbehaving state agents. Starting in the late 1980s, more than 3,600 local procuratorate offices established centers for citizens to report on corruption.[15] Telephone hotlines and public awareness campaigns disseminating information on how to make complaints have also been created. In 1998, the party recruited more than 100,000 prosecutors all over China to canvas neighborhoods and provide legal advice to citizens on how to report corruption. In all of these efforts, citizens were guaranteed anonymity and protection.[16] Between 1996 and June 2008, the government received almost 14 million reports from citizens of corruption, embezzlement, bribery, inappropriate handling of public funds, and dereliction of duty.[17]

Village elections, often interpreted as the implementation of limited democratic rights for citizens to choose their own local officials, might in fact be more accurately viewed as a channel for citizens to report on the behavior of local officials to higher levels. As Edin observes, "[v]illage elections are in my view part of the same trend to delegate evaluation and monitoring functions to the local community." Because the township government continues to appoint the village party secretary, the outcome of village elections does not change the entire village leadership. Instead, voting acts as "client rating" which "is intended to improve governance and efficiency," not as the exercise of democratic rights.[18]

In a fire-alarm system of accountability, what citizens believe about the commitment of higher levels to punishing corruption and malfeasance becomes critical for whether they believe that it is worth their time and effort to monitor lower levels and make complaints about poor performance. Unless higher levels actually punish poorly performing agents, there is no reason for citizens to participate in monitoring and reporting misbehavior. Given that higher levels provide these channels for citizen complaints, as Cai notes, "if people's claims and demands are legitimate, the

---

[14] Wenfang Tang, *Populist Authoritarianism: Chinese Political Culture and Regime Sustainability*, Oxford University Press, 2016.

[15] Yongshun Cai, *State and Agents in China: Disciplining Government Officials*, Stanford University Press, 2014.

[16] Carolyn L. Hsu, "Political Narratives and the Production of Legitimacy: The Case of Corruption in Post-Mao China," *Qualitative Sociology* 24, no. 1 (2001): 46–47.

[17] Yongshun Cai, *State and Agents in China: Disciplining Government Officials*, Stanford University Press, 2014.

[18] Maria Edin, "Remaking the Communist Party-State: The Cadre Responsibility System at the Local Level in China," *China: An International Journal* 1, no. 1 (2003): 9.

high-level officials may need to respond either symbolically or substantively to maintain their own legitimacy."[19]

Retributive Justice and Anti-Corruption under Xi Jinping

Since becoming president in 2012, Xi Jinping has clearly heightened the salience of retributive justice for public opinion. But as we have seen through previous chapters, Xi's governance strategies build on long-standing institutional legacies and political culture rooted in imperial China that have made strategies of retributive justice an effective tool for mobilizing public support. A 2018 newspaper report estimated that more than 1.4 million officials have been investigated by the anti-corruption campaign during the five years since Xi became president.[20] Consistent with a model of retributive justice, regulations promulgated in 2014 on the appointment and promotion of government officials stress that moral character as well as ability should be a key criterion for evaluating the performance of public officials. Leading party and government cadre promotions and appointments are to follow the "principle of having both ability and integrity, and putting virtue first."[21] Government-controlled media under Xi have also increasingly described misbehavior by officials in terms of their moral failings. Javed notes that many officials prosecuted for corruption are often also accused of paying prostitutes for sex to reinforce the public depiction of their turpitude. These "sensationalized accounts of moral wrongdoing" help to mobilize public support for a campaign that could otherwise be dismissed as a campaign against potential political competitors.[22]

Xi's regime has also made a point of providing credible signals that government authorities are willing to punish corruption and malfeasance.

[19] Yongshun Cai, "The Resistance of Chinese Laid-off Workers in the Reform Period," *The China Quarterly* 170 (June 25, 2002): 329.

[20] Josh Rudolph, "New Anti-Graft Ministry Heightens Rights Concerns," *China Digital Times*, February 23, 2018, citing Katsuji Nakazawa, "Welcome to the Club: Xi Takes Anti-Corruption Hunt to All Chinese," *Nikkei Asian Review*, January 29, 2018; see also Reuters, "China's Xi: We Can't Be 'Blindly Optimistic' on Corruption Inside the Communist Party," *Newsweek*, July 2017.

[21] Anne Henochowicz, "Work Regulations for Leading Party and Government Cadre Promotions and Appointments," *China Digital Times*, February 4, 2014.

[22] Jeffrey A. Javed, *Righteous Revolutionaries: Morality, Mobilization, and Violence in the Making of the Chinese State (Manuscript Draft)*, forthcoming, citing Eva Li, "Ex-Aide to China's Personnel Chief Sacked for 'Corrupt Political Morals,'" *South China Morning Post*, August 3, 2017.

For more than a year after the announcement of the anti-corruption campaign in late 2012, 500 cases of dismissals of government officials were published on the website of the Central Commission for Disciplinary Inspection (CCDI), averaging almost one dismissal a day.[23] Though high-profile cases reported in the media not surprisingly focus on leaders at the top, data collected by Xi et al. for the period 2013–2016 show that officials at municipal and provincial levels are also being investigated and charged, and that municipal officials are even more frequently charged than provincial officials. During fieldwork conducted in 2016 and 2017, both citizens and local officials at township and village levels viewed national anti-corruption campaigns as affecting the political climate and oversight coming from above, and local officials reporting fearing for their positions.

Not surprisingly, the anti-corruption campaign also takes advantage of historical legacies that prioritize retributive justice over procedural justice. Suspects can be held under *shuanggui*, a secret detention system overseen by the CCP's Central Commission for Discipline Inspection (CCDI), which has been criticized for the use of torture. Although Xi announced at the 19th Party Congress in October 2017 that *shuanggui* would be abolished and replaced by formal regulations, critics believe these initiatives simply codify many of its practices into law.[24]

Xi's strategy of retributive justice is clearly centralized, but it remains unclear how institutionalized it will be. Some view the 2018 establishment of the National Supervision Commission as the creation of a "fourth branch of government" that formalizes and extends the anti-corruption drive. The new bureaucracy is empowered to supervise, detain, and investigate around 200 million people working in the public sector as civil servants, employees at state-owned enterprises, as well as doctors, nurses, teachers, and academics at public institutions.[25] Despite the fact that the

[23] Wenfang Tang, *Populist Authoritarianism: Chinese Political Culture and Regime Sustainability*, Oxford University Press, 2016.

[24] "People's Republic of China Supervision Law (Draft)," *China Law Translate*, 2017, www .chinalawtranslate.com/en/peoples-republic-of-china-supervision-law-draft/; Josh Rudolph, "New Anti-Graft Ministry Heightens Rights Concerns," *China Digital Times*, February 23, 2018; Samuel Wade, "Party Tightens Rule Over Law with Supervisory Reforms," *China Digital Times*, January 25, 2018.

[25] Katsuji Nakazawa reviewed measures in Xi's anti-party corruption drive, and described the campaign's significant potential expansion and empowerment of an effective "fourth branch of government" following the expected passing of the supervision law: "Now, by using the national supervisory commission, the crusade will be expanded to cover some 200 million people, including nonparty members, working in the public sector."

new supervision law is currently still in draft form, provincial and muni-
cipal-level supervision commissions have already been set up in several
regions as nascent local branches of the new bureaucracy.[26]

Others see Xi's anti-corruption initiatives as a return to the ad-hoc
approach to retributive justice of Maoist-era mass campaigns. Like the
work teams of the Maoist period, the central government has deployed
surprise inspection teams to all levels of government as well as state-
owned enterprises and universities. The Central Commission for
Discipline Inspection said in an October 16, 2014 statement on its website
that such teams are intended to "achieve an intimidating effect."

Xi's regime has also shown a renewed interest in mobilizing citizen
participation in the monitoring and identification of corrupt officials.
Guidelines published by the CCDI direct its new anti-graft inspection
teams to conduct surprise investigations of government offices by "des-
cending on the inspection target" and then publicly announcing their
contact details, including a hotline and mail box, to encourage whistleblowers, whose contact details should be discarded when the team with-
draws. The media has also publicized cases of successful whistleblowers.
Liu Tienan, the former deputy head of the National Development and
Reform Commission, a powerful economic planning agency, was sentenced to life in prison in 2014 after a journalist accused him of graft.[27]

Top officials have even hinted at reinstating citizen participation in
sanctioning, although there appears to be conflict about this issue within
the CCP.[28] In April 2018, Premier Li Keqiang delivered a speech to the
State Council calling for ordinary citizens to use social media and the
internet to exert oversight over officials and discourage them from
engaging in corruption. Li's comments were subsequently censored, possibly in part to dissuade groups like the New Citizens' Movement, which
was founded in 2010 to promote civil society and government

Katsuji Nakazawa, "Welcome to the Club: Xi Takes Anti-Corruption Hunt to All
Chinese," *Nikkei Asian Review*, January 29, 2018.

[26] Gao notes that despite the fact that the law has yet to be passed, provincial and municipal-
level supervision commissions have already been appointed in several regions across
China. Charlotte Gao, "While Law Unpassed, Provincial Supervision Commissions
Already Established in China," *The Diplomat*, February 2018, cited in Josh Rudolph,
"New Anti-Graft Ministry Heightens Rights Concerns," *China Digital Times*,
February 23, 2018.

[27] David Lague, Benjamin Kang Lim, and Charlie Zhu, "Special Report: Fear and
Retribution in Xi's Corruption Purge," *Reuters*, December 23, 2014.

[28] Josh Rudolph, "Premier's Call for Supervision of Government Censored," *China Digital
Times*, May 2, 2018.

transparency, but possibly also in part from apprehension about even the remotest possibility of the uncontrollable citizen mobilization that characterized the Cultural Revolution.[29]

In any case, the salience of retributive justice in local governance and public opinion has increased under Xi Jinping. The regime has increasingly made use of a variety of strategies for signaling their commitment to punishing corruption and malfeasance, although the formal cadre evaluation system continues to be the most common everyday mechanism for supervising the performance of village officials at the grassroots level. At the same time, township authorities have discretion over if or when to enforce penalties when village officials misbehave or underperform. In some places, there are no penalties for village officials who fail to accomplish their responsibilities on paper, much less in reality. Based on a theory of retributive justice concerns, we would expect citizens in these localities to be less likely to evaluate the moral character of local authorities positively. Conversely, citizens in localities that ensure implementing performance contracts with penalties should be more likely to view higher-level authorities as well intentioned and to believe that authorities share their values. We should also expect citizens in these localities to be more likely to engage in conventional participation through formal mechanisms such as village elections and complaint channels, as well as more likely to comply voluntarily with government authorities.

PATTERNS AT THE OUTSET OF THE XI PERIOD: FINDINGS FROM 2017 RURAL BEIJING SURVEY

Do citizens look at the actual institutions for top-down punishment implemented by higher levels in their communities and read them as signals about the state's commitment to retributive justice? A retributive justice model of citizen engagement posits that disciplinary institutions shape behavior and attitudes toward government authorities, not only by changing incentives or the allocation of resources, but also by providing signals about the intentions and moral commitments of authorities. Based on a retributive justice model, we should expect that citizens in localities that enforce top-down performance contracts with penalties should have higher moral character evaluations of higher-level authorities (the

---

[29] Sophie Beach, "20,000 Officials Punished for Violating Discipline," *China Digital Times*, December 3, 2013; Samuel Wade, "New Trial for New Citizen Transparency Activists," *China Digital Times*, December 3, 2013.

principals overseeing the agents) and should be more likely to engage in local governance, both in terms of political participation and in terms of voluntary compliance. Unlike the experimental findings discussed in the previous chapter, however, the observational analyses in this section cannot evaluate the causal impact of top-down institutions for retributive justice. Nevertheless, it is important to look at whether real-world top-down institutions are at least correlated with citizen attitudes about their actual government officials in the ways that a retributive justice model posits.

To assess whether these expectations are borne out, we first look at the "most likely" case of the Xi Jinping period and draw on data from a 2017 field survey conducted on 892 randomly sampled respondents from two counties in rural Beijing. In addition to the conjoint experiment administered through this in-person survey discussed in Chapter 4, respondents also answered a short questionnaire on local governance and their political attitudes and behaviors. In collaboration with a Chinese academic, we surveyed 892 individuals selected through a multistage sampling process from two rural counties within Beijing municipality, which spans a jurisdiction slightly larger than the state of Connecticut. While urban Beijing is highly developed, rural Beijing is relatively poor, with per capita consumption about the same as the national average (see chapter appendix).

Top-Down Punishment. To measure the existence of bureaucratic institutions for top-down discipline, respondents were asked whether they thought township authorities signed performance contracts with village officials and whether they thought these contracts included penalties when village officials failed to meet performance targets for development and public goods provision. A dichotomous measure for the existence of top-down punishment for poor performance was constructed to equal one when respondents answered yes to both questions, and zero otherwise.

While this indicator is not a perfect measure for the existence of retributive justice institutions as failure to meet these kinds of targets can result from lack of capacity as well as malfeasance, nevertheless, the cadre evaluation system and its performance contracts serve as the central means for detecting and punishing corruption as well as underperformance. We also know from comments made by survey respondents to interviewers and our survey pretesting interviews that anti-corruption was on their minds when the survey asked about top-down punishment and bureaucratic supervision, and in fact, these questions about township

TABLE 5.1 *Summary statistics from the 2017 rural Beijing survey*

Variable	Mean
Age	46.99
	(se = 0.23; n = 888)
Age >= 40	0.7
	(se = 0.03; n = 888)
Female	0.52
	(se = 0.02; n = 889)
Education >= High school	0.38
	(se = 0.02; n = 891)
Party member	0.16
	(se = 0.01; n = 890)
Household consumption	3301.24
	(se = 108.51; n = 880)
N	897

penalizing of village officials were the closest questions we could push to ask about anti-corruption punishment. The survey did not ask citizens directly about their evaluation of Xi's anti-corruption measures as local officials giving permission for the survey indicated that we could not explicitly ask respondents to evaluate Xi's decisions or policies.

Citizen Behavior and Evaluations of Government. To measure citizen evaluations of the intentions and moral character of township officials and their willingness to comply voluntarily with local government authorities, the survey asked three questions. The first question was whether respondents agreed or disagreed with the following statement: "When township officials punish village officials for misusing public funds, villagers are more likely to think that township officials share their values." As Table 5.2 shows, when citizens think that township officials implement performance contracts with penalties for village officials, they are indeed more likely to believe that township punishment of corruption and malfeasance signals that township authorities share their values.

Second, the survey also asked citizens how satisfied they were with the *process* of how public projects are organized, independently of how they felt about the *result* of the public project construction. Even when a road or other infrastructural project does not directly benefit the respondent, he

TABLE 5.2 *Bivariate regression results from the 2017 rural Beijing survey*

	Dependent variable		
	Officials share citizens' values	Satisfied with process of organizing public projects	Willing to contribute to public projects
Belief about contracts with penalties	0.494*** (0.145)	0.565*** (0.179)	0.338** (.132)
Constant	3.100*** (0.058)	3.262*** (0.072)	3.690*** (0.053)
Observations	656	323	652
R^2	0.017	0.030	0.010

Note: *$p<0.1$; **$p<0.05$; ***$p<0.01$
Standard errors are in parentheses.

or she may still believe that the project's finances and logistics were handled with responsibility and integrity. Again, we see that when citizens think that township authorities penalize village officials using the cadre evaluation system, they are more likely to express satisfaction with the process of public project construction.[30]

Finally, the survey asked citizens about their willingness to contribute resources to public projects. In rural China, citizens are often asked to provide voluntary contributions of labor and money to projects such as the construction of roads, school buildings, and irrigation infrastructure to supplement investments and materials provided by the government. Since village officials lack access to formal coercive resources, such contributions are generally voluntary in practice as well as by law. If citizens see top-down punishment by township authorities as signal of their commitment to retributive justice, we should expect them to be more willing to cooperate with requests for such voluntary donations since they have stronger beliefs in the good intentions of authorities. Data from the survey are consistent with this expectation. Citizens express higher willingness to comply with contributions to public

[30] After each section of the survey, respondents were given the option to terminate the survey if they felt it was taking too long, though they were not informed what types of questions were in the remaining sections. This question was in the last section of the survey, which accounts for why we see far fewer respondents answering this question.

projects when higher levels have implemented performance contracts and formal mechanisms for supervising village officials and punishing malfeasance.

PATTERNS UNDER WEN JIABAO: FINDINGS FROM 2008 SURVEY DATA

We might expect that retributive justice concerns would of course exist due to Xi Jinping's anti-corruption campaign, but have they only become salient in recent years? Survey data from a nationally representative survey administered in 2008 even before Xi came to power suggest that ordinary people in rural China were already expressing concern about retributive justice and top-down discipline. We again see that when government authorities signal that they are committed to bureaucratic supervision and retributive justice by implementing penalties for lower-level officials through the cadre evaluation system's performance contracts, citizens are more likely to believe that authorities uphold their moral values and are more likely to engage in local governance. Seeing these relationships in a time period when there is no government anti-corruption campaign that makes voicing support for retributive justice salient (and politically correct) helps to increase our confidence that retributive justice concerns are generally important for citizen attitudes and behavior.

These data come from a nationally representative survey (with the exception of Xizang province, also known as Tibet) administered in collaboration with the Chinese Center for Agricultural Policy to 2,000 households and the local officials of 100 villages in 25 counties across 5 provinces. One province was randomly selected from each of China's major agroecological zones: Jiangsu from the eastern coastal region, Sichuan from the southwest, Shaanxi from the northwest, Hebei from the central region, and Jilin from the northeast. Through a stratified clustering strategy, five counties were randomly selected from each province, two townships from each county, two villages from each township, and twenty households from each village.[31]

---

[31] Per capita gross value of industrial output was used for stratification since it is often more reliable than official Chinese statistics on rural net per capita income and is one of the best predictors of standard of living. See Scott Rozelle, "Stagnation without Equity: Patterns of Growth and Inequality in China's Rural Economy," *The China Journal* 35 (January 1996): 63–92.

Top-Down Punishment. In this study, both township and village authorities were surveyed about local economic development and local governance. Both township and village authorities were asked whether the township signed performance contracts with village officials that identified village development as the most important target and enforced penalties on village officials for substandard performance.

In contrast to the 2017 survey discussed earlier, which asked ordinary citizens about their beliefs about the existence of such performance contracts, this measure reflects the actual existence of such contracts, as corroborated by surveys administered to township officials as well as village officials. At the township level, one of the leading township officials – the township party secretary or township head – was asked whether the highest priority target was village development and whether the salary of village officials was conditional on the achievement of this target. At the village level, one of the leading village officials – the village party secretary or village head – was similarly asked whether the highest priority target for both the village party secretary and the village head was village development, and whether the salaries of these village officials were conditional on the achievement of this target. A dichotomous measure for the existence of performance contracts with penalties for poor performance was constructed to equal one when both township and village officials answered yes to these questions, and zero otherwise.

Again, this measure is not a perfect reflection of the existence of retributive justice institutions as failure to meet performance targets can result from lack of capacity as well as from corruption and malfeasance. But since performance contracts are the primary means of township supervision that are visible to ordinary villagers, they serve as an important signal of whether or not township authorities care about top-down discipline and retributive justice. Township authorities that do not bother to enforce bureaucratic performance contracts with penalties are unlikely to take stronger measures to ensure that village officials are doing their jobs properly.

These data allow us to assess whether citizens are more likely to have positive evaluations of the moral character of township officials and to engage in local governance when township authorities actually do implement institutions for top-down punishment of village officials, rather than when citizens simply think that they do. Because we ask both township and village officials, we can corroborate the existence of these institutions from both sides independently, thus reducing any potential reporting biases.

Controls. As with the rural Beijing survey discussed in the previous section, the data from this 2008 survey only allow us to examine whether top-down bureaucratic institutions are correlated with citizen attitudes and behaviors in the way that a retributive justice model posits. This survey, however, did include a richer set of village- and individual-level covariates so we can further examine the results from both bivariate and controlled regressions to probe the robustness of correlations. Village characteristics that might confound the relationship between the existence of top-down institutions for bureaucratic discipline and citizen engagement include the size of the village, how rural or peripherally located the village is, and the level of village development. We thus control for 2007 village population; geographical dispersion of village as measured by the distance between the two furthest settlements within the village; the distance from the village to the township; the number of kindergartens and nursery schools in the village in 2004; the number of enterprises in the village in 2004; and the average wage for men and women in 2004. Individual-level controls include age, sex, party membership, and *hukou* status (whether the respondent is registered as a rural or urban resident).

Attitudinal and Behavioral Outcomes. We assess the relationship between township institutions of top-down punishment and three outcomes: citizen evaluations of the moral character of township authorities; citizen participation in local governance; and citizen willingness to take complaints about the performance of village officials to authorities. Based on a model of retributive justice concerns, we should expect citizens in places where township authorities have implemented top-down institutions for disciplining village officials to believe that township authorities have better moral character, as well as to be more likely to participate and complain to authorities about governmental performance.

Our index of citizen evaluations of township moral character is based on the six questions in the survey that ask respondents about the benevolence of township authorities. In rural China, the vast majority of villagers have little or no direct interaction with township officials. Their evaluations of township officials are thus inferences they make based on what they hear and see of township policies and regulations toward villages and village officials. As a result, some of the survey questions ask citizens directly about what they believe of the intentions of township officials, while others measure beliefs about intentions by asking citizens to speculate about how they think township officials might interact with villagers.

An overall additive index of township moral character evaluations is constructed by summing the answers to the following questions: (1) Do you think the policies made by the township government really, truly reflect caring about villagers? (2) Do you think township officials care more about the interests of ordinary villagers or the policies of higher levels of governments? (3) Do you think township officials respect and take into account the views of villagers? (4) Do you think the township government welcomes villagers to come and complain about problems? (5) Do you think township officials give villagers a chance to express their views when making decisions? (6) Do you think township officials give villagers opportunities to participate in making decisions about the village's affairs?

As with the findings from the rural Beijing survey, when township authorities implement performance contracts with penalties for village officials, citizens are more likely to have positive evaluations of their moral character and benevolence. Both naïve and controlled regression analyses (Table 5.3) show a significant positive relationship between the existence of top-down disciplinary institutions and belief in the moral character of township authorities.

REGRESSION ANALYSIS

A model of retributive justice concerns also implies that citizens are more likely to engage in political participation when they believe that higher-level authorities are upholding retributive justice through the implementation of top-down disciplinary institutions. In this context, when township officials seem to be morally upstanding, citizens are more likely to believe that they are not just colluding with malfeasant village officials and that their implementation of village elections is genuine and the outcomes are not simply rigged behind the scenes.

To evaluate whether there is a relationship between top-down discipline and higher levels of citizen participation through formal channels, we can look at how many of the following actions a respondent has taken: (1) personally filled out and cast his or her own ballot in the last village election; (2) worked to persuade or mobilize others to vote for or against a particular candidate in the last village election; (3) nominated a candidate for the most recent village election;[32] (4) complained to village officials about problems with public goods provision. A simple additive

---

[32] This could include the respondent nominating himself or herself.

TABLE 5.3 *Regression results from the representative 2008 rural survey*

	Dependent variable					
	Belief in moral character		Level of participation in public projects		Willingness to engage in public projects	
Contracts with penalties	0.377**	0.331*	0.172*	0.173*	0.091**	0.071**
	(0.161)	(0.172)	(0.089)	(0.090)	(.032)	(0.030)
Constant	1.920***	2.317***	1.249***	1.278***	0.366***	0.292***
	(0.073)	(0.345)	(0.037)	(0.154)	(0.016)	(0.053)
Controls	No	Yes	No	Yes	No	Yes
Observations	704	683	1,952	1,846	1,894	1,831
R^2	0.007	0.041	0.005	0.099	0.005	0.039

Note: * $p<0.1$; ** $p<0.05$; *** $p<0.01$. Controls include 2007 village population; geographical dispersion of village as measured by the distance between the two furthest settlements within the village; distance from the village to the township; hukou status of respondent; sex of respondent; age of respondent; party membership status of respondent.
Standard errors clustered at village level are in parentheses. "Don't know" answers are coded as missing

index for the level of political participation is constructed by summing the responses to these four yes/no questions.

Consistent with a model of retributive justice concerns, we can see from *Table 5.3* that there is a positive relationship between township institutions for top-down punishment and higher levels of conventional participation. As with citizen evaluations of the moral character of township authorities, both naïve and controlled regression analyses (Table 5.3) show a significant positive relationship between the existence of top-down disciplinary institutions and the level of citizen participation in local governance.

Finally, we also examine the relationship between top-down institutions of bureaucratic discipline and the willingness of citizens to engage in "higher-risk" participation as measured by their willingness to complain to township authorities about poor implementation of village elections. Specifically, this survey question asks respondents whether or not they would complain to township officials if higher levels decided to cancel the next round of village elections. Registering complaints with township officials is an action that entails both higher costs and higher risks.

Villages can be located far from township government offices, which means that villagers have to go out of their way to travel to the township to make the complaint and to pay for transportation costs. Complaining to the township also indicates that the villager considers the issue a serious one. Because this action can imply more serious criticism of government authorities, it potentially entails more risk and fear on the part of would-be complainants.

Again, consistent with a retributive justice theory that hypothesizes that citizens will be more likely to engage with authorities when they believe that officials are committed to upholding retributive justice, we can see from Table 5.3 that citizens are more willing to engage even in higher-cost, higher-risk political participation when they see township authorities implementing top-down disciplinary institutions. Both naïve and controlled regression analyses (Table 5.3) show a significant positive relationship between the existence of top-down disciplinary institutions and citizen willingness to go to township authorities to complain about poor implementation of village elections.

Placebo Tests. One concern is that in places with stronger, top-down institutions of bureaucratic discipline, political coercion and repression are also stronger. It may thus be that respondents in places with top-down punishment are simply more likely to give politically desirable responses – more positive evaluations of township moral character, more participation through conventional channels – because they fear repercussions for saying the wrong thing. This possibility seems unlikely given the willingness of respondents in places with more top-down punishment to say that they would engage in higher-risk complaining to the township. Nevertheless, we can assess this possibility by looking at the relationship between township institutions for the enforcement of birth control and tax collection – more unpopular and coercive targets – to see if politically desirable responses are more common in places where there is clearly more control and coercion exerted over citizens.

A dichotomous measure for top-down control and coercion of citizens is constructed from similar questions to the measure for top-down supervision of village officials. Both township and village leading officials were asked to report the highest priority target on township performance contracts for village officials and whether the salary of village officials was conditional on the achievement of this target. If this target was birth control or tax collection, and there were salary penalties for failing to

TABLE 5.4 *Placebo regression result from the representative 2008 rural survey using top-down citizen control as the main independent variable*

	Dependent variable					
	Belief of moral character		Level of participation in public projects		Willingness to engage in public projects	
Top-down citizen control	0.050	0.059	0.005	0.015	−0.013	−0.010
	(0.139)	(0.135)	(0.068)	(0.071)	(.029)	(0.028)
Constant	1.937***	2.077***	1.292***	1.293***	0.388***	0.305***
	(0.080)	(0.372)	(0.044)	(0.159)	(0.020)	(0.064)
Controls	No	Yes	No	Yes	No	Yes
Observations	688	667	1,850	1,786	1,834	1,771
R^2	0.0002	0.030	0.0001	0.095	0.0002	0.035

Note: $*p<0.1$; $**p<0.05$; $***p<0.01$
Standard errors clustered at village level are in parentheses. "Don't know" answers are coded as missing

achieve the target, the dichotomous measure for top-down control of citizens equals one, and zero otherwise.

As we see in Table 5.4, there is no relationship between top-down citizen control and citizen behavior or attitudes about local authorities. Individuals who live in places where township authorities make coercive targets like the enforcement of birth control or tax collection, the top priority for village officials is no more likely to express positive moral character evaluations of township authorities than individuals who live in places where top-down citizen control is lower. They are also no less likely to engage in political participation or to be willing to take the higher-risk action of complaining to township officials about poorly implemented village elections. The fact that respondents are not more likely to give politically correct responses in places where local officials exert more top-down control or coercion can somewhat alleviate concerns about desirability bias.

Overall, the analyses in this section suggest that actual top-down institutions of bureaucratic discipline are correlated with citizen attitudes and behaviors in the ways expected by a retributive justice model of citizen engagement. These data have important limitations. With only 100 villages in the sample, our ability to detect statistically significant relationships is limited. We also cannot use these data to identify causal relationships. These correlations might reflect an equilibrium where more citizen engagement makes higher-level township authorities feel like it is more critical for them to implement top-down bureaucratic discipline of village officials, which then leads to more positive citizen evaluations of township moral character and sustains high levels of citizen engagement. Finally, even with these correlations, unobserved confounders could very well account for these patterns.

Nevertheless, these results serve as a plausibility probe into the external validity of the experimental findings reported in the previous chapter. Not only are ordinary people more likely to prefer hypothetical township authorities that enforce top-down institutions of bureaucratic discipline and to see them as having more moral character, but ordinary people are also more likely to view their actual township authorities as having more moral character and more likely to engage in local governance when their township authorities enforce top-down institutions to discipline their village officials.

INVESTIGATING THE RELATIONSHIP BETWEEN RETRIBUTIVE JUSTICE AND VOLUNTARY CITIZEN COMPLIANCE IN URBAN CHINA

The findings discussed in the previous sections are suggestive, but they increase our confidence that a retributive justice model of citizen evaluations of government is generalizable to real-world contexts beyond the survey experimental evidence presented in Chapter 4. In this section, we turn to evaluating the impact of retributive justice on voluntary compliance behavior among urban citizens.

Retributive Justice and Tax Compliance in Urban China

If the retributive justice model of citizen engagement is correct, citizens should be more likely to view government authorities as moral and committed to the public good when they enforce top-down institutions for discipline and punishment. When citizens believe that government authorities are moral, well-intentioned, and likely to pursue the public interest, they should be more willing to interact constructively with the government, not only by participating in formal channels for monitoring and sanctioning village officials, but also by complying voluntarily when government authorities ask them to pay taxes and contribute to public projects. When citizens believe that government authorities are genuinely committed to the public good, they themselves may also feel a greater sense of duty to the public good as well as more confidence that government authorities will use their payments to produce public goods.

To assess the impact of top-down institutions of discipline and punishment on voluntary compliance, I conducted a study in 2016 in collaboration with Xiaobo Lü to investigate citizen preferences for hypothetical property tax regimes and citizen willingness to comply with property taxation.[33] This study took advantage of the increasing salience of property taxation for urban Chinese residents. Property taxation has become a policy priority for the Chinese government, which has been seeking to develop new sources of revenue as economic growth slows and traditional sources of local fiscal revenue become depleted. In pursuit of this objective, the State Council issued provisional regulations on real estate registration, which took effect March 2015.[34] Pilot experiments with property taxes in Shanghai and Chongqing have been ongoing since 2011. Not surprisingly, however, the prospect of property taxation is contentious as real estate makes up nearly three-quarters of the assets of Chinese households.[35] The conditions under which people will comply voluntarily with property taxation are thus a looming question for both government and the public.

To study this question, we designed a conjoint survey experiment that was administered to an online sample of 895 urban Chinese respondents aged 25 and above. This experiment assesses the impact of top-down institutions for punishing lower-level misuse of tax revenue along with other factors that might influence citizen preferences for particular property tax regimes such as the inclusion of institutions for citizen input on how tax revenues should be used, the existence of penalties for late payment of taxation, and an exemption from taxation on the first property owned. We commissioned two survey firms with large respondent pools in China, Qualtrics and Survey Sampling International (SSI), to implement identical surveys. Using a quota sampling strategy based on age and gender, and targeting the adult urban population, Qualtrics and SSI collected data from 464 respondents and 431 respondents, respectively, in May and June 2016.

[33] Xiaobo Lü and Lily L. Tsai, "When Do Citizens Want Representation in Exchange for Taxation? An Experimental Study on Property Tax in Urban China," *MIT Political Science Department Research Paper No. 2016-36*, 2016.

[34] Xinhua, "China Issues Real Estate Registration Rules," 2014, https://www.globaltimes.cn/content/898050.shtml.

[35] Keith Bradsher, "China's Housing Market Is Like a Casino. Can a Property Tax Tame It?" *New York Times*, January 22, 2018.

The conjoint experiment presented each respondent with four rounds of choices, selecting between two profiles of hypothetical property tax regimes in each round. The order of attributes was randomized for each respondent, and the levels of each attribute were randomly assigned in each round.

Each profile contained four attributes that theories of voluntary compliance suggest are important for willingness to comply with taxation (see Table 5.5). To evaluate the importance of retributive justice concerns, one attribute was whether or not the property tax regime included top-down institutions for the punishment of corruption and malfeasance. Specifically, respondents were told whether or not the tax regime included institutions for provincial government supervision of lower-level government use of tax revenue and punishment for misuse. To evaluate the importance of procedural justice concerns, the second attribute was whether or not the tax regime included institutions for citizen input on how tax revenues should be used. The remaining two attributes evaluated factors that economic theories of compliance have shown are important for compliance – the economic costs and benefits of the tax regime for the individual. Including these two attributes help us to benchmark the magnitude of the impact of retributive justice and procedural justice on citizen preferences and willingness to comply.

We looked at two outcomes. After each pair of tax regime profiles, we asked respondents to choose which profile he or she preferred and to indicate their willingness to comply with taxation under each regime on a five-point Likert scale (on which one was equal to "never comply" and five was equal to "always comply").

Findings from these data are again consistent with a retributive justice model of citizen evaluations and engagement. The existence of top-down

TABLE 5.5 *Conjoint experiment attributes*

Tax policy profile attribute	Possible value
Top-down provincial government supervision of lower-level government use of tax revenue and punishment for misuse	Yes or No
Channels for citizen input into use of tax revenue	Yes or No
Penalty for late payment of taxation	15 percent or 3 percent interest rate for late payment
Exemption of the first apartment from taxation	Yes or No

institutions for punishment of lower-level corruption and malfeasance had a significant positive effect on both citizen willingness to comply voluntarily with taxation and citizen preferences for a particular tax regime.

The most direct measure of our outcome of interest was citizen willingness to comply with taxation. We found that the estimated impact of the existence of top-down institutions of punishment was on par with the impact of the existence of channels for citizen input. It was also larger than the effect of increasing the penalty for late payment of taxes from an interest rate of 3 percent to a hefty 15 percent.

The second outcome was simply the respondent's choice or preference of tax regime. We look at both outcomes because the choice outcome may be a slightly less direct measure of voluntary compliance. Willingness to comply voluntarily with a property tax regime is likely to be one of the inputs into an individual's selection of tax regime but might not be the only one. Individuals, for example, may decide to select tax regimes that have more exemptions or lower tax rates, even if other aspects of the regime make them less likely to comply voluntarily. In other words, it is possible that individuals prioritize one set of variables when they reflect on whether they are willing to comply with something voluntarily but another set of variables when they think about what they would prefer as a policy.

Results are nevertheless similar when we look at the impact of top-down institutions on citizen selection of tax regimes. The existence of top-down institutions had an estimated impact on citizen selection of a tax regime that was close to the effect of the existence of channels for citizen input and an exemption for the first property owned. Including institutions for top-down auditing and sanctioning of corruption increased support for a tax policy by 9.8 percentage points.

These findings suggest that a theory of retributive justice concerns is useful for explaining both attitudinal and behavioral measures of citizen engagement with government in both rural and urban China. The remaining question is whether the salience of retributive justice is unique to China, or does the importance of retributive justice concerns extend beyond the Chinese context?

CROSS-NATIONAL PATTERNS IN RETRIBUTIVE JUSTICE AND TAX COMPLIANCE

To answer this question, this section discusses findings from a survey experiment that I conducted in fifty countries in collaboration with a research team at the World Bank.[36] This survey experiment evaluated the importance of retributive justice and procedural justice concerns in the formation of citizen beliefs about their responsibilities for paying government taxes.[37] In 2017, we administered an online study to evaluate the impact of top-down institutions of bureaucratic discipline and bottom-up institutions for citizen participation on tax morale, or the belief that citizens have a responsibility to pay their taxes. The importance of bureaucratic institutions for punishing corruption and malfeasance for tax morale was assessed along with the importance of democratic institutions for citizen input on how public monies should be spent.

To evaluate the impact of top-down disciplinary institutions and bottom-up democratic institutions, we designed a survey experiment that was administered to online respondents in fifty countries in June 2017 (see chapter appendix for a full list of countries). Using an online survey platform (Riwi), internet users who enter a frequently occurring typo in an internet search (e.g., "googel.com") were asked if they would like to take the survey. Respondents could decide whether or not to accept and were able to opt out at any time. Compared to traditional survey methods, platforms such as Riwi have advantages in terms of cost, speed, and geographical coverage. They, however, are more prone to issues such as attrition since respondents were not expecting to take a survey in the first place.

The questionnaire was translated into local languages by professional translators and then double-checked by researchers who were native speakers. Respondents in multilingual countries were able to select their preferred language. A total of 151,096 subjects answered the first substantive question (after the age and gender questions) and 65,471 respondents completed all 9 questions of the survey.

Respondents were randomly assigned to one of three treatment conditions in Table 5.6. In all three conditions, respondents were presented with an introduction that poses a question to them. Respondents assigned to the control group were provided information about the use of search engines and asked how positively or negatively they feel about advertising on search engines. Respondents assigned to the top-down discipline

---

[36] Fredrik M. Sjoberg, Jonathan Mellon, Tiago Peixoto, Johannes Hemker, and Lily L. Tsai, "Voice and Punishment: A Global Survey Experiment on Tax Morale," *Policy Research Working Paper No. 8855*, Washington, DC: World Bank, 2019, https://openknowledge .worldbank.org/handle/10986/31713, License: CC BY 3.0 IGO.

[37] This team included Fredrik Sjoberg, Hannes Hemker, Jonathan Mellon, and Tiago Peixoto.

TABLE 5.6 *Treatments*

Control group	Top-down accountability intervention	Bottom-up participation intervention
There are many popular search engines in the world, with different designs and functions. Search engines are used every day by over 1 billion people worldwide	When government money is misused, it is very important to find and punish those responsible. Your government has a national agency, the (AGENCY NAME), that helps to punish the misuse of government funds	You have been selected to be part of the Online Citizen Assembly: a national conversation about how the government of (COUNTRY NAME) should spend money. The results of the Online Citizen Assembly will be presented to the government
Many people say they are annoyed by all the advertising on search engines. How much does this apply to you?	The (AGENCY NAME) has investigated many cases of government corruption. Many people who misused government funds have been punished. Do you think it is good to have an agency that investigates government corruption?	What should your government spend more money on? The results of the Online Citizen Assembly will be presented to the government
Not at all	Yes	Defense and police
A bit	No	Education
Quite a bit		Transportation
Very much		Welfare
		Health
		Environment

condition were provided with information about the investigative and punitive functions of the anti-corruption agency in their respective country and asked how positively or negatively they feel about anti-corruption agencies. Respondents assigned to the bottom-up democratic conditions were provided information about an online initiative to collect citizen input about preferences for public investment and present it to the government, and then asked for their preferences.

To measure tax morale, we used two outcome questions, one from the General Social Survey (GSS) and another seeking to measure tax morale more concretely. The GSS question asks: "If a taxpayer does not report all of their income in order to pay less income taxes, do you feel that it is not wrong, a bit wrong, wrong, or seriously wrong?" Our question asks: "If a taxpayer does not report all of their income in order to pay less income taxes, what percentage of their income should they pay as a penalty? None (0 percent), 1–10 percent, 11–20 percent, or more than 20 percent?" Both of these questions provide measures of tax morale. The first question, however, is framed as a moral issue, while the second question is more specific and integrates the moral issue with policy considerations. The main outcome variable was a sum of these two outcome questions.

Findings. We find that both treatments have a large and significant effect on the main outcome variable, the sum of the two outcome questions. Consistent with a retributive justice theory, tax morale is highest in the top-down condition where the mean score on tax morale on a scale from 1 to 8 was 5.299, compared to the control group where the mean tax morale score was 5.068. Priming citizens to think about top-down discipline resulted in an increase of 0.124 standard deviations above the control group. The effect of priming citizens to think about top-down discipline was also greater than the effect of priming citizens to think about bottom-up democratic channels. The mean score on tax morale was 5.225 for the bottom-up condition.

When we look separately at the two component questions of the tax index, the rank order between the treatment conditions remains the same, although the difference between the two treatment conditions is larger for the morally framed GSS tax morale question than for the tax fine question. Effect estimates are similar when we estimate treatment effects using linear regression models with and without covariate adjustments on our main outcome variable and the two component questions. In models with covariate adjustment, we include the pretreatment covariates: age categories, gender, and employment status.

Robustness Checks. To assess the robustness of our findings, for each of the three outcome measures, we estimated models on the following subsets of countries: (1) only countries where we cannot reject balance for any covariate; (2) only countries where treatment status does not predict completing the survey; (3) only countries where, jointly with covariates, treatment status does not predict completing the survey; (4)

only countries where we can reject the hypothesis that the bottom-up procedural justice treatment had no effect on the corresponding manipulation check question; (5) only countries where we can reject the hypothesis that the top-down retributive justice treatment had no effect on the corresponding manipulation check question. For both the combined tax morale index measure and the two component questions, the estimated treatment effects remain remarkably stable when restricting the sample in these various ways. If anything, effect sizes are larger when discarding observations from countries where treatment assignment predicts attrition. An examination of attrition suggested that it is not differentially affecting subgroups we can measure. Instead, the most likely cause seemed to be that the control condition was slightly less taxing than the treatment conditions so that there was a general tendency across all subgroups to drop out of treatment groups at a slightly higher rate.

Summary. The results from this study suggest that top-down institutions of discipline and punishment for corruption are indeed important for many contexts beyond China. Despite the fact that this survey experiment was only able to assess the importance of top-down institutions through a relatively weak prime, we see remarkably consistent evidence for a global treatment effect on tax morale and the belief that citizens should comply with government taxation. This top-down treatment had a positive effect on forty out of the fifty countries in our sample.

Heterogeneous Effects: Where Does Retributive Justice Matter Most?

One final question we might have is where retributive justice concerns are more important or salient to ordinary people? What types of countries have stronger top-down treatment effects? The theory outlined in Chapter 2 posited that individuals who live in environments with more uncertainty may care more about retributive justice. This section draws on work conducted in collaboration with Paige Bollen that suggests citizens in countries that are experiencing greater economic uncertainty or socioeconomic diversity react more strongly to a top-down retributive justice prime.

For this analysis, we utilized nonparametric causal forests, a machine learning method using iterative algorithms to discover relevant subpopulations and their corresponding conditional average treatment effects in the data (see chapter appendix for more details).[38] Although we are underpowered with only fifty countries in the sample, Figures 5.1 and 5.2 suggest trends in treatment effects across values of country-level covariates that are consistent with a retributive justice model.

Change in Unemployment Rates

Countries with larger increases in the unemployment rate between 2016 and 2017 were more likely to have stronger treatment effects for the top-down retributive justice prime (Figure 5.1). As Chapter 2 notes, citizens in countries with higher levels of economic instability may experience more uncertainty, which may increase their need for a sense of social order and make retributive justice concerns more salient. (Though not directly germane to the focus of this book, it is interesting to note that citizens in countries with more economic uncertainty in terms of higher levels of change in unemployment seem to care less about the bottom-up democratic participation prime.)

As Figure 5.2 suggests, countries with higher levels of ethnolinguistic fractionalization (ELF) are also likely to have stronger treatment effects for the top-down retributive justice prime.[39] Countries that have higher levels of ethnic and linguistic diversity may find it more difficult to establish a sense of shared moral values across society and the state. Citizens in these countries may thus have a stronger desire for government authorities that establish and uphold a stable social order by punishing corruption and wrongdoing within their ranks. In contrast, there is little association between ethnic diversity and the bottom-up democratic participation prime.

CONCLUSION

Empirical investigations of data collected from rural and urban China, offline and online populations, and in countries beyond China, all consistently illustrate the importance of retributive justice and anti-corruption punishment for citizen engagement and evaluations of

---

[38] Stefan Wager and Susan Athey, "Estimation and Inference of Heterogeneous Treatment Effects Using Random Forests," *Journal of the American Statistical Association* 113, no. 523 (June 6, 2018): 1228–42.

[39] We utilize the ELF data from Fearon. James D. Fearon, "Ethnic and Cultural Diversity by Country," *Journal of Economic Growth* 8, no. 2 (2003): 195–222.

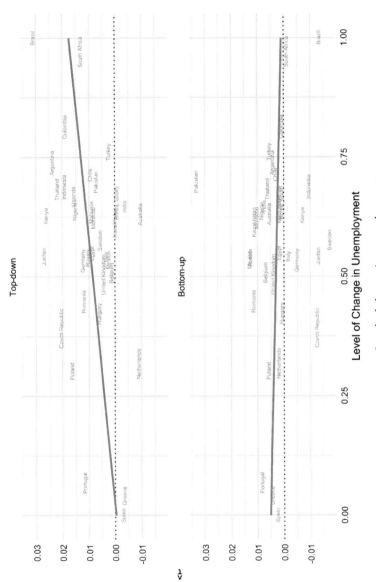

FIGURE 5.1 Level of change in unemployment.

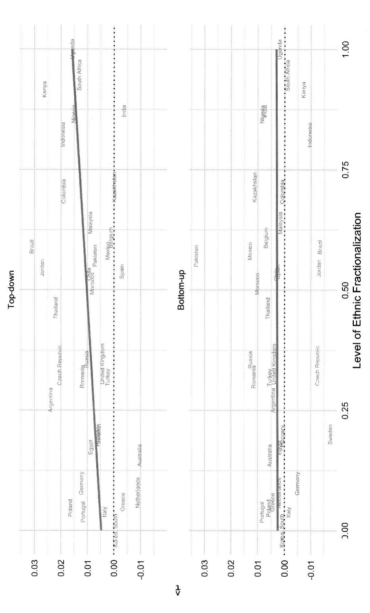

FIGURE 5.2 Level of ethnolinguistic fractionalization (ELF).

government authorities. All told, findings from a broad range of data sources and empirical investigations provide remarkably consistent support for the theory that retributive justice concerns and anti-corruption punishment play a role in the formation of citizen attitudes and beliefs about government authorities, their level of engagement with local governance and politics, and their willingness to comply voluntarily with government regulations. Retributive justice can help us understand attitudinal and behavioral outcomes that are central to mass political behavior and state–society relations.

The findings discussed in this chapter suggest that ordinary people in a range of contexts care about whether government authorities uphold moral and social order by punishing wrongdoers among their own. When ordinary people look at the institutions and initiatives for discipline and punishment that are implemented by higher levels, they make inferences about the moral character of those in power. These inferences influence their decisions about whether to engage in the institutions that government leaders have provided for participation and engagement and whether to comply with the government in areas like taxation where authorities would most like their cooperation.

Understanding when citizens engage in these ways has important implications for government responsiveness both to citizen concerns and to regime stability. If we want to understand when citizens in hybrid regimes and developing democracies take action to provide local authorities with feedback on their performance – an objective of many internationally funded development interventions that seek to promote better public services through "social accountability" and "citizen empowerment" – we need to understand whether government authorities are signaling through their actions and institutions that they care about retributive justice and punishing corruption. A retributive justice model posits that unless citizens think that government authorities care about their concerns and well-being, they may feel there is little point in going to the trouble of voicing these concerns.

It is worth noting that these forms of citizen engagement are motivated by the desire for better policy implementation, rather than the desire to participate in policymaking. In contrast to normative democratic theory, which focuses on representation and the aggregation of individual policy preferences into a choice of policy that represents the public as a whole, the forms of political participation discussed in this chapter constitute citizen participation in governance and accountability – the monitoring and sanctioning of government actors for performance and public goods provision. Although political scientists often focus far more attention on participation in elections and policymaking, participation that aims for better policy implementation and government accountability occurs and is important to citizens in all types of regimes.

Though retributive justice clearly influences political behavior across a range of contexts, it may be more salient for citizen monitoring behavior in authoritarian regimes. In consolidated democracies, citizens can, at least in theory, both monitor and sanction officials. Elections give citizens a direct role in retributive justice because they can punish wrongdoers by voting them out of office. In authoritarian regimes, however, citizens generally lack the ability to sanction government authorities formally. They can only participate by monitoring the behavior of officials in "fire-alarm accountability." Since it makes no sense to monitor and report misbehavior unless higher levels actually demonstrate that they will respond to these reports with punishment, retributive justice evaluations are likely to have a large impact on levels of citizen monitoring.

It is also worth noting that citizen engagement in governance and accountability is participation that reinforces regime stability. Citizens engage under the assumption that the system is not broken. Instead, it simply has bad apples or individuals that need to be weeded. In this type of system, government leaders welcome help in this endeavor from members of the public, and citizens participate by helping leaders through the channels that leaders have condoned.

A retributive justice model of citizen engagement helps us understand the role of top-down accountability and anti-corruption initiatives in authoritarian popularity. Can it also help us understand global trends in democratic dissatisfaction and backsliding? Is there anything we can learn from authoritarian popularity that can help us promote liberal democracy? In the next and final chapter, we turn to these questions.

CHAPTER 5 APPENDIX

List of countries in cross-national survey experiment

Algeria
Egypt
Iraq
Jordan
Morocco
Saudi Arabia
Sudan
Syria
Tunisia
Bangladesh
China
Hong Kong
Taiwan
Czech Republic
The Netherlands
Belgium
Australia
India
Kenya
Nigeria
Philippines
Singapore
South Africa
Uganda
The United Kingdom
The United States
Canada
Iran
France
Austria
Germany
Greece
Hungary
Indonesia
Italy
Japan

(continued)

(continued)

Kazakhstan
South Korea
Malaysia
Poland
Angola
Brazil
Portugal
Romania
Russia
Serbia
Slovakia
Argentina
Chile
Colombia
Mexico
Peru
Spain
Venezuela
Sweden
Thailand
Turkey
Ukraine
Pakistan
Vietnam

Nonparametric Causal Forests Analysis

Causal forests consist of a number of causal trees. Causal trees start by randomly dividing the data into two subgroups. The first subgroup (we will call this the training dataset) is used to partition the covariate space, while the second subgroup (we will call this the testing dataset) is used to estimate the average treatment effect for the subset corresponding to each of these partitions. We can similarly think of estimating causal trees as a two-step process. In the first step, a causal tree uses the training dataset to create relevant subgroups by finding the locally optimal partition of the covariate space by finding the partition with the largest difference in treatment effects. This process occurs at each division of the data, conditioning on previous partitions to estimate the locally optimal partition at each step. In the second step, the algorithm divides the testing dataset into these identified partitions and estimates the corresponding conditional average treatment effects for each of these partitions.

We split the data to estimate causal trees into two subgroups – one for creating partitions and the other for estimating conditional average treatment effects – because it allows us to draw valid statistical inferences about the estimated effects; using a different sample for inference allows us to treat that partition as if exogenously given. However, causal trees still tend to overfit the data, and their partitions and estimates are therefore variable. To address this variability, we estimate a large number of causal trees to create a causal forest. Causal forests reduce the variance of estimates by averaging over a number of causal trees. Additionally, each causal tree in a causal forest randomly chooses a subset of covariates to input in the algorithm (to address potentially highly correlated predictors) and randomly chooses a subset of the data with which to create the causal tree.

Causal forests have many advantages, particularly for exploratory analyses. By relying on the data to discover relevant subgroups, researchers can identify heterogeneity in treatment effects without having to prespecify hypotheses about this heterogeneity. Moreover, given that these analyses do not require prespecified hypotheses about when treatment effects may vary across covariates, they similarly do not require adjusting p-values for multiple hypothesis testing. Given these advantages and the exploratory nature of our analysis, we use the "grf" R package by Wagner and Athey (2018) to estimate conditional average treatment effects for both bottom-up and top-down treatments using a nonparametric random forest.[40]

---

[40] Stefan Wager and Susan Athey, "Estimation and Inference of Heterogeneous Treatment Effects Using Random Forests," *Journal of the American Statistical Association* 113, no. 523 (June 6, 2018): 1228–42.

6

Democratic Dissatisfaction, Punitive Populism, and the Rise of the "Benevolent" Dictator

Good governments, as Levi notes, provide public goods that "the populace needs and desires."[1] Retributive justice is one of these public goods. Ordinary people can desire retributive justice more than education, good roads, or any of the other public services that typically come to mind. And retributive justice can trump procedural and distributive justice in citizen evaluations of government legitimacy.[2] Indeed, without retributive justice, it is difficult to guarantee procedural and distributive justice. When wrongdoers are not always punished, how can citizens know whether decision making procedures are fair or whether resources will be distributed equitably?

We may not always want citizens to care so much about retributive justice. Our desire to punish wrongdoers can lead us down the illiberal and authoritarian paths. But we need to recognize when and why retributive justice concerns come to the fore so that we can understand how best to work toward the political outcomes that we deem normatively desirable. Instead of indulging in the comfortable assumption that democracy naturally results in effective governance, we need to look empirically at

---

[1] Margaret Levi, "Why We Need a New Theory of Government," *Perspectives on Politics* 4, no. 1 (March 24, 2006): 5.

[2] Bruce Gilley, "The Determinants of State Legitimacy: Results for 72 Countries," *International Political Science Review* 27, no. 1 (January 29, 2006): 47–71; Bruce Gilley, *The Right to Rule: How States Win and Lose Legitimacy*, Columbia University Press, 2009. See also Stefan Dahlberg and Sören Holmberg, "Democracy and Bureaucracy: How Their Quality Matters for Popular Satisfaction," *West European Politics* 37, no. 3 (May 4, 2014): 515–37.

how regimes succeed or fail and to learn from these successes and failures regardless of where they occur.

PUNITIVE POPULISM AND THE RISE OF "BENEVOLENT" DICTATORS

This book argues that our concerns about retributive justice help account for the popularity of authoritarian leaders and regimes. But retributive justice is something that we always want. So why do we sometimes find benevolent dictators who promote punitive populism more appealing than at other times?

Lessons from China under Xi Jinping

What we currently see in China under Xi Jinping suggests a two-part answer to this question. In China, citizen concerns about retributive justice have come to a head as (1) structural changes threaten people's economic security and social status, and (2) political leaders respond by making moral order and anti-corruption initiatives their top priority. China is facing its lowest levels of economic growth in thirty years. In 2014, Xi Jinping started using the term the "New Normal" to refer to policy adjustments in response to this economic slowdown. In contrast to the previous two presidents before him, Xi Jinping does not identify GDP growth as the government's primary objective and on several occasions has asserted that it should not be used as the only basis for performance evaluations and promotions.[3]

Instead, the Chinese Communist Party under Xi has increased the salience of retributive justice in order to diversify their sources of legitimacy and "recession-proof" the regime. In 2013, the Central Committee put forward a plan to build a system to punish and prevent corruption, announcing that "public satisfaction should be achieved" on this issue within five years.[4] In their research on Xi Jinping's anti-corruption campaign, Xi et al. observe that "the official media has begun to propagate a strong populist agenda to reinstall a clean

[3] Tianyang Xi, Yang Yao, and Qian Zhang, "Dilemmas of Autocratic Governance: Evidence from the Anti-Corruption Campaign in China," unpublished manuscript, Peking University, 2018.
[4] Cindy A. Nguyen, "Public Satisfaction on Graft 'Within Five Years,'" *China Digital Times*, December 26, 2013.

government for the people" and that "[i]t is clear that, from the view of the current leadership under Xi, the reputation of a clean government superseded performance as the most critical component of popular consent for the regime."[5]

Democratic Dissatisfaction and Authoritarian Politicians

Self-styled benevolent dictators are not only popular in authoritarian regimes – over the last decade, we have also seen their appeal in Hungary, Brazil, India, Peru, Poland, the Philippines, Nigeria, and the United States. In all these places, voters have elected leaders who portray themselves as champions of moral and social order, even as these leaders undermine liberal democracy and dismantle institutions painstakingly constructed over many years.

As with China under Xi Jinping, the appeal of politicians in democratic systems who style themselves as benevolent dictators or "avenging angels" often stems from a similar combination of structural dislocations and politicians who take political advantage of these uncertainties. Cross-national research suggests that retributive justice can become more salient in places facing economic, social, and political challenges. Gelfand et al., for example, find that societies facing resource scarcity, high population density, and territorial threats are more likely to develop strong norms, attitudes of low tolerance for behavior that deviates from these norms, and harsh punishment for norm violations.[6] Janoff-Bulman and Carnes observe that societies experiencing these challenges are more likely to develop a group morality based on social order, while societies facing relatively few of these challenges are more likely to have civil liberties and to tolerate deviant behavior.[7]

Trump's rise to power in the United States is a case in point. Anxieties about globalization, increasing inequality, migration, and the demographic and cultural decline have mounted, especially among the white

---

[5] Tianyang Xi, Yang Yao, and Qian Zhang, "Dilemmas of Autocratic Governance: Evidence from the Anti-Corruption Campaign in China," unpublished manuscript, Peking University, 2018.

[6] M. J. Gelfand, J. L. Raver, L. Nishii, L. M. Leslie, J. Lun, B. C. Lim, L. Duan, et al., "Differences between Tight and Loose Cultures: A 33-Nation Study," *Science* 332, no. 6033 (May 27, 2011): 1100–04.

[7] See Ronnie Janoff-Bulman and Nate C. Carnes, "Social Justice and Social Order: Binding Moralities Across the Political Spectrum," edited by Asim Zia, *PLOS ONE* 11, no. 3 (March 31, 2016): e0152479.

majority in wide swathes of the United States, while the government has failed to implement policies and practices that reassure these groups that their economic and social standing is secure. In 2016, Trump accepted the Republican Party's nomination for president by announcing: "In this race for the White House, I am the Law and Order candidate." Trump's speech, however, did not focus on upholding the rule of law. Arguing that the political system making and enforcing the laws was itself corrupt, Trump instead underscored the importance of using government power to identify and punish wrongdoers, that is, a promise to uphold retributive justice. Drawing our attention to the "violence in our streets and the chaos in our communities," Trump vowed to establish order not only in terms of predictability but also in terms of moral and social certainty: "When innocent people suffer, because our political system lacks the will, or the courage, or the basic decency to enforce our laws – or worse still, has sold out to some corporate lobbyist for cash – I am not able to look the other way." In this narrative, his challenger Hillary Clinton played the part of the quintessential bad apple rotting government from the inside: "When a Secretary of State illegally stores her emails on a private server, deletes 33,000 of them so the authorities can't see her crime, puts our country at risk, lies about it in every different form and *faces no consequence* (emphasis added) – I know that corruption has reached a level like never before."[8]

Over the last ten years, this story has become a familiar one around the world. Authoritarian populists have gained support in Austria, Britain, France, Germany, Italy, the Netherlands, Sweden, and other developed democracies. Orban in Hungary campaigns, as he says, for "illiberal democracy." Bolsonaro in Brazil has made statements such as, "I am in favour of torture, you know that. And the people are in favour as well," and "The Congress today is useless … let's do the coup already. Let's go straight to the dictatorship."[9] Similar sentiments have been echoed by Duterte in the Philippines, Buhari in Nigeria, Modi in India, and Kaczynski in Poland. In all these places, voters have come to believe that they need strongmen leaders who are willing to take the necessary actions, no matter how drastic, to restore order and morality, at least as defined by the majority. "Democratic deconsolidation," as Foa and Mounk have

---

[8] Politico Staff, "Full Text: Donald Trump 2016 RNC Draft Speech Transcript," *Politico*, July 2016.
[9] Mariana Simões, "Brazil's Polarizing New President, Jair Bolsonaro, in His Own Words," *New York Times*, October 28, 2018.

noted, is now a grave reality.[10] Coups used to be the primary threat to democracy, but Kendall-Taylor and Franza point out that democratically elected populist parties, or what they call "populist-fueled authoritarianization," accounted for 40 percent of democratic failures between 2000 and 2010, matching coups in frequency.

How Politicians Make Retributive Justice Salient in Democracies: The Expropriation of Uncertainty

Trump's speech accepting the nomination of the Republican Party worked as a textbook example of the ways in which politicians strategically expropriate the concerns that people have about the social order and whether their place in it is secure and respected. Crafted to heighten anxieties about the crumbling of moral order, both within society and within the state, it reminded ordinary people of their precarious positions and social status within this disintegrating order. As Jonathan Rauch comments, "Trump didn't cause the chaos. The chaos caused Trump."[11] Against this backdrop of uncertainty and insecurity, Trump presented himself as the moral hero of the people, committed to doing whatever it takes to beat this chaos back, in much the same way as Chinese rulers have channeled the noble figure of Judge Bao for centuries.

Retributive justice concerns mean that populist leaders benefit from both punishing those who contribute to disorder and the perpetuation of disorder itself. Just as the Chinese state makes it difficult for local officials not to engage in activity that is technically defined as corruption, Trump seeks to define public demonstrations as civil unrest. David Frum, for example, has observed, "[civil unrest] will be a resource. Trump will likely want not to repress it, but to publicize it. Immigration protesters marching with Mexican flags; Black Lives Matter demonstrators bearing antipolice slogans – these are the images of the opposition that Trump will wish his supporters to see."[12] The social psychology of retributive justice means that leaders like Trump benefit from both how "quashing unrest" signals their commitment to upholding moral order and also how harsh responses may stir up even more unrest from protesters, enabling the "hero" to

---

[10] Roberto Stefan Foa and Yascha Mounk, "The Signs of Deconsolidation," *Journal of Democracy* 28, no. 1 (2017): 5–15.

[11] Jonathan Rauch, "How American Politics Went Insane," *The Atlantic*, 2016.

[12] David Frum, "How to Build an Autocracy," *The Atlantic*, March 2017.

continue painting his opponents as forces of disorder and himself as a force for good.

The case of Brazil serves as another example. Judges, prosecutors, and other horizontal accountability actors have come to play the role of national retributive justice heroes (as with Judge Bao in China, they have their own popular television series in Brazil). Over the last decade, the Brazilian public has come to see corruption as the country's most important problem and judges, prosecutors, and policemen as the ones with solutions to this problem. In this narrative, unelected officials and populist leaders frame themselves as heroes who stand outside the dirty game of politics, while painting elected officials and conventional politicians as the villains. Judge Sérgio Moro who accepted Bolsonaro's invitation to become the Minister of Justice is a case in point.

THE SLIPPERY SLOPE OF POLITICIZING RETRIBUTIVE JUSTICE

Ideally, retributive justice is provided by institutionalizing the rule of law. This is ideal, in terms of both protecting liberal rights and perhaps also guaranteeing political and social stability. When public institutions for punishing crime and corruption are long-standing and durable, when they are fairly and reliably enforced, citizens can be confident that government authorities are providing retributive justice and upholding moral order.

In contrast, making retributive justice a political or partisan issue to consolidate power or campaign for elections can take citizens and politicians down a slippery slope, one that is particularly dangerous for democratic participation and democratic institutions.

The Dangers of Anti-Corruption Politics for Democracy

On the citizen side, focusing politics and elections on anti-corruption is dangerous because it moves the attention of voters away from policy considerations and toward aspects of government behavior about which they have limited or no information. It is hard for ordinary people to know how much corruption there is in government. They may sometimes directly encounter corrupt officials if they interact with frontline service providers or street-level bureaucrats asking for petty bribes. During elections, they may see politicians engaging in vote-buying.

Perhaps far more important, however, in the formation of citizen beliefs about the prevalence of corruption are the claims of party elites that draw their attention to corruption and make it politically salient. Politicians who run on anti-corruption platforms spend much of the run-up to elections accusing each other of wrongdoing. Media follows suit, dramatizing these accusations and uncovering corruption scandals.

In the midst of these political dramas, international anti-corruption campaigns and transparency interventions can inadvertently exacerbate the problem by encouraging unrealistically high expectations for clean government while at the same time providing information about how dirty it actually is. When expectations are unmet, the result can be disillusionment, disengagement from political participation, and despair with democracy.[13]

The Case of Anti-Corruption Initiatives in Eastern Europe

Beginning with the fall of communism in Eastern Europe, a number of initiatives spearheaded by governments and organizations based in the United States and Western Europe have sought to set up institutions and run international advocacy campaigns to promote anti-corruption and "open government" in developing democracies. Ranging from the European Union's accession norms, the Open Government Partnership (OGP), the Extractive Industries Transparency Initiative (EITI), and the World Bank's turn to "good governance" and "social accountability" to the creation of Transparency International and an array of public rankings on corruption and corruption perceptions, international actors have sought to pressure domestic elites to fight corruption and to encourage domestic public to pressure their elites to do so.

Whether these initiatives have reduced actual corruption remains unclear.[14] In their review of studies since 1990, Andersson and Heywood concluded: "Overall the results of the major efforts to fight corruption over the last 20 years have yielded rather meagre results."[15] Even when there seems to be political will at the top, and these efforts succeed in leading to

---

[13] David J. Samuels and Cesar Zucco, *Partisans, Antipartisans, and Nonpartisans: Voting Behavior in Brazil*, Cambridge University Press, 2018.

[14] One exception is a paper on EITI in Zambia. Ana Rita Sequeira, Mark P. McHenry, Angus Morrison-Saunders, Hudson Mtegha, and David Doepel, "Is the Extractive Industry Transparency Initiative (EITI) Sufficient to Generate Transparency in Environmental Impact and Legacy Risks? The Zambian Minerals Sector," *Journal of Cleaner Production* 129 (August 2016): 427–36.

[15] Paul M. Heywood and Staffan Andersson, "Anti-Corruption as a Risk to Democracy: On the Unintended Consequences of International Anti-Corruption Campaigns," in *Governments, NGOs and Anti-Corruption*, edited by Luís de Sousa, Peter Larmour,

legislation or the establishment of anti-corruption agencies, government authorities fail to monitor agents effectively. As a result, agents may simply replace more visible corruption with less visible activities, as Bussell notes in India and Wedeman notes in China.[16] Rix has observed the same for nineteenth-century Britain where anti-corruption legislation starting in 1841 triggered a shift from direct to indirect bribery.[17]

What is clear is that these initiatives have heightened the political salience of retributive justice concerns for politicians and citizens. Andersson and Heywood argue that the obsession with "cleanliness" rather than policy issues in the former Communist countries of Eastern and Central Europe have led to a focus on politician morality rather than policy positions and representation. "The danger with emphasizing corruption," they caution,

is that it serves to legitimize its use as a proxy for other forms of explanation. Thus, politics starts to be played out in terms of mutual accusation of corruption: the politics of *kompromat* which involves looking for ways to discredit opponents through finding (or often inventing) compromising material and damaging allegations about them. This in turn further reinforces the sense of corruption being everywhere, and feeds perceptions about the scale of the problem.[18]

Consistent with this diagnosis are reports of a mismatch between citizen perceptions about the severity of corruption and their actual direct experiences of it.[19]

---

and Barry Hindess, Routledge, 2012, 33–50; see also Patrick Keuleers, "Corruption, Poverty and Development," *Background Paper (Plenary 2)*, 2005.

[16] See Jennifer Bussell, *Corruption and Reform in India: Public Services in the Digital Age*, Cambridge University Press, 2012. In China, Wedeman argues that it is low-level corruption that has been deterred, rather than high-level corruption. Andrew Wedeman, "Anticorruption Campaigns and the Intensification of Corruption in China," *Journal of Contemporary China* 14, no. 42 (February 2005): 106.

[17] K. Rix, "'The Elimination of Corrupt Practices in British Elections'? Reassessing the Impact of the 1883 Corrupt Practices Act," *The English Historical Review* 123, no. 500 (February 1, 2008): 65–97.

[18] Staffan Andersson and Paul M. Heywood, "Anti-Corruption as a Risk to Democracy: On the Unintended Consequences of International Anti-Corruption Campaigns," in *Governments, NGOs and Anti-Corruption: The New Integrity Warriors*, edited by Luís De Sousa, Barry Hindess, and Peter Larmour, 42, Routledge, 2012.

[19] William L. Miller, Åse B. Grødeland, and Tatyana Y. Koshechkina, "Confessions: A Model of Officials' Perspectives on Accepting Gifts from Clients in Post-Communist Europe," *Political Studies* 49, no. 1 (March 29, 2001): 1–29, cited in Staffan Andersson and Paul M. Heywood, "The Politics of Perception: Use and Abuse of Transparency International's Approach to Measuring Corruption," *Political Studies* 57, no. 4 (December 2009): 752.

At the macro-level, anti-corruption initiatives can inadvertently encourage a national politics of accusation and a "race to the bottom" between politicians and parties that constantly attack each other for crimes against the public. At the microlevel, such initiatives may lead to citizen disillusionment and political disengagement. Government transparency initiatives that deliver information about corruption without delivering information about effective punishment of corruption may often have the opposite effect of what they intend. Instead of stimulating citizens to take action, such information can lead citizens to believe that the political system is hopelessly broken and that there is no point in doing anything about it. Research on directed motivated reasoning suggests that those who already believe that the government is corrupt will hold these beliefs more strongly, while positive information about the government will not lead them to update their beliefs.[20] And because group identity shapes information processing, if the groups to which I belong think there is no point in doing anything, then I am likely to follow suit.[21]

[20] Angus Campbell, Philip E. Converse, Warren E. Miller, and Donald E. Stokes, *The American Voter*, University of Chicago Press, 1980; Jennifer Jerit and Jason Barabas, "Partisan Perceptual Bias and the Information Environment," *The Journal of Politics* 74, no. 3 (July 2012): 672–84; Dan M. Kahan, "Ideology, Motivated Reasoning, and Cognitive Reflection," *Judgment and Decision Making* 8, no. 4 (2013): 407–24; Dan M. Kahan, David Hoffman, Danieli Evans, Neal Devans, Eugene Lucci, and Katherine Cheng, "Ideology or Situation Sense: An Experimental Investigation of Motivated Reasoning and Professional Judgment," *University of Pennsylvania Law Review* 164 (2015): 349; Shanto Iyengar and Kyu S. Hahn, "Red Media, Blue Media: Evidence of Ideological Selectivity in Media Use," *Journal of Communication* 59, no. 1 (March 2009): 19–39; Brendan Nyhan and Jason Reifler, "When Corrections Fail: The Persistence of Political Misperceptions," *Political Behavior* 32, no. 2 (June 30, 2010): 303–30; Brendan Nyhan, Jason Reifler, and Peter A. Ubel, "The Hazards of Correcting Myths about Health Care Reform," *Medical Care* 51, no. 2 (February 2013): 127–32; Brian F. Schaffner and Cameron Roche, "Misinformation and Motivated Reasoning: Responses to Economic News in a Politicized Environment," *Public Opinion Quarterly*, 81, no. 1 (March, 2017): 86–110; Natalie Jomini Stroud, *Niche News: The Politics of News Choice*, Oxford University Press on Demand, 2011; David P. Redlawsk, "Hot Cognition or Cool Consideration? Testing the Effects of Motivated Reasoning on Political Decision Making," *The Journal of Politics* 64, no. 4 (November 2002): 1021–44; Cass R. Sunstein, Sebastian Bobadilla-Suarez, Stephanie C. Lazzaro, and Tali Sharot, "How People Update Beliefs about Climate Change: Good News and Bad News," *Cornell Law Review* 102 (2016): 1431.
[21] Christopher H. Achen and Larry M. Bartels, *Democracy for Realists: Why Elections Do Not Produce Responsive Government*, Princeton University Press, 2017; Larry M. Bartels, "No Title," *Political Behavior* 24, no. 2 (2002): 117–50; Pamela Johnston Conover, Stanley Feldman, and Kathleen Knight, "The Personal and Political Underpinnings of Economic Forecasts," *American Journal of Political Science* 31, no. 3 (1987): 559–83; Alan S. Gerber and Gregory A. Huber, "Partisanship, Political Control, and Economic Assessments," *American Journal of Political Science* 54, no. 1 (2010):

Electoral competition can, ironically, exacerbate these dynamics of increasing polarization and declining trust. The experience of Eastern Europe again proves instructive. As a requirement for accession to the European Union, Romania and Bulgaria were required to establish anti-corruption commissions. While these reforms initially raised public aware-ness about corruption, citizens eventually grew tired and cynical as it became clear that corruption investigations were simply a tool used by politicians to discredit each other.[22] Before Romania's accession to the European Union, the president spearheaded anti-corruption initiatives. After accession, opposition parties banded together to accuse the president of corruption and launch impeachment proceedings. Despite high-profile investigations of senior party leaders on both sides, no convictions were made, leading to declining public trust in the political process.[23] In Bulgaria, each election has introduced a new and different populist anti-corruption challenger, leading to the perception that all of the major parties are corrupt.[24] Elections in post-communist states, as Heywood and Krastev note, have become about "corrupt government versus clean opposition."[25]

These cases suggest that external actors have to be very careful about making anti-corruption and retributive justice politically salient, espe-cially when anti-corruption campaigns and interventions do not also provide effective and visible punishment. Sometimes politicians them-selves exploit opportunities to expropriate uncertainty and promote anti-corruption politics. But for international actors, even those with the best of intentions, it is worth remembering that the ordinary people who are the intended beneficiaries of these initiatives have little recourse when such initiatives have negative impacts on their political systems and societies.

153–73; Alan Hamlin and Colin Jennings, "Expressive Political Behaviour: Foundations, Scope and Implications," *British Journal of Political Science* 41, no. 3 (2011): 645–70; Danielle Shani, *On the Origins of Political Interest*, Princeton University, 2009.

[22] Daniel Smilov, "Anti-Corruption Bodies as Discourse-Controlling Instruments: Experiences from South-East Europe," in *Governments NGOs, and Anti-Corruption: The New Integrity Warriors*, edited by Luis de Sousa, Peter Larmour, and Barry Hindess, Routledge, 86, 2012.

[23] Steven Sampson, "Corruption and Anti-Corruption in Southeast Europe," in *Governments, NGOs, and Anti-Corruption: The New Integrity Warriors*, edited by Luis de Sousa, Peter Larmour, and Barry Hindess, Routledge 180, 2012; see also Daniel Smilov, ibid., 95.

[24] Ibid.

[25] Paul Heywood and Ivan Krastev, "Political Scandals and Corruption," in *Developments in European Politics*, edited by Heywood, Paul M., Jones, Erick, Rhodes, Martin, and Sedelmeier, Ulrich, Palgrave Macmillan, 2006, 157–77.

The Dangers of Anti-Corruption Politics for Politicians

Even for politicians, anti-corruption politics can lead them down a slippery slope. Anti-corruption politics in democratic systems tends to pit political parties and factions against each other, taking the form of "he said, she said" accusations and counteraccusations between parties campaigning intensely to win elections. Both because people find it difficult to verify the truth of these accusations and because they often absorb only the information that is already consistent with their prior beliefs, anti-corruption politics in democratic regimes can exacerbate partisan conflict and polarization among citizens, while leading to public distrust in institutions and fatigue with political engagement.

Once the public develops the perception that anti-corruption investigations simply mirror political battles for power among elites, it may be difficult to persuade citizens that leaders are genuinely committed to retributive justice and upholding a social and moral order. When Buhari failed to investigate members of his own party or administration for the first two years after taking power in 2015, he was widely criticized for pursuing a "selective war."[26] Protest-vote democracies and anti-system populism can take hold.[27] In Brazil, Bolsonaro's rise was preceded by the political circus around Rousseff's 2016 impeachment. As a politics of accusation took hold during the end of Rousseff's presidency, it became difficult for citizens to know who, if anyone, was authentically committed to upholding social order and basic moral values. During this period, citizen confidence in the government plummeted.[28] In 2015, approval of leadership was at 15 percent.[29] Support of democracy reportedly dropped 22 percent between 2015 and 2016, and "by 2016 only 32 percent of

---

[26] BBC News Staff, "Nigeria's Dasuki 'Arrested over $2bn Arms Fraud,'" *BBC News*, December 1, 2015; John Campbell, "Resistance to President Buhari's Anticorruption Campaign," *Council on Foreign Relations*, October 2017; Garba Shehu, "Nigeria: Executive Order 6 – Buhari Acquires a Big Stick against Corruption," *All Africa*, July 6, 2018.

[27] Staffan Andersson and Paul M. Heywood, "Anti-Corruption as a Risk to Democracy: On the Unintended Consequences of International Anti-Corruption Campaigns," in *Governments, NGOs and Anti-Corruption: The New Integrity Warriors*, edited by Luís De Sousa, Barry Hindess, and Peter Larmour, 42, Routledge, 2012.

[28] Paul F. Lagunes and Susan Rose-Ackerman, "Why Brazil Is Winning Its Fight against Corruption," *The Conversation*, February 2, 2017.

[29] Jesus Rios and Julie Ray, "Brazilian's Trust in Country's Leadership at Record Low," 2015, https://news.gallup.com/poll/190481/brazilians-trust-country-leadership-record-low.aspx.

Brazilians agreed that 'democracy is preferable to all other forms of government.'"[30]

RETRIBUTIVE JUSTICE POLITICS AND DEMOCRATIC DE-INSTITUTIONALIZATION

Once populist politicians come to power, they are increasingly more likely to lead to concentration of power in the hands of what Weber called a charismatic leader who derives his authority not from traditional or legal-rational sources but from the perceived endowment of exceptional personal qualities.[31] Kendall-Taylor and Franza find that between 1946 and 1999, 46 percent of cases of authoritarianization led to the establishment of personalist dictatorships, but from 2000 to 2010, 75 percent of such cases did. Democratically elected "benevolent dictators" who succeed in maintaining public support after coming to power may then seek to consolidate their power through a process of what Kendall-Taylor and Frantz call "authoritarianization." Leaders who are voted into power leverage citizen support for upholding social order through retributive justice and punishment of wrongdoers to eliminate institutional constraints on their authority, while increasing restrictions on civil society and political opposition.[32] If they follow the approach that Chávez, Putin, and Erdogan have pursued, they then install their supporters in the judiciary, military, and security services and neutralize the media by buying it and/or legislating against it.[33] When this process of democratic backsliding is incremental, Kendall-Taylor and Frantz warn that there may be no "focal point around which an opposition can coalesce."[34]

Citizens in democratic systems may also be fundamentally disinclined and slow to take political action. In the United States, Hibbing and Theiss-Morse have argued that the majority of citizens want a "stealth democracy." Most Americans, they find, do not want to participate in the democratic process on an everyday basis. Instead, people only want to

---

[30] Data from the Latinobarometro cited in David J. Samuels and Cesar Zucco, *Partisans, Antipartisans, and Nonpartisans: Voting Behavior in Brazil*, Cambridge University Press, 2018, 2.

[31] Maximilian Weber, "Theory of Social and Economic Organization," in *The Nature of Charismatic Authority and Its Routinization*, Translated by A. R. Anderson and Talcott Parsons, Free Press 1947.

[32] Steven Levitsky and Daniel Ziblatt, *How Democracies Die*, Crown, 2018.

[33] Andrea Kendall-Taylor and Erica Frantz, "Foreign Affairs," *Foreign Affairs*, December 2016.

[34] Ibid.

be able to take action in the (unlikely) event that they feel moved to do so: "[People] want to be certain that if they ever did deign to get involved, if an issue at some point in the future happened to impinge so directly on their lives that they were moved to ask the system for something, elected officials would respond to their request with the utmost seriousness."

Seen through the lens of a retributive justice model, their findings have important implications for democratic backsliding. Often, when we see low levels of participation, we interpret these low levels as indicative of political alienation. Hibbing and Theiss-Morse's work implies that ordinary people can exhibit low levels of participation and behavioral engagement even as they continue to believe in government responsiveness and channels for citizen voice. We have seen that when populist politicians exploit retributive justice concerns, they can sustain citizen beliefs in government responsiveness to their needs. To the extent that citizens in places like the United States assume the continued existence of a "stealth democracy" and are reassured about government responsiveness through retributive justice strategies, it may be possible to dismantle democratic institutions before the majority of citizens are aware of these institutional changes and organize to oppose them.

COSTLY SIGNALING AND PUNISHING YOUR OWN

One tactic that aspiring benevolent dictators can use to build public support through retributive justice is the strategy of "punishing their own." Magufuli in Tanzania, for example, has used this strategy effectively. Upon coming to power, Magufuli fired groups of high-level officials and became known for being directed and efficient at removing wrongdoers within his own party.[35] After winning election to the presidency in 2015 with just over 50 percent of the vote, his approval rating one year later was around 90 percent.[36] In Brazil, Rousseff also started her presidency in 2011 with a similar process of "cleaning house." Firing a series of cabinet ministers as well as her own chief of staff for corruption during her

---

[35] Antonio Andreoni, "Anti-Corruption in Tanzania: A Political Settlements Analysis," *Anti-Corruption Evidence (ACE) Research Consortium Working Paper 01*, 2017; Lukiko Lukiko, "Exploring a Sustainable Anti-Corruption Regime for Tanzania," University of the Western Cape, 2017.

[36] Carolyn Del Vecchio, "The Political Participation, Engagement, and Perceptions of President Magufuli among Students at the College of African Wildlife Management," 2016. *Independent Study Project (ISP) Collection.* 2351. https://digitalcollections.sit.edu /isp_collection/2351

first year, Rousseff maintained an approval rating of around 70 percent for several years.[37] After winning the 2015 elections in Nigeria, Buhari focused his anti-corruption efforts on eliminating his political opponents, which drew widespread criticism from the media and civil society. When he finally fired two of his own high-ranking officials in 2017, public evaluations rose accordingly. In 2017, 59 percent of Nigerians in the Afrobarometer survey reported that the government was performing "fairly well" or "very well" in fighting corruption, a huge rise from the 21 percent reported in 2015.[38]

The strategy of punishing your own can be effective for several reasons. One is that it is virtually impossible for ordinary citizens to know the true number of corrupt officials and how these officials are distributed across parties or factions.[39] Because citizens cannot know the denominator of actual corruption, they focus on the information that leaders provide about the numerator of prosecutions. If that number seems to be changing and increasing rapidly, they may conclude that leaders are genuinely serious and effective about rooting out corruption and wrongdoing.

Another reason punishing your own builds credibility is leaders voluntarily seem to be taking actions that run counter to their self-interest. Since their actions do not seem to result from external incentives or individual self-interest, observers infer that they must be intrinsically motivated by altruism or a commitment to collective good.[40]

All other things being equal, this strategy may be easier for leaders in authoritarian regimes. Because autocrats are not subject to competitive

---

[37] Paul F. Lagunes and Susan Rose-Ackerman, "Why Brazil Is Winning Its Fight against Corruption," *The Conversation*, February 2, 2017; Joe Weisenthal, "Brazilian President's Popularity Takes Breathtaking Nosedive – And That Should Worry Investors," *Business Insider*, July 16, 2013.

[38] John P. Frinjuah, "A 'Cry for Change' and President Buhari's Fight against Corruption," *Afro Barometer*, February 2018.

[39] Staffan Andersson and Paul M. Heywood, "Anti-Corruption as a Risk to Democracy: On the Unintended Consequences of International Anti-Corruption Campaigns," in *Governments, NGOs and Anti-Corruption: The New Integrity Warriors*, edited by Luís De Sousa, Barry Hindess, and Peter Larmour, 44, Routledge, 2012.

[40] Adam J. Berinsky, "Rumors and Health Care Reform: Experiments in Political Misinformation"; see also Lily L. Tsai, Benjamin S. Morse, and Robert A. Blair, "Building Credibility and Cooperation in Low-Trust Settings: Persuasion and Source Accountability in Liberia During the 2014–2015 Ebola Crisis," *Comparative Political Studies* 53, no.10–11 (September 1, 2020): 1582–1618; Rebecca Weitz-Shapiro and Matthew S. Winters, "Can Citizens Discern? Information Credibility, Political Sophistication, and the Punishment of Corruption in Brazil," *The Journal of Politics* 79, no. 1 (January 2017): 60–74.

elections, they may be more willing and able to punish those within their parties or factions without fear of losing power in the short term. They may have the benefit of a longer time horizon than politicians in democracies.

Moreover, as the case of China illustrates, leaders in authoritarian regimes can also target local officials as the "bad guys" in their anti-corruption campaigns. In contrast to democracies where political parties try to paint each other as the bad guy, authoritarian leaders can conveniently pick on their underlings. This is how anti-corruption politics has long been framed – and institutionalized – in China, and how Kagame is currently framing anti-corruption in Rwanda. By structuring politics as a battle against corrupt government agents, anti-corruption heroes can build trust in their regime and its institutions rather than undermining it.

Yet even in authoritarian regimes, the temptation for leaders is to use anti-corruption not just to build public support but to eliminate rivals. On the one hand, Xi Jinping has been acutely aware of the need to combat perceptions that his anti-corruption initiatives are politically motivated. Upon taking power in 2013, Xi immediately announced that his campaign would go after officials at the top of the Party, not just a token few low-ranking local officials, saying: "We must uphold the fighting of tigers and flies at the same time, resolutely investigating law-breaking cases of leading officials and also earnestly resolving the unhealthy tendencies and corruption problems which happen all around people."[41] As public speculation about the factional struggles within the CCP mounted in the run-up to the 19th Party Congress in 2017 – held every five years to elect the CCP's top leadership and unveil the national policy plan – Xi explicitly acknowledged and bluntly denied these criticisms. In a January 2016 speech that Xi gave to the Central Committee for Discipline Inspection, he referenced a popular American TV series about the dark dealings of a fictional American president who stops at nothing, including murder, to stay on top: "[We] need to make it clear that our party's fight against corruption is not a snobbish affair that discriminates between different people, and it is not a House of Cards power struggle."[42]

On the other hand, there is good reason to suspect that Xi's campaign is indeed motivated by strategic considerations. Although the campaign has resulted in arrests of high-ranking officials from competing political

---

[41] Reuters Staff, "China's Xi Urges Swatting of Lowly 'Flies' in Fight on Everyday Graft," *Reuters*, January 22, 2013.

[42] Bianji Yuan Can, "Xi Warns of Party 'Cabals and Cliques,'" *Xinhua Net*, May 3, 2016.

factions,[43] recent research suggests that provincial and prefectural officials with political connections to Xi are less likely to be investigated. Based on official government data published for over 1,000 prefectural mayors and party secretaries and 91 provincial governors and secretaries, Xi et al. found that officials with stronger connections to current incumbent superiors were less likely to be investigated, while officials with connections to the previous superiors were more vulnerable to investigation.[44] Whether Xi's campaign represents a genuine commitment to retributive justice or simply provides a convenient façade for his consolidation of power remains to be seen.

WHAT CAN LIBERAL DEMOCRATS LEARN FROM AUTHORITARIANS?

Populist authoritarian leaders have strategically rallied public support in countries that are rich and poor, democratic as well as authoritarian. In places like China and Rwanda, government authorities are developing models of governance and development that seem stable, successful, and popular. These cases powerfully challenge the claim that liberal democracy is always the most admired form of government. As a liberal democrat, I fear that we often fail to make an effective case for liberal democracy, in part because our biases blind us to seeing the strengths that nondemocratic systems can have and the ways in which they can respond effectively to citizen needs.

What can we learn from "successful" authoritarians? For ordinary citizens and advocates of liberal democracy, one lesson that emerges from effective authoritarians is that we need to do a better job of acknowledging and addressing concerns about retributive justice in addition to advocating for liberal rights. We need to do so because some of our fellow citizens may prioritize retributive justice over liberal rights. When people

---

[43] Reuters Staff, "China's Xi: We Can't Be 'Blindly Optimistic' on Corruption inside the Communist Party," *Newsweek*, July 2017; David Lague, Benjamin Kang Lim, and Charlie Zhu, "Special Report: Fear and Retribution in Xi's Corruption Purge," *Reuters*, December 23, 2014; Brian Spegele, "China's Investigation of Ex-President's Aide Marks New Phase in War on Corruption," *Wall Street Journal*, December 23, 2014; Cindy A. Nguyen, "Ousted Chinese Officials 'Plotted to Overthrow Xi,'" *China Digital Times*, October 21, 2017. See also ChinaFile Team, "Visualizing China's Anti-Corruption Campaign," *ChinaFile*, January 21, 2016.

[44] Tianyang Xi, Yang Yao, and Qian Zhang, "Dilemmas of Autocratic Governance: Evidence from the Anti-Corruption Campaign in China," unpublished manuscript, Peking University, 2018.

are worried about their status and being respected, talk about protecting human rights sounds like giving attention to others that they cannot afford. Unless their concerns about moral and social order are alleviated, they may be unable to turn their attention to questions of rights. Rather than focusing only on what people should do, we need to accept what they actually do as an empirical fact and use that as a point of departure for designing institutions that alleviate these worries.

We may also need to address retributive justice concerns first because we in fact need the fair and just implementation of punishment in order to ensure individual liberties. In a liberal democracy, it is the rule of law that provides retributive justice. Defending the rule of law is as important as defending liberal rights because without a rule of law to which everyone, including the most powerful, is subject, we cannot protect every individual's rights.

We also need to recognize these realities when we seek to promote liberal democracy as external interveners in developing contexts. The hard truth is that building state institutions and constructing a robust rule of law may be necessary before liberal democracy can really be constructed. As we now know from decades of democracy promotion work, instituting elections – even genuinely competitive ones – are no guarantee that the political system has effective institutions to identify and punish corruption and wrongdoing and provide retributive justice. Elections, as Fearon has noted, are actually poor mechanisms for accountability.[45] And to the extent that elections encourage politicians to focus on minimum winning coalitions rather than the good of the public as a whole, there may be few incentives to build long-standing institutions for the provision of retributive justice and other public goods – and many incentives to engage in corruption if electoral competition makes time horizons short.

What about lessons for political leaders in liberal democracies? For example, do liberal democrats need to imitate authoritarians in identifying and punishing bad apples to signal the provision of retributive justice to the public? I think the answer is no, though we do need to stress the importance of the rule of law more explicitly, and to communicate more clearly the difference between rule of law and "law and order" politics.

---

[45] James D. Fearon, "Electoral Accountability and the Control of Politicians: Selecting Good Types versus Sanctioning Poor Performance," in *Democracy, Accountability, and Representation*, edited by Adam Przeworski, Susan C. Stokes, and Bernard Manin, Cambridge University Press, 1999, 55–97.

And there is a critical way in which leaders in liberal democracies should indeed imitate effective authoritarians in identifying targets for punishment: We should make a habit of punishing our own. In order to sustain – or, as is too often the case, rebuild – public trust in the political system, leaders in liberal democracies have to show that they are willing to punish wrongdoers among their political supporters and within their political parties. In the case of the United States, as the public conversation about money in politics has highlighted, this would mean politicians taking initiative to investigate wrongdoing by those who campaign for them, donate money to you, promote you to higher positions, and do them favors. When individual politicians are willing to bear the costs of losing donors, important institutions – such as our political parties – and public trust in these institutions benefit. The findings in this book suggest that punishing your own builds public confidence in the commitment of leaders to upholding retributive justice. Leaders who communicate this commitment enjoy higher levels of support and regime-reinforcing citizen engagement – which are essential for a vibrant democracy.

Another lesson to take from authoritarian China is the importance of civic education that inculcates participation in governance and politics as a moral responsibility and an ideal of public service and public servants as morally motivated. Imperial China, as Perry has noted, was able to administer an expansive empire with a remarkably small cadre of bureaucratic officials in large part because classical Confucian education institutionalized through state examinations and reinforced by family, community, and state rituals created a literary and moral order of intellectuals and officials, to which ordinary people aspired.[46] Public service was for the most morally virtuous. Civic education was part of moral education, and moral education was civic education. And this was reinforced in school, in public life, as well as in the home.

In its ideal form, civic education makes it clear that punishing the bad apples is not the only thing necessary for upholding moral order. The question becomes not just who the bad apples are but how to keep yourself from becoming a bad apple. We need to create education and institutions that encourage people and officials to be their best selves in a shared moral and political community, and that revive an ideal of the public official as a moral exemplar to which ordinary people ought to aspire.

[46] Elizabeth Perry, "Cultural Governance in Contemporary China: 'Re-Orienting' Party Propaganda," in *To Govern China: Evolving Practices of Power*, edited by Vivienne Shue and Patricia M. Thornton, Cambridge University Press, 2017, 29–55.

Authoritarians do not take regime support and durability for granted. Neither should liberal democrats. In the United States, we have assumed that liberal democracy, once "consolidated," is inherently stable. But we are seeing now that structural changes can lead to tribalization and polarization. Because those of us in the United States are steeped in the discourse of neoliberalism, we tend only to think about how such changes affect income and employment, and how economic interests lead to political conflict. Taking citizen concerns about social order and retributive justice seriously means that we need to pay attention to how structural and demographic changes affect not only the economic well-being but also the social and psychological well-being of ordinary people.

As with authoritarianism, public support for liberal democracy cannot be assumed – *it must be strategically constructed and continuously maintained*. Authoritarian popularity, in the United States as well as the rest of the world, suggests that we need to pay attention to how these changes create uncertainty, insecurity, and the desire to see government authorities to provide a sense of order. Liberalism claimed, as Glerum notes, that a village could raise a child, but it "never got around to building the village." Older generations in the United States lament the loss of community, religion, and nation they feel they used to have, and millennials feel they have been "born into a desert of meaning."[47] Although we idealize elections as expressing the voice of the people, electoral competition can exacerbate these dynamics, especially when we lack political parties, unions, social organizations, and other intermediaries that bring diverse individuals together in ways that cut across identity-based loyalties. As people come to distrust elites as well as each other, it becomes easier to dismantle public institutions.

Effective authoritarians persuade the public that they uphold a moral order. Liberal democrats need to do the same. We must make the case for liberal democracy as a *moral order* that is not simply a set of shared values but a system that provides security and certainty in our daily lives and reliably punishes those who disrupt this order. We cannot succeed in building a consensus for liberal democracy if we dismiss retributive justice as concerns that only apply to people with conservative values or authoritarian personalities. We need to demonstrate that liberal democratic government authorities provide retributive justice, not just procedural and distributive justice.

---

[47] Angela Nagle, "The Lost Boys," *The Atlantic*, December 2017.

When the body politic is "corrupted," people perceive it as a problem of moral disintegration and decay. They look to government authorities to find the bad apple and throw it out before it spoils the lot. This book has shown that citizens can view leaders, even those who are illiberal or authoritarian, as just, fair, and committed to the public good when they address citizen concerns about retributive justice by punishing wrong-doers within the government and signaling to citizens that they are moral leaders and genuinely care about the public good. Many of us would rather have benevolent dictators that seem to respond to these needs than dirty democrats that seem unaware of them. The question now is whether we will be able to articulate a compelling alternative to the dirty democrat or the benevolent dictator. The answer may very well determine the world order to come.

Bibliography

Abelson, Robert P., Donald R. Kinder, Mark D. Peters, and Susan T. Fiske. 1982. "Affective and Semantic Components in Political Person Perception." *Journal of Personality and Social Psychology* 42 (4): 619–30. https://doi.org/10.1037/0022-3514.42.4.619.

Abrams, Philip. 2006. "Notes on the Difficulty of Studying the State." *The Anthropology of the State: A Reader* 1: 12–130.

Acharya, Avidit, Matthew Blackwell, and Maya Sen. 2018. "Analyzing Causal Mechanisms in Survey Experiments." *Political Analysis* 26 (4): 357–78. https://doi.org/10.1017/pan.2018.19.

Achen, Christopher H. and Larry M. Bartels. 2017. *Democracy for Realists: Why Elections Do Not Produce Responsive Government*. Princeton University Press.

Adams, Gabrielle S. and Elizabeth Mullen. 2013. "Increased Voting for Candidates Who Compensate Victims Rather than Punish Offenders." *Social Justice Research* 26 (2): 168–92. https://doi.org/10.1007/s11211-013-0179-x.

Ahlers, Anna. 2014. *Rural Policy Implementation in Contemporary China: New Socialist Countryside*. Routledge.

Akker, L. V., Leonie Heres, Karin Lasthuizen, and F. E. Six. 2009. "Ethical Leadership and Trust: It's All about Meeting Expectations." www.regent.edu/acad/global/publications/ijls/new/vol5iss2/IJLS_vol5_iss2_akker_ethical_leadership.pdf

Allais, Lucy. 2011. "Restorative Justice, Retributive Justice, and the South African Truth and Reconciliation Commission." *Philosophy & Public Affairs* 39 (4): 331–63. https://doi.org/10.1111/j.1088-4963.2012.01211.x.

Anagnost, Ann. 1997. *National Past-Times: Narrative, Representation, and Power in Modern China*. Duke University Press.

Andersson, Staffan and Paul M. Heywood. 2009. "The Politics of Perception: Use and Abuse of Transparency International's Approach to Measuring Corruption." *Political Studies* 57 (4): 746–67. https://doi.org/10.1111/j.1467-9248.2008.00758.x.

Andreoni, Antonio. 2017. "Anti-Corruption in Tanzania: A Political Settlements Analysis." http://eprints.soas.ac.uk/24853/1/ACE-WorkingPaper001-TZ-A ntiCorruption-171102finalrevised.pdf.

Ang, Yuen Yuen and Nan Jia. 2014. "Perverse Complementarity: Political Connections and the Use of Courts among Private Firms in China." *The Journal of Politics* 76 (2): 318–32. https://doi.org/10.1017/ S0022381613001400.

Antony, Robert J. 2002. "Subcounty Officials, the State, and Local Communities in Guangdong Province, 1644-1860." *Cornell East Asia Series* 114: 27–60.

Arriola, Leonardo R. 2009. "Patronage and Political Stability in Africa." *Comparative Political Studies* 42 (10): 1339–62. https://doi.org/10.1177/ 0010414009332126.

Arvey, Richard D. and Allen P. Jones. 1985. "The Use of Discipline in Organizational Settings: A Framework for Future Research." *Research in Organizational Behavior* 7: 367–408.

Aston, Margaret E. 1960. "Lollardy and Sedition 1381-1431." *Past & Present* 17: 1–44.

Baker, Wayne E. and Nathaniel Bulkley. 2014. "Paying It Forward vs. Rewarding Reputation: Mechanisms of Generalized Reciprocity." *Organization Science* 25 (5): 1493–510. https://doi.org/10.1287/ orsc.2014.0920.

Bartels, Larry M., J. Eric Oliver, and Wendy M. Rahn. 2016. "Rise of the Trumpenvolk: Populism in the 2016 Election." *The ANNALS of the American Academy of Political and Social Science* 667 (1): 189–206. http s://doi.org/10.1177/0002716216662639.

Bateman, Thomas S. and Dennis W. Organ. 1983. "Job Satisfaction and the Good Soldier: The Relationship between Affect and Employee 'Citizenship.'" *Academy of Management Journal* 26 (4): 587–95. https:// doi.org/10.5465/255908.

Bayart, Jean-Francois. 1993. *The State in Africa: The Politics of the Belly.* Longman.

BBC News Staff. 2015. *Nigeria's Dasuki "Arrested over $2bn Arms Fraud."* www.bbc.com/news/world-africa-34973872.

Beach, Sophie. 2013. *20,000 Officials Punished for Violating Discipline.* China Digital Times. The following is the link to the news article: https://chinadigi taltimes.net/2013/12/20000-officials-punished-violating-discipline/

Beijing Municipal Bureau of Statistics. 2016. *Beijing Statistical Yearbook 2016.* Beijing Municipal Bureau of Statistics.

Bell, Daniel. 2008. *China's New Confucianism: Politics and Everyday Life in a Changing Society.* Princeton University Press.

Berinsky, Adam J. 2015. "Rumors and Health Care Reform: Experiments in Political Misinformation." *British Journal of Political Science* 47 (2): 1–22. https://doi.org/10.1017/S0007123415000186.

Bernstein, Thomas P. and Xiaobo Lü. 2003. *Taxation without Representation in Contemporary Rural China.* Vol. 37. Cambridge University Press.

Bianco, Lucien. 1986. "Peasant Movements." *The Cambridge History of China* 13 (Part 2): 311–12.

Bies, Robert J. 1987. "The Predicament of Injustice: The Management of Moral Outrage." *Research in Organizational Behavior* 9: 289–319.

Bies, Robert J. and Thomas M. Tripp. 1996. "Beyond Distrust: 'Getting Even' and the Need for Revenge." In *Trust in Organizations*, edited by R. M. Kramer and T. R. Tyler Sage Publications, 246–60.

Boehringer, Gill. 2017. "Asia-Pacific: Duterte's Drug War: Violating Rights for a Quick Fix." *Alternative Law Journal* 42 (3): 233–36. https://doi.org/10.1 177/1037969X17730700.

Bohm, Robert M. 1992. "Retribution and Capital Punishment: Toward a Better Understanding of Death Penalty Opinion." *Journal of Criminal Justice* 20 (3): 227–36. https://doi.org/10.1016/0047-2352(92)90047-D.

Boone, Catherine. 2003. "Decentralization as Political Strategy in West Africa." *Comparative Political Studies* 36 (4): 355–80.

Booth, D. and F. Golooba-Mutebi. 2012. "Developmental Patrimonialism? The Case of Rwanda." *African Affairs* 111 (444): 379–403. https://doi.org/10.1 093/afraf/ads026.

Bradsher, Keith. 2018. *China's Housing Market Is Like a Casino. Can a Property Tax Tame It?* www.nytimes.com/2018/01/22/business/china-housing-prop erty-tax.html

Braithwaite, John. 1999. "Restorative Justice: Assessing Optimistic and Pessimistic Accounts." *Crime and Justice* 25 (January): 1–127. https://doi.o rg/10.1086/449287.

Bratton, Michael and Nicholas Van de Walle. 1997. *Democratic Experiments in Africa: Regime Transitions in Comparative Perspective*. Cambridge University Press.

Brief, Arthur P. and Stephan J. Motowidlo. 1986. "Prosocial Organizational Behaviors." *Academy of Management Review* 11 (4): 710–25. https://doi.or g/10.5465/amr.1986.4283909.

Brokaw, Cynthia Joanne. 2014. *The Ledgers of Merit and Demerit: Social Change and Moral Order in Late Imperial China*. Vol. 1180. Princeton University Press.

Brower, Holly H., F. David Schoorman, and Hwee Hoon Tan. 2000. "A Model of Relational Leadership." *The Leadership Quarterly* 11 (2): 227–50. https://d oi.org/10.1016/S1048-9843(00)00040-0.

Brown, Michael E., Linda K. Treviño, and David A. Harrison. 2005. "Ethical Leadership: A Social Learning Perspective for Construct Development and Testing." *Organizational Behavior and Human Decision Processes* 97 (2): 117–34. https://doi.org/10.1016/j.obhdp.2005.03.002.

Brownlee, Jason. 2007. *Authoritarianism in an Age of Democratization*. Cambridge University Press.

Bussell, Jennifer. 2012. *Corruption and Reform in India: Public Services in the Digital Age*. Cambridge University Press.

Cai, Yongshun. 2002. "The Resistance of Chinese Laid-off Workers in the Reform Period." *The China Quarterly* 170 (June): 327–44. https://doi.org/10.1017/ S0009443902000219.

Cai, Yongshun. 2014. *State and Agents in China: Disciplining Government Officials*. Stanford University Press.

Calhoun, Craig J. 1997. *Neither Gods Nor Emperors: Students and the Struggle for Democracy in China.* University of California Press, 249.

Campbell, Angus, Philip E. Converse, Warren E. Miller, and Donald E. Stokes. 1980. *The American Voter.* University of Chicago Press.

Campbell, John. 2017. "Resistance to President Buhari's Anticorruption Campaign." *Council on Foreign Relations*, October. www.cfr.org/blog/resist ance-president-buharis-anticorruption-campaign.

Carlsmith, Kevin M. and John M. Darley. 2008. "Psychological Aspects of Retributive Justice." *Advances in Experimental Social Psychology*, 40: 193–236. https://doi.org/10.1016/S0065-2601(07)00004-4.

Carlsmith, Kevin M., John M. Darley, and Paul H. Robinson. 2002. "Why Do We Punish?: Deterrence and Just Deserts as Motives for Punishment." *Journal of Personality and Social Psychology* 83 (2): 284–99. https://doi.org/10.1037// 0022-3514.83.2.284.

Cavaillé, Charlotte and Kris-Stella Trump. 2015. "The Two Facets of Social Policy Preferences." *The Journal of Politics* 77 (1): 146–60. https://doi.org/10.1086/ 678312.

Chen, Chi-yun. 1990. "Orthodoxy as a Mode of Statecraft: The Ancient Concept of Cheng." In *Orthodoxy in Late Imperial China*, edited by Liu Kwang-ching, University of California Press, 27–52.

Chen, Feng. 2000. "Subsistence Crises, Managerial Corruption and Labour Protests in China." *The China Journal* 44 (July): 41–63. https://doi.org/10.2 307/2667476.

Chen, Jie. 2004. *Popular Political Support in Urban China.* Woodrow Wilson Center Press.

Chen, Jie, Yang Zhong, and Jan William Hillard. 1997. "The Level and Sources of Popular Support for China's Current Political Regime." *Communist and Post-Communist Studies* 30 (1): 45–64. https://doi.org/10.1016/S0967-067 X(96)00022-0.

Chêne, Marie. 2011. *What Makes New Zealand, Denmark, Finland, Sweden and Others 'Cleaner' than Most Countries?* Transparency International.

Chiao, Vincent. 2016. "What Is the Criminal Law For?" *Law and Philosophy* 35 (2): 137. https://doi.org/10.1007/s10982-015-9247-8.

ChinaFile Team. 2016. *Visualizing China's Anti-Corruption Campaign.* https:// www.chinafile.com/infographics/visualizing-chinas-anti-corruption-campaign

Chou, Bill K. P. 2005. "Implementing the Reform of Performance Appraisal in China's Civil Service." *China Information* 19 (1): 39–65. https://doi.org/10 .1177/0920203X05051019.

Clarke, Harold D., Nitish Dutt, and Allan Kornberg. 1993. "The Political Economy of Attitudes toward Polity and Society in Western European Democracies." *The Journal of Politics* 55 (4): 998–1021. https://doi.org/10 .2307/2131945.

Clear, Todd R. and Natasha A. Frost. 2013. *The Punishment Imperative: The Rise and Failure of Mass Incarceration in America.* NYU Press.

Conover, Pamela Johnston, Stanley Feldman, and Kathleen Knight. 1987. "The Personal and Political Underpinnings of Economic Forecasts." *American Journal of Political Science*, 31(3): 559–83.

Cook, Linda J. 1993. *The Soviet Social Contract and Why It Failed: Welfare Policy and Workers' Politics from Brezhnev to Yeltsin.* Vol. 86. Harvard University Press.

Corrigan, Philip and Derek Sayer. 1985. *The Great Arch: English State Formation as Cultural Revolution.* Blackwell.

Corstange, Daniel. 2009. "Sensitive Questions, Truthful Answers? Modeling the List Experiment with LISTIT." *Political Analysis* 17 (1): 45–63. https://doi .org/10.1093/pan/mpn013.

Crook, Richard C., James Manor, and A. Sinha. 2000. "Democracy and Decentralization in South Asia and West Africa: Participation, Accountability and Performance." *Comparative Political Studies* 33 (1): 144–47.

Cushman, Fiery, Rachel Sheketoff, Sophie Wharton, and Susan Carey. 2013. "The Development of Intent-Based Moral Judgment." *Cognition* 127 (1): 6–21. https://doi.org/10.1016/j.cognition.2012.11.008.

Dahl, Robert Alan. 1973. *Polyarchy: Participation and Opposition.* Yale University Press.

Dahlberg, Stefan and Sören Holmberg. 2014. "Democracy and Bureaucracy: How Their Quality Matters for Popular Satisfaction." *West European Politics* 37 (3): 515–37. https://doi.org/10.1080/01402382.2013.830468.

Dahlberg, Stefan, Jonas Linde, and Sören Holmberg. 2015. "Democratic Discontent in Old and New Democracies: Assessing the Importance of Democratic Input and Governmental Output." *Political Studies* 63 (1_suppl): 18–37. https://doi.org/10.1111/1467-9248.12170.

Dalton, Russell J. 2013. *Citizen Politics: Public Opinion and Political Parties in Advanced Industrial Democracies.* Cq Press.

Da Qing Luli Huitong Xinzuan. 1966. Wenhai chubanshe.

Darley, John M., Kevin M. Carlsmith, and Paul H. Robinson. 2000. "Incapacitation and Just Deserts as Motives for Punishment." *Law and Human Behavior* 24 (6): 659–83. https://doi.org/10.1023/A:1005552203727.

Davidson, Jamie S. 2007. "Politics-as-Usual on Trial: Regional Anti-Corruption Campaigns in Indonesia." *The Pacific Review* 20 (1): 75–99. https://doi.org/ 10.1080/09512740601133237.

Davis, Deborah and Stevan Harrell. 1993. *Chinese Families in the Post-Mao Era.* Vol. 17. University of California Press.

De Sousa, Luís, Barry Hindess, and Peter Larmour, eds. 2012. *Governments, NGOs and Anti-Corruption: The New Integrity Warriors.* Routledge, 42.

Del Vecchio, Carolyn. 2016. "The Political Participation, Engagement, and Perceptions of President Magufuli among Students at the College of African Wildlife Management." *Independent Study Project (ISP) Collection.* 2351. http://digitalcollections.sit.edu/isp_collection/2351/.

Deutsch, Morton. 1975. "Equity, Equality, and Need: What Determines Which Value Will Be Used as the Basis of Distributive Justice?" *Journal of Social Issues* 31 (3): 137–49. https://doi.org/10.1111/j.1540-4560.1975.tb01000.x.

Deutsch, Morton. 1983. "Conflict Resolution: Theory and Practice." *Political Psychology* 4 (3): 431. https://doi.org/10.2307/3790868.

Deutsch, Morton. 1985. *Distributive Justice: A Social-Psychological Perspective.* Yale University Press.

Deutsch, Morton, Peter T. Coleman, and Eric C. Marcus. 2011. *The Handbook of Conflict Resolution: Theory and Practice.* John Wiley & Sons.

Dickson, Bruce. 2016. *The Dictator's Dilemma: The Chinese Communist Party's Strategy for Survival.* Oxford University Press.

Dietz, Graham and Deanne N. Den Hartog. 2006. "Measuring Trust inside Organisations." Edited by Karin Sanders. *Personnel Review* 35 (5): 557–88. https://doi.org/10.1108/00483480610682299.

Doorenspleet, Renske. 2012. "Critical Citizens, Democratic Support and Satisfaction in African Democracies." *International Political Science Review* 33 (3): 279–300. https://doi.org/10.1177/0192512111431906.

Duara, Prasenjit. 1988. "Superscribing Symbols: The Myth of Guandi, Chinese God of War." *The Journal of Asian Studies* 47 (4): 778. https://doi.org/10.2 307/2057852.

Duckett, Jane and Hua Wang. 2013. "Extending Political Participation in China: New Opportunities for Citizens in the Policy Process." *Journal of Asian Public Policy* 6 (3): 263–76. https://doi.org/10.1080/17516234.2013.850221.

Duff, Antony. 2001. *Punishment, Communication, and Community.* Oxford University Press.

Dugan, Christopher F. and Vladimir Lechtman. 1997. "The FCPA in Russia and Other Former Communist Countries." *The American Journal of International Law* 91 (2): 378. https://doi.org/10.2307/2954220.

Durkheim, Emile. 1964. *The Division of Labour in Society.* Free Press (first published 1893).

Economist Intelligence Unit. 2017. *Senegal.*

Edin, Maria. 1998. "Why Do Chinese Local Cadres Promote Growth? Institutional Incentives and Constraints of Local Cadres." *Forum for Development Studies* 25 (1): 97–127. https://doi.org/10.1080/08039410.1998.9666077.

Edin, Maria. 2003a. "Remaking the Communist Party-State: The Cadre Responsibility System at the Local Level in China." *China: An International Journal* 1 (1): 1–15. https://doi.org/10.1353/chn.2005.0013.

Edin, Maria. 2003b. "State Capacity and Local Agent Control in China: CCP Cadre Management from a Township Perspective." *The China Quarterly* 173 (March): 35–52. https://doi.org/10.1017/S0009443903000044.

Elias, Norbert. 1978. *The Civilizing Process.* Vol. 1, translated by Edmund Jephcott. Blackwell.

Ellickson, R. C. 2001. "The Market for Social Norms." *American Law and Economics Review* 3 (1): 1–49. https://doi.org/10.1093/aler/3.1.1.

Ellsworth, Phoebe C. and Samuel R. Gross. 1994. "Hardening of the Attitudes: Americans' Views on the Death Penalty." *Journal of Social Issues* 50 (2): 19–52. https://doi.org/10.1111/j.1540-4560.1994.tb02409.x.

Ellsworth, Phoebe C. and Lee Ross. 1983. "Public Opinion and Capital Punishment: A Close Examination of the Views of Abolitionists and Retentionists." *Crime & Delinquency* 29 (1): 116–69. https://doi.org/10.11 77/001112878302900105.

Elvin, M. 1998. "Who Was Responsible for the Weather? Moral Meteorology in Late Imperial China." *Osiris* 13: 213–237. https://www.journals.uchicago .edu/doi/abs/10.1086/649286?journalCode=osiris

Enke, Benjamin. 2018. *Moral Values and Voting: Trump and Beyond*. National Bureau of Economic Research. https://doi.org/10.3386/w24268.

Fairbank, John King. 1987. *China Watch*. Harvard University Press.

Fearon, James D. 1999. "Electoral Accountability and the Control of Politicians: Selecting Good Types versus Sanctioning Poor Performance." In *Democracy, Accountability, and Representation*, edited by Adam Przeworski, Susan C. Stokes, and Bernard Manin, 55–97. Cambridge University Press.

Feather, N. T. 1999. "Judgments of Deservingness: Studies in the Psychology of Justice and Achievement." *Personality and Social Psychology Review* 3 (2): 86–107. https://doi.org/10.1207/s15327957pspr0302_1.

Fehr, Ernst and Urs Fischbacher. 2004. "Third-Party Punishment and Social Norms." *Evolution and Human Behavior* 25 (2): 63–87. https://doi.org/10 .1016/S1090-5138.

Fehr, Ernst and Simon Gächter. 2000. "Cooperation and Punishment in Public Goods Experiments." *American Economic Review* 90 (4): 980–94.

Feldman, D. C. 1984. "The Development and Enforcement of Group Norms." *Academy of Management Review* 9 (1): 47–53. https://doi.org/10.5465/ AMR.1984.4277934.

Festinger, Leon. 1950. "Informal Social Communication." *Psychological Review* 57 (5): 271–82. https://doi.org/10.1037/h0056932.

Finkel, Steven E., Edward N. Muller, and Mitchell A. Seligson. 1989. "Economic Crisis, Incumbent Performance and Regime Support: A Comparison of Longitudinal Data from West Germany and Costa Rica." *British Journal of Political Science* 19 (3): 329. https://doi.org/ 10.1017/S0007123400005512.

Foa, Roberto Stefan and Yascha Mounk. 2017. "The Signs of Deconsolidation." *Journal of Democracy* 28 (1): 5–15. https://doi.org/10.1353/jod.2017.0000.

Folger, Robert G. 2012. *The Sense of Injustice: Social Psychological Perspectives*. Springer Science & Business Media.

Folger, Robert, Tom R. Tyler, Robert J. Boeckmann, Heather J. Smith, and Yuen J. Huo. 1999. "Social Justice in a Diverse Society." *Administrative Science Quarterly* 44 (4): 839. https://doi.org/10.2307/2667063.

Forero, Juan. 2011. *In Her First Year, Brazilian President Dilma Rousseff Cleans House*. www.washingtonpost.com/world/americas/in-her-first-year-brazil-p resident-dilma-rousseff-cleans-house/2011/12/12/gIQAOMnStO_story.htm l?noredirect=on&utm term=.5203c504a271.

Fox, Jonathan A. 2015. "Social Accountability: What Does the Evidence Really Say?" *World Development* 72: 346–61.

Freedom House. 2010. "Freedom in the World." https://freedomhouse.org/sites/ default/files/2020-03/FIW_2010_Complete_Book_Scan.pdf

Friedland, Paul. 2012. *Seeing Justice Done: The Age of Spectacular Capital Punishment in France*. Oxford University Press.

Frinjuah, John P. 2018. "A 'Cry for Change' and President Buhari's Fight against Corruption." *Afro Barometer*, February. http://afrobarometer.org/blogs/cry-change-and-president-buharis-fight-against-corruption.

Fritz, Heider. 1958. "The Psychology of Interpersonal Relations." *The Journal of Marketing* 56: 322.

Frum, David. 2017. "How to Build an Autocracy." *The Atlantic*, March. www.theatlantic.com/magazine/archive/2017/03/how-to-build-an-autocracy/513872/.

Gaddis, Isis, Waly Wane, and Jacques Morisset. 2013. *Youth in Tanzania: A Growing Uneducated Labor Force*. The World Bank. http://blogs.worldbank.org/africacan/youth-in-tanzania-a-growing-uneducated-labor-force.

Galbiati, Fernando. 1985. *P'eng P'ai and the Hai-Lu-Feng Soviet*. Stanford University Press.

Gandhi, Jennifer. 2008. "Dictatorial Institutions and Their Impact on Economic Growth." *European Journal of Sociology* 49 (1): 3–30. https://doi.org/10.1017/S0003975608000015.

Gandhi, Jennifer and Ellen Lust-Okar. 2009. "Elections under Authoritarianism." *Annual Review of Political Science* 12 (1): 403–22. https://doi.org/10.1146/annurev.polisci.11.060106.095434.

Gao, Charlotte. 2018. "While Law Unpassed, Provincial Supervision Commissions Already Established in China." *The Diplomat*, February. https://thediplomat.com/2018/02/while-law-unpassed-provincial-supervision-commissions-already-established-in-china/

Gaventa, John and Rosemary McGee. 2013. "The Impact of Transparency and Accountability Initiatives." *Development Policy Review* 31 (July): s3–s28. https://doi.org/10.1111/dpr.12017.

Gawthrop, Louis C. 1997. "Democracy, Bureaucracy, and Hypocrisy Redux: A Search for Sympathy and Compassion." *Public Administration Review*, 57(3), 205–10. https://doi.org/10.2307/976650

Geddes, Barbara. 2006. "Stages of Development in Authoritarian Regimes." In *World Order after Leninism*, edited by V. Tismaneanu, Marc Howard Morje, and Rudra Sil, 149–70. University of Washington Press.

Geertz, Clifford. 1980. *Negara*. Princeton University Press.

Gelfand, M. J., J. L. Raver, L. Nishii, L. M. Leslie, J. Lun, B. C. Lim, L. Duan, et al. 2011. "Differences between Tight and Loose Cultures: A 33-Nation Study." *Science* 332 (6033): 1100–04. https://doi.org/10.1126/science.1197754.

Génaux, Maryvonne. 2004. "Social Sciences and the Evolving Concept of Corruption." *Crime, Law and Social Change* 42 (1): 13–24. https://doi.org/10.1023/B:CRIS.0000041034.66031.02.

Gerber, Alan S. and Gregory A. Huber. 2010. "Partisanship, Political Control, and Economic Assessments." *American Journal of Political Science* 54 (1): 153–73.

Gilley, Bruce. 2006. "The Determinants of State Legitimacy: Results for 72 Countries." *International Political Science Review* 27 (1): 47–71. https://doi.org/10.1177/0192512106058634.

Gilley, Bruce. 2009. *The Right to Rule: How States Win and Lose Legitimacy*. Columbia University Press.

Gingerich, Daniel W. 2010. "Understanding Off-the-Books Politics: Conducting Inference on the Determinants of Sensitive Behavior with Randomized Response Surveys." *Political Analysis* 18 (3): 349–80. https://doi.org/10.1093 /pan/mpq010.

Glinkina, Svetlana P. 1998. "The Ominous Landscape of Russian Corruption." *Transitions* 5 (3): 16–23.

Global Integrity. 2009. *Global Integrity Report 2009*. Global Integrity.

Goenka, Himanshu. 2016. *Philippine Drug War: President Duterte Launches Corruption Purge*. www.ibtimes.com/philippine-drug-war-president-dutert e-launches-corruption-purge-2398555.

Gollwitzer, Mario, Milena Meder, and Manfred Schmitt. 2011. "What Gives Victims Satisfaction When They Seek Revenge?" *European Journal of Social Psychology* 41 (3): 364–74. https://doi.org/10.1002/ejsp.782.

Goodwin, Geoffrey P. and Dena M. Gromet. 2014. "Punishment." *Wiley Interdisciplinary Reviews: Cognitive Science* 5 (5): 562. https://doi.org/10.1 002/wcs.1301.

Greenberg, Gerald R. 1984. "Left Dislocation, Topicalization, and Interjections." *Natural Language and Linguistic Theory* 2 (3): 283–87. https://doi.org/10.1 007/BF00133789.

Greenberg, Jerald. 1990. "Organizational Justice: Yesterday, Today, and Tomorrow." *Journal of Management* 16 (2): 399–432. https://doi.org/10.1 177/014920639001600208.

Gromet, Dena M. 2012. "Restoring the Victim: Emotional Reactions, Justice Beliefs, and Support for Reparation and Punishment." *Critical Criminology* 20 (1): 9–23. https://doi.org/10.1007/s10612-011-9146-8.

Gromet, Dena M. and John M. Darley. 2011. "Political Ideology and Reactions to Crime Victims: Preferences for Restorative and Punitive Responses." *Journal of Empirical Legal Studies* 8 (4): 830–55. https://doi.org/10.1111/j.1740-14 61.2011.01242.x.

Gross, Samuel R. and Phoebe C. Ellsworth. 2001. "Second Thoughts: Americans' Views on the Death Penalty at the Turn of the Century," *SSRN Electronic Journal*, working paper. http://dx.doi.org/10.2139/ssrn.264018

Grzymala-Busse, Anna. 2008. "Beyond Clientelism." *Comparative Political Studies* 41 (4–5): 638–73. https://doi.org/10.1177/0010414007313118.

Guo, Gang. 2007. "Retrospective Economic Accountability under Authoritarianism." *Political Research Quarterly* 60 (3): 378–90. https:// doi.org/10.1177/1065912907304501.

Gurr, Ted Robert. 1970. *Why Men Rebel*. Princeton University Press.

Hainmueller, Jens, Daniel J. Hopkins, and Teppei Yamamoto. 2013. "Causal Inference in Conjoint Analysis: Understanding Multidimensional Choices via Stated Preference Experiments." *Political Analysis* 22 (1): 1–30.

Hamilton, V. Lee. 1978. "Who Is Responsible? Toward a Social Psychology of Responsibility Attribution." *Social Psychology* 41 (4): 316. https://doi.org/1 0.2307/3033584.

Hamlin, Alan and Colin Jennings. 2011. "Expressive Political Behaviour: Foundations, Scope and Implications." *British Journal of Political Science* 41 (3): 645–70.

Hampton, Jean. 1992. "Correcting Harms vs. Righting Wrongs: The Goal of Retribution." *UCLA Law Review* 39(6): 1659–1702.

Hanlon, Joseph. 1985. *Mozambique: The Revolution under Fire*, Zed, 144, 208.

Hart, Herbert Lionel Adolphus and Leslie Green. 2012. *The Concept of Law*. Oxford University Press.

Haslam, S. Alexander, Craig Mcgarty, and John C. Turner. 1996. "Salient Group Memberships and Persuasion: The Role of Social Identity in the Validation of Beliefs." In *What's Social about Social Cognition? Research on Socially Shared Cognition in Small Groups*, edited by Judith L. Nye and Aaron M Brower, 29–56. Sage. https://doi.org/10.4135/9781483327648.n2.

Hegel, G. W. F. 1991. *Elements of the Philosophy of Right*. Edited by Allen W. Wood. Cambridge University Press.

Hellman, Joel S., Geraint Jones, and Daniel Kaufmann. 2000. *Seize the State, Seize the Day: State Capture, Corruption, and Influence in Transition*. The World Bank.

Henochowicz, Anne. 2014. *Work Regulations for Leading Party and Government Cadre Promotions and Appointments*. https://chinadigitaltimes.net/2014/02/work-regulations-leading-party-government-cadre-promotions-appointments/

Heywood, Paul and Ivan Krastev. 2006. "Political Scandals and Corruption." In *Developments in European Politics,* edited by Heywood, Paul M., Jones, Erick, Rhodes, Martin, Sedelmeier, Ulrich, 157–77. http://hdl.handle.net/1814/7349

Heywood, Paul M. and Staffan Andersson. 2012. "Anti-Corruption as a Risk to Democracy: On the Unintended Consequences of International Anti-Corruption Campaigns." In *Governments, NGOs and Anti-Corruption*, edited by Luís de Sousa, Peter Larmour, and Barry Hindess, 33–50. Routledge.

Hibbing, John R. and Elizabeth Theiss-Morse. 2002. *Stealth Democracy: Americans' Beliefs about How Government Should Work*. Cambridge University Press.

Hirschberger, Gilad, Tom Pyszczynski, and Tsachi Ein-Dor. 2015. "Why Does Existential Threat Promote Intergroup Violence? Examining the Role of Retributive Justice and Cost-Benefit Utility Motivations." *Frontiers in Psychology* 6 (November). https://doi.org/10.3389/fpsyg.2015.01761.

Ho, Alfred Tat-Kei and Meili Niu. 2013. "Rising with the Tide without Flipping the Boat - Analyzing the Successes and Challenges of Fiscal Capacity Building in China." *Public Administration and Development* 33 (1): 29–49. https://doi.org/10.1002/pad.1613.

Hofferbert, Richard I. and Hans-Dieter Klingemann. 1999. "Remembering the Bad Old Days: Human Rights, Economic Conditions, and Democratic Performance in Transitional Regimes." *European Journal of Political Research* 36 (2): 155–74. https://doi.org/10.1111/1475-6765.00466.

Hogg, Michael A. 1993. "Group Cohesiveness: A Critical Review and Some New Directions." *European Review of Social Psychology* 4 (1): 85–111. https://doi.org/10.1080/14792779343000031.

Hogg, Michael A. and Deborah I. Terry. 2000. "Social Identity and Self-Categorization Processes in Organizational Contexts." *Academy of Management Review* 25 (1): 121–40. https://doi.org/10.5465/amr.2000.2791606.

Holmberg, Sören and Bo Rothstein. 2012. *Good Government: The Relevance of Political Science.* Edward Elgar Publishing.

Holmes, Leslie. 1993. *The End of Communist Power: Anti-Corruption Campaigns and Legitimation Crisis (Europe and the International Order).* 204. Oxford University Press.

Holmes, Leslie. 2003. "Political Corruption in Central and Eastern Europe." In *Corruption in Contemporary Politics*, edited by Martin J. Bull and James L. Newell, 193–206. Palgrave Macmillan.

Holmes, Stephen. 1997. "Crime and Corruption after Communism. Introduction." *East European Constitutional Review* 6 (4): 69–70.

Howard, Marc Morjé. 2002. "The Weakness of Postcommunist Civil Society." *Journal of Democracy* 13 (1): 157–69.

Hsu, Carolyn L. 2001. "Political Narratives and the Production of Legitimacy: The Case of Corruption in Post-Mao China." *Qualitative Sociology* 24 (1): 25–54. https://doi.org/10.1023/A:1026691329912.

Huang, Philip C. C. 1985. *The Peasant Economy and Social Change in North China.* Stanford University Press.

Huang, Philip C. C. 1996. *Civil Justice in China: Representation and Practice in the Qing.* Stanford University Press.

Huang, Philip C. C. 2001. *Code, Custom, and Legal Practice in China: The Qing and the Republic Compared (Law, Society, and Culture in China).* Stanford University Press.

Huang, Yasheng. 1995. "Administrative Monitoring in China." *The China Quarterly* 143 (September): 828. https://doi.org/10.1017/S0305741000015071.

Huangshan Shi Difang Zhi Bianzuan Weiyuanhui, Huangshan Municipal Gazetteer. 1992. Huangshan Shushe.

Huddleston, R. Joseph and Nicholas Weller. 2017. "Unintended Causal Pathways: Probing Experimental Mechanisms through Mediation Analysis." *SSRN Electronic Journal.* https://doi.org/10.2139/ssrn.2964336.

Hung, Ho-fung. 2013. *Protest with Chinese Characteristics: Demonstrations, Riots, and Petitions in the Mid-Qing Dynasty.* Columbia University Press.

Huntington, H. B. 1968. "Driving Forces for Thermal Mass Transport." *Journal of Physics and Chemistry of Solids* 29 (9): 1641–51. https://doi.org/10.1016/0022-3697(68)90106-6.

Huntington, S. P. 1968. *Political Order in Changing Societies.* Yale University Press.

Hurst, William and Kevin J. O'Brien. 2002. "China's Contentious Pensioners." *The China Quarterly* 170 (June): 345–60. https://doi.org/10.1017/S0009443902000220.

Hyden, Goran. 2012. *African Politics in Comparative Perspective.* Cambridge University Press.

Idema, Wilt L. 2010. *Judge Bao and the Rule of Law: Eight Ballad-Stories from the Period 1250–1450.* World Scientific.

Idema, Wilt L. 2010. "Judge Bao Selling Rice in Chenzhou." In *Judge Bao and the Rule of Law: Eight Ballad-Stories from the Period 1250–1450*, 31–66. World Scientific. https://doi.org/10.1142/9789814277587_0002.

Imai, Kosuke, Dustin Tingley, and Teppei Yamamoto. 2013. "Experimental Designs for Identifying Causal Mechanisms." *Journal of the Royal Statistical Society: Series A (Statistics in Society)* 176 (1): 5–51. https://doi.org/10.1111/j.1467-985X.2012.01032.x.

Iyengar, Shanto and Kyu S. Hahn. 2009. "Red Media, Blue Media: Evidence of Ideological Selectivity in Media Use." *Journal of Communication* 59 (1): 19–39. https://doi.org/10.1111/j.1460-2466.2008.01402.x.

Janoff-Bulman, Ronnie and Nate C. Carnes. 2016. "Social Justice and Social Order: Binding Moralities across the Political Spectrum." Edited by Asim Zia. *PLOS ONE* 11 (3): e0152479. https://doi.org/10.1371/journal.pone.0152479.

Javed, Jeffrey A. n.d. *Righteous Revolutionaries: Morality, Mobilization, and Violence in the Making of the Chinese State (Manuscript Draft)*.

Jennings, M. Kent. 1997. "Political Participation in the Chinese Countryside." *American Political Science Review* 91 (2): 361–72. https://doi.org/10.2307/2952361.

Jensen, Jacob and Terry Anderson. 2016. "A Qualitative Comparison of Anti-Corruption Measures in Guatemala and Brazil." *Journal of Politics and Democratization* 1 (2): 1–20. https://gipa.ge/JPD/files/JensenandAnderson1-2.pdf.

Jerit, Jennifer and Jason Barabas. 2012. "Partisan Perceptual Bias and the Information Environment." *The Journal of Politics* 74 (3): 672–84. https://doi.org/10.1017/S0022381612000187.

Jowitt, Ken. 1992. *New World Disorder: The Leninist Extinction*. University of California Press.

Kahan, Dan M. 2013. "Ideology, Motivated Reasoning, and Cognitive Reflection." *Judgment and Decision Making* 8 (4): 407–24.

Kahan, Dan M., David Hoffman, Danieli Evans, Neal Devans, Eugene Lucci, and Katherine Cheng. 2015. "Ideology or Situation Sense: An Experimental Investigation of Motivated Reasoning and Professional Judgment." *University of Pennsylvania Law Review* 164: 349.

Kahneman, Daniel, Jack L. Knetsch, and Richard H. Thaler. 1986. "Fairness and the Assumptions of Economics." *Journal of Business*, 59(4): S285–S300.

Kalinin, Kirill. 2016. "The Social Desirability Bias in Autocrat's Electoral Ratings: Evidence from the 2012 Russian Presidential Elections." *Journal of Elections, Public Opinion and Parties* 26 (2): 191–211. https://doi.org/10.1080/17457289.2016.1150284.

Kanfer, Ruth. 1990. "Motivation Theory and Industrial and Organizational Psychology." *Handbook of Industrial and Organizational Psychology* 1 (2): 75–130.

Kendall-Taylor, Andrea and Erica Frantz. 2016. "Foreign Affairs." *Foreign Affairs*, December. www.foreignaffairs.com/articles/2016-12-05/how-democracies-fall-apart.

Kennedy, Scott. 2009. "Comparing Formal and Informal Lobbying Practices in China." *China Information* 23 (2): 195–222. https://doi.org/10.1177/0920203X09105125.

Kerr, Norbert L., Robert W. Hymes, Alonzo B. Anderson, and James E. Weathers. 1995. "Defendant-Juror Similarity and Mock Juror Judgments." *Law and Human Behavior* 19 (6): 545.

Kesebir, Pelin and Tom Pyszczynski. 2012. "The Role of Death in Life: Existential Aspects of Human Motivation." In *Oxford Library of Psychology. The Oxford Handbook of Human Motivation*, edited by Richard M. Ryan. Oxford University Press, 43–64.

Keuleers, Patrick. 2005. "Corruption, Poverty and Development." In *Background Paper (Plenary 2)*. ABD/OECD Anti-Corruption Initiative for Asia and the Pacific. http://www.oecd.org/site/adboecdanti-corruptioninitiative/regional seminars/35593188.pdf

Kinder, Donald R., Mark D. Peters, Robert P. Abelson, and Susan T. Fiske. 1980. "Presidential Prototypes." *Political Behavior* 2 (4): 315–37. https://doi.org/10.1007/BF00990172.

King, Gary, Jennifer Pan, and Margaret E. Roberts. 2013. "How Censorship in China Allows Government Criticism but Silences Collective Expression." *American Political Science Review* 107 (2): 326–43. https://doi.org/10.1017/S0003055413000014.

Klitgaard, Robert. 1988. *Controlling Corruption*. University of California Press.

Kosack, Stephen and Archon Fung. 2014. "Does Transparency Improve Governance?" *Annual Review of Political Science* 17 (1): 65–87. https://doi.org/10.1146/annurev-polisci-032210-144356.

Krebs, Hanna B. 2014. *Responsibility, Legitimacy, Morality: Chinese Humanitarianism in Historical Perspective*. Humanitarian Policy Group, Overseas Development Institute.

Krishna, Anirudh. 2002. "Enhancing Political Participation in Democracies: What Is the Role of Social Capital?" *Comparative Political Studies* 35 (4): 437–60.

Kruks-Wisner, Gabrielle K. 2013. *Claiming the State: Citizen-State Relations and Service Delivery in Rural India*. Massachusetts Institute of Technology. https://dspace.mit.edu/handle/1721.1/83760

Lague, David, Benjamin Kang Lim, and Charlie Zhu. 2014. *Special Report: Fear and Retribution in Xi's Corruption Purge*. https://www.reuters.com/article/us-china-corruption-purge-specialreport/special-report-fear-and-retribution-in-xis-corruption-purge-idUSKBN0K200320141224

Lagunes, Paul F. and Susan Rose-Ackerman. 2017. *Why Brazil Is Winning Its Fight Against Corruption*. http://theconversation.com/why-brazil-is-winning-its-fight-against-corruption-71968.

Lam, Wai-man. 2016. *Political Legitimacy in Hong Kong: A Hybrid Notion*. Cambridge University Press.

Landry, Pierre F. 2008. *Decentralized Authoritarianism in China: The Communist Party's Control of Local Elites in the Post-Mao Era*. Cambridge University Press.

Landry, Pierre F., Deborah Davis, and Shiru Wang. 2010. "Elections in Rural China: Competition without Parties." *Comparative Political Studies* 43 (6): 763–90. https://doi.org/10.1177/0010414009359392.

Lane, Christel. 1981. *The Rites of Rulers: Ritual in Industrial Society-the Soviet Case*. Cambridge University Press.

Larmour, Peter. 2012. "Populist Anti-Corruption and Military Coups: The Clean-up Campaign in Fiji 2006–07." In *Governments, NGOs and Anti-Corruption*, edited by Luís de Sousa, Barry Hindess, and Peter Larmour,146–158. Routledge.

Lasthuizen, Karin M. 2008. "Leading to Integrity: Empirical Research into the Effects of Leadership on Ethics and Integrity." https://research.vu.nl/en/publi cations/leading-to-integrity-empirical-research-into-the-effects-of-leade

Latham, Richard J. 1985. "The Implications of Rural Reforms for Grass-Roots Cadres." in *The Political Economy of Reform in Post-Mao China*, edited by Elizabeth J. Perry and Christine Wong, 169. Harvard University Asia Center.

Le Monde. 2017. *Accusé de « détournement de Fonds », Le Maire de Dakar a Été Inculpé et Écroué*. https://www.lemonde.fr/afrique/article/2017/03/08/accus e-de-detournement-de-fonds-le-maire-de-dakar-a-ete-inculpe-et-ecrou e_5090873_3212.html

Lee, Ching Kwan. 2000. "The 'Revenge of History'." *Ethnography* 1 (2): 217–37. https://doi.org/10.1177/14661380022230741.

Lee, Ching Kwan. 2002. "From the Specter of Mao to the Spirit of the Law: Labor Insurgency in China." *Theory and Society* 31 (2): 213. https://doi.org/10.10 23/A:1015083610306.

Lee, Ching Kwan. 2003. "Pathways of Labour Insurgency." In *Chinese Society: Change, Conflict and Resistance*, edited by Elizabeth Perry and Mark Selden, 87–109. Routledge.

Leonard, Jane Kate and John Robertson Watt. 1992. "Introduction." In *To Achieve Security and Wealth: The Qing Imperial State and the Economy*, edited by Jane Kate Leonard and John R. Watt, *1644–1911*, 2. 56. Cornell University East Asia Program.

Lerner, Melvin J. 1980. "The Belief in a Just World." In *The Belief in a Just World*, 9–30. Springer US. https://doi.org/10.1007/978-1-4899-0448-5_2.

Levi, Margaret. 1989. *Of Rule and Revenue*. Vol. 13. University of California Press.

Levi, Margaret. 1997. *Consent, Dissent, and Patriotism*. Cambridge University Press.

Levi, Margaret. 2003. "Organizing Power: The Prospects for an American Labor Movement." *Perspective on Politics* 1 (1): S1537592703000045. https://doi .org/10.1017/S1537592703000045.

Levi, Margaret. 2006. "Why We Need a New Theory of Government." *Perspectives on Politics* 4 (1): 5. https://doi.org/10.1017/S1537592706060038.

Levi, Margaret. 2019. "Trustworthy Government and Legitimating Beliefs." In *Political Legitimacy: NOMOS LXI*, edited by Jack Knight and Melissa Schwartzberg, 362–84. New York University Press.

Levi, Margaret and Audrey Sacks. 2009. "Legitimating Beliefs: Sources and Indicators." *Regulation & Governance* 3 (4): 311–33.

Levi, Margaret and Institut Universitaire Européen Centre Robert Schuman. 1996. *A State of Trust*. Citeseer.

Levi, Margaret and Richard Sherman. 1997. "Rationalized Bureaucracies and Rational Compliance." In *Institutions and Economic Development: Growth and Governance in Less Developed and Post-Socialist Countries*, edited by Christopher Clague, 316–40. Johns Hopkins University Press.

Levine, John M. 1989. "Reaction to Opinion Deviance in Small Groups." *Psychology of Group Influence* 2: 187–231.

Levitsky, Steven and Lucan A. Way. 2010. *Competitive Authoritarianism: Hybrid Regimes after the Cold War.* Cambridge University Press.

Lewicki, Roy J., Edward C. Tomlinson, and Nicole Gillespie. 2006. "Models of Interpersonal Trust Development: Theoretical Approaches, Empirical Evidence, and Future Directions." *Journal of Management* 32 (6): 991–1022. https://doi.org/10.1177/0149206306294405.

Lewis-Beck, Michael S. and Mary Stegmaier. 2007. *Economic Models of Voting.* Oxford University Press. https://doi.org/10.1093/oxfordhb/9780199270125.003.0027.

Li, Eva. 2017. *Ex-Aide to China's Personnel Chief Sacked for "Corrupt Political Morals."* https://www.scmp.com/news/china/policies-politics/article/2105330/ex-aide-chinas-personnel-chief-sacked-corrupt-political

Li, Lianjiang. 2001. "Support for Anti-Corruption Campaigns in Rural China." *Journal of Contemporary China* 10 (29): 573–86. https://doi.org/10.1080/10670560120075019.

Li, Lianjiang. 2003. "The Empowering Effect of Village Elections in China." *Asian Survey* 43 (4): 648–62. https://doi.org/10.1525/as.2003.43.4.648.

Li, Lianjiang and Kevin J. O'Brien. 1996. "Villagers and Popular Resistance in Contemporary China." *Modern China* 22 (1): 28–61. https://doi.org/10.1177/009770049602200102.

Liberman, Peter. 2013. "Retributive Support for International Punishment and Torture." *Journal of Conflict Resolution* 57 (2): 285–306.

Lind, E. Allan and Tom R. Tyler. 1988. *The Social Psychology of Procedural Justice.* Springer. https://books.google.com/books?hl=en&id=oyXZ5IMoJ8MC&oi=fnd&pg=PA1&dq=lind+and+tyler+1988&ots=QsFCtPyY6o&sig=9UBoMxC81ndqF7SpV2QmcPYBWAo#v=onepage&q=lindandtyler1988&f=false.

Link, Perry. 2000. *The Uses of Literature: Life in the Socialist Chinese Literary System.* Princeton University Press.

Lipovsek, Varja and Lily L. Tsai. 2018. *What Do We Know about Transparency and Non-Electoral Accountability? Synthesizing the Evidence from the Last Ten Years.* MIT Governance Lab.

Lipset, Seymour Martin. 1960. *Political Man.* Vintage Books.

Lipsky, Michael. 1993. "Street-Level Bureaucracy: An Introduction." In *The Policy Process: A Reader*, edited by Hill, Michael 381–85. Harvester Wheatsheaf.

Lisheng, Dong. 2006. "Direct Township Elections in China: Latest Developments and Prospects." *Journal of Contemporary China* 15 (48): 503–15. https://doi.org/10.1080/10670560600736533.

Lloyd-Bostock, Sally M. 1983. *Attributions of Cause and Responsibility as Social Phenomena.* Academic Press.

Lü, Xiaobo. 2000. *Cadres and Corruption: The Organizational Involution of the Chinese Communist Party.* Stanford University Press.

Lü, Xiaobo and Lily L. Tsai. 2016. "When Do Citizens Want Representation in Exchange for Taxation? An Experimental Study on Property Tax in Urban China." *MIT Political Science Department Research Paper No. 2016–36.*

Luce, R. Duncan and John W. Tukey. 1964. "Simultaneous Conjoint Measurement: A New Type of Fundamental Measurement." *Journal of Mathematical Psychology* 1 (1): 1–27. https://doi.org/10.1016/0022-2496(64)90015-X.

Lukiko, Lukiko. 2017. *Exploring a Sustainable Anti-Corruption Regime for Tanzania*. University of the Western Cape. http://etd.uwc.ac.za/xmlui/handle/11394/5692.

Macauley, Melissa. 1998. *Social Power and Legal Culture: Litigation Masters in Late Imperial China (Law, Society, and Culture in China)*. Stanford University Press.

MacCoun, Robert J. 1993. "Drugs and the Law: A Psychological Analysis of Drug Prohibition." *Psychological Bulletin* 113 (3): 497.

Magalhães, Pedro C. 2014. "Government Effectiveness and Support for Democracy." *European Journal of Political Research* 53 (1): 77–97. https://doi.org/10.1111/1475-6765.12024.

Magaloni, Beatriz. 2006. *Voting for Autocracy: Hegemonic Party Survival and Its Demise in Mexico*. Cambridge University Press.

Malesky, Edmund and Paul Schuler. 2011. "The Single-Party Dictator's Dilemma: Information in Elections without Opposition." *Legislative Studies Quarterly* 36 (4): 491–530. https://doi.org/10.1111/j.1939-9162.2011.00025.x.

Manion, Melanie. 2006. "Democracy, Community, Trust: The Impact of Elections in Rural China." *Comparative Political Studies* 39 (3): 301–24. https://doi.org/10.1177/0010414005280852.

Marques, José M. , Vincent Y. Yzerbyt, and Jacques-Philippe Leyens. 1988. "The 'Black Sheep Effect': Extremity of Judgments towards Ingroup Members as a Function of Group Identification." *European Journal of Social Psychology* 18 (1): 1–16. https://doi.org/10.1002/ejsp.2420180102.

Mayer, Roger C., James H. Davis, and F. David Schoorman. 1995. "An Integrative Model Of Organizational Trust." *Academy of Management Review* 20 (3): 709–734. https://doi.org/10.5465/amr.1995.9508080335.

McWalters, Ian, David Fitzpatrick, and Andrew Bruce. 2015. *Bribery and Corruption Law in Hong Kong*. LexisNexis.

Meindl, James R. and Melvin J. Lerner. 1983. "The Heroic Motive: Some Experimental Demonstrations." *Journal of Experimental Social Psychology* 19 (1): 1–20. https://doi.org/10.1016/0022-1031(83)90002-1.

Metzger, Thomas A. 1973. *The Internal Organization of Ch'ing Bureaucracy: Legal, Normative, and Communication Aspects*. Vol. 7. Harvard University Press.

Meyer, Alexander and Leah R. Rosenzweig. 2016. "Conjoint Analysis Tools for Developing Country Contexts." *The Political Methodologist* 23(2): 2–6. https://polmeth.org/files/polmeth/files/tpm_v23_n2.pdf#page=2.

Miller, Dale T. 2001. "Disrespect and the Experience of Injustice." *Annual Review of Psychology* 52 (1): 527–53.

Miller, Dale T. and Neil Vidmar. 1981. "The Social Psychology of Punishment Reactions." In *The Justice Motive in Social Behavior: Adapting to Times of Scarcity and Change*, edited by Melvin J. Lerner and Sally C. Lerner, 145–72. Springer US. https://doi.org/10.1007/978-1-4899-0429-4_8.

Ministry of Organization. 1988. "Notice Regarding Implementation of the Annual Job Evaluation System for Leading Cadres of Local Party and Government Organs (Guanyu Shixing Defang Dangzeng Lingdao Ganbu Niandu Gongzuo Kaohe Zhidu de Tongzhi)."

Mishler, William and Richard Rose. 2001. "What Are the Origins of Political Trust?" *Comparative Political Studies* 34 (1): 30–62. https://doi.org/10.1177/0010414001034001002.

Moehler, Devra C. 2008. *Distrusting Democrats: Outcomes of Participatory Constitution Making*. University of Michigan Press.

Monroe, Andrew E. and Glenn D. Reeder. 2011. "Motive-Matching: Perceptions of Intentionality for Coerced Action." *Journal of Experimental Social Psychology* 47 (6): 1255–61. https://doi.org/10.1016/j.jesp.2011.05.012.

Moore Jr, Barrington. 2016. *Injustice: The Social Bases of Obedience and Revolt: The Social Bases of Obedience and Revolt*. Routledge.

Moriarty, Jeffrey. 2003. "Against the Asymmetry of Desert." *Nous* 37 (3): 518–36. https://doi.org/10.1111/1468-0068.00449.

Munro, Neil M. I., Jane Duckett, Kate Hunt, and Matt Sutton. 2013. "Does China's Regime Enjoy 'Performance Legitimacy'? An Empirical Analysis Based on Three Surveys from the Past Decade." http://ssrn.com/abstract=2302982.

Murphy, Colleen. 2016. "Transitional Justice, Retributive Justice and Accountability for Wrongdoing." In *Theorizing Transitional Justice*, edited by Claudio Corradetti and Nir Eisikovits, 59–68. Routledge.

Nacoste, Rupert Barnes. 1990. "Sources of Stigma: Analyzing the Psychology of Affirmative Action." *Law & Policy* 12 (2): 175–95. https://doi.org/10.1111/j.1467-9930.1990.tb00046.x.

Nadelhoffer, Thomas, Saeideh Heshmati, Deanna Kaplan, and Shaun Nichols. 2013. "Folk Retributivism and the Communication Confound." *Economics and Philosophy* 29 (2): 235–61. https://doi.org/10.1017/S0266626711300021 7.

Nadler, Arie and Nurit Shnabel. 2008. "Instrumental and Socioemotional Paths to Intergroup Reconciliation and the Needs-Based Model of Socioemotional Reconciliation." In *The Social Psychology of Intergroup Reconciliation*, edited by Arie Nadler, Thomas Malloy, and Jeffrey D. Fisher, 37–56. Oxford University Press.

Nagle, Angela. 2017. *The Lost Boys*. www.theatlantic.com/magazine/archive/2017/12/brotherhood-of-losers/544158/.

Nakazawa, Katsuji. 2018. *Welcome to the Club: Xi Takes Anti-Corruption Hunt to All Chinese*. https://asia.nikkei.com/Editor-s-Picks/China-up-close/Welcome-to-the-club-Xi-takes-anti-corruption-hunt-to-all-Chinese

Nguyen, Cindy A. 2013. *Public Satisfaction on Graft "Within Five Years."* https://chinadigitaltimes.net/2013/12/china-unveils-5-year-anti-corruption-plan/.

Nguyen, Cindy A. 2017. *Ousted Chinese Officials "Plotted to Overthrow Xi."* https://chinadigitaltimes.net/2017/10/outsted-chinese-officials-plotted-overthrow-xi-jinping/

Norris, Pippa. 2012. *Making Democratic Governance Work: How Regimes Shape Prosperity, Welfare, and Peace*. Cambridge University Press.

Nossiter, Adam. 2015. *Nigerian President-Elect Muhammadu Buhari Sets Out His Agenda.* https://www.nytimes.com/2015/04/02/world/africa/nigerian-pr esident-elect-muhammadu-buhari-sets-out-his-agenda.html

Nyhan, Brendan and Jason Reifler. 2010. "When Corrections Fail: The Persistence of Political Misperceptions." *Political Behavior* 32 (2): 303–30. https://doi .org/10.1007/s11109-010-9112-2.

Nyhan, Brendan, Jason Reifler, and Peter A. Ubel. 2013. "The Hazards of Correcting Myths about Health Care Reform." *Medical Care* 51 (2): 127–32. https://doi.org/10.1097/MLR.0b013e318279486b.

O'Brien, Kevin J. and Lianjiang Li. 1999a. "Selective Policy Implementation in Rural China." *Comparative Politics* 31 (2): 167. https://doi.org/10.2307/ 422143.

O'Brien, Kevin J. and Lianjiang Li. 1999b. "Campaign Nostalgia in the Chinese Countryside." *Asian Survey* 39 (3): 375–93. https://doi.org/10.2307/3021204.

Office of the Ombudsman. 2014. "Annual Report July 2013–June 2014." OMB, Kigali. https://www.minijust.gov.rw/fileadmin/user_upload/Minijust/Public ations/Reports/MOJ_reports/Annual_Report_2013-2014.pdf

Oi, Jean C. 1989. *State and Peasant in Contemporary China: The Political Economy of Village Government.* Vol. 30. University of California Press.

Oi, Jean C., Kim Singer Babiarz, Linxiu Zhang, Renfu Luo, and Scott Rozelle. 2012. "Shifting Fiscal Control to Limit Cadre Power in China's Townships and Villages." *The China Quarterly* 211 (September): 649–75. https://doi.o rg/10.1017/S0305741012000823.

Okimoto, Tyler G. and Michael Wenzel. 2009. "Punishment as Restoration of Group and Offender Values Following a Transgression: Value Consensus through Symbolic Labelling and Offender Reform." *European Journal of Social Psychology* 39 (3): 346–67. https://doi.org/10.1002/ejsp.537.

Okimoto, Tyler G. , Michael Wenzel, and N. T. Feather. 2012. "Retribution and Restoration as General Orientations towards Justice." *European Journal of Personality* 26 (3): 255–75. https://doi.org/10.1002/per.831.

Okimoto, Tyler G. , Michael Wenzel, and Michael J. Platow. 2010. "Restorative Justice: Seeking a Shared Identity in Dynamic Intragroup Contexts." In *Fairness and Groups (Research on Managing Groups and Teams, Vol. 13)*, edited by E. A. Mannix, M. A. Neale, and E. Mullen, 205–42. Emerald Group. https://doi.org/10.1108/S1534-0856(2010)0000013011.

Ong, Lynette H. 2012. *Prosper or Perish: Credit and Fiscal Systems in Rural China.* Cornell University Press.

Organ, Dennis W. 1988. "A Restatement of the Satisfaction-Performance Hypothesis." *Journal of Management* 14 (4): 547–57.

Organ, Dennis W. 1990. "The Motivational Basis of Organizational Citizenship Behavior." *Research in Organizational Behavior* 12 (1): 43–72.

Organ, Dennis W. and Mary Konovsky. 1989. "Cognitive versus Affective Determinants of Organizational Citizenship Behavior." *Journal of Applied Psychology* 74 (1): 157–64. https://doi.org/10.1037/0021-9010.74.1.157.

Ottervik, Mattias. 2013. "Conceptualizing and Measuring State Capacity: Testing the Validity of Tax Compliance as a Measure of State Capacity." https://core .ac.uk/download/pdf/43558814.pdf

Oyamada, Eiji. 2017. "Combating Corruption in Rwanda: Lessons for Policy Makers." *Asian Education and Development Studies* 6 (3): 249–62. https://doi.org/10.1108/AEDS-03-2017-0028.

Panksepp, Jaak. 1998. *Affective Neuroscience: The Foundations of Human and Animal Emotions.* Oxford University Press.

Panksepp, Jaak and Lucy Biven. 2012. *The Archeology of Mind: Neurorevolutionary Origins of Human Emotions.* W. W. Norton.

People's Republic of China Supervision Law (Draft). 2017. https://www.china lawtranslate.com/en/peoples-republic-of-china-supervision-law-draft/

Perry, Elizabeth. 2002. "Moving the Masses: Emotion Work in the Chinese Revolution." *Mobilization: An International Quarterly* 7 (2): 111–28.

Perry, Elizabeth. 2017. "Cultural Governance in Contemporary China: 'Re-Orienting' Party Propaganda." In *To Govern China: Evolving Practices of Power*, edited by Vivienne Shue and Patricia M. Thornton, 29–55. Cambridge University Press.

Perry, Elizabeth J. 2010. "Popular Protest in China: Playing by the Rules." In *China Today, China Tomorrow: Domestic Politics, Economy and Society*, edited by Joseph Fewsmith, 11–28. Rowman & Littlefield. http://nrs.harvard .edu/urn-3:HUL.InstRepos:30827732

Perry, Elizabeth J. 2011. "From Mass Campaigns to Managed Campaigns: 'Constructing a New Socialist Countryside'." In *Mao's Invisible Hand : The Political Foundations of Adaptive Governance in China*, edited by Sebastian Heilmann and Elizabeth J. Perry, 31. Harvard University Asia Center .

Perry, Elizabeth J. 2018. "Making Communism Work: Sinicizing a Soviet Practice." *MIT Sloan China Seminar Series.* https://www.cambridge.org/cor e/services/aop-cambridge-core/content/view/B46222FDEBF05BA314191 D56AF429F89/S0010417519000227a.pdf/div-class-title-making-commun ism-work-sinicizing-a-soviet-governance-practice-div.pdf

Persson, Anna, Bo Rothstein, and Jan Teorell. 2013. "Why Anticorruption Reforms Fail–Systemic Corruption as a Collective Action Problem." *Governance* 26 (3): 454–55. https://doi.org/10.1111/j.1468-0491.2012.01604.x.

Piaget, Jean. 1965. *The Moral Judgment of the Child.* Free Press. (Original work published 1932).

Piaget, Jean. 2006. "The Stages of the Intellectual Development of the Child." In *Educational Psychology in Context: Readings for Future Teachers*, edited by Bruce A. Marlowe and Alan S. Canestrari, 98–106. Sage Publications.

Plato. 1961. "The Laws." In *The Collected Dialogues of Plato*, edited by Edith Hamilton and Huntington Cairns, 1225–1514. Princeton University Press.

Plato. 2016. *The Republic.* Edited by Allan Bloom and Adam Kirsch. Basic Books.

Polimedio, Chayenne. 2017. "Brazilians Are Losing Faith in Democracy and Considering a Return to Military Rule." *Vox*, September. www.vox.com/p olyarchy/2017/9/19/16333360/brazilians-losing-faith-democracy.

Politico Staff. 2016. *Full Text: Donald Trump 2016 RNC Draft Speech Transcript.* www.politico.com/story/2016/07/full-transcript-donald-trump-nomination-acceptance-speech-at-rnc-225974.

Pop-Eleches, Grigore and Joshua A. Tucker. 2011. "Communism's Shadow: Postcommunist Legacies, Values, and Behavior." *Comparative Politics* 43 (4): 379–408. https://doi.org/10.5129/001041511796301588.

Przeworski, Adam. 1991. *Democracy and the Market: Political and Economic Reforms in Eastern Europe and Latin America*. Cambridge University Press.

Przeworski, Adam, Susan C. Stokes, and Bernard Manin. 1999. *Democracy, Accountability, and Representation*. Cambridge University Press.

Pye, Lucian W. 1992. *The Spirit of Chinese Politics*. 2nd ed. Harvard University Press.

Pyszczynski, Tom, Sheldon Solomon, and Jeff Greenberg. 2015. "Thirty Years of Terror Management Theory." *Advances in Experimental Social Psychology*, 52: 1–70. https://doi.org/10.1016/bs.aesp.2015.03.001.

Rauch, Jonathan. 2016. "How American Politics Went Insane." *The Atlantic*. www.theatlantic.com/magazine/archive/2016/07/how-american-politics-went-insane/485570/.

Rawls, John. 1971. *A Theory of Justice*. Cambridge University Press, 314–15.

Rawls, John. 1999. *A Theory of Justice, Revised Edition*. Cambridge University Press.

Redlawsk, David P. 2002. "Hot Cognition or Cool Consideration? Testing the Effects of Motivated Reasoning on Political Decision Making." *The Journal of Politics* 64 (4): 1021–44. https://doi.org/10.1111/1468-2508.00161.

Reed, Bradly. 2000. *Talons and Teeth: County Clerks and Runners in the Qing Dynasty*. Stanford University Press.

Reichle, Barbara, Angela Schneider, and Leo Montada. 1998. "How Do Observers of Victimization Preserve Their Belief in a Just World Cognitively or Actionally?" In *Responses to Victimizations and Belief in a Just World*, edited by Leo Montada and Melvin J. Lerner, 55–64. Springer US. https://doi.org/10.1007/978-1-4757-6418-5_4.

Reuter, Ora John and Jennifer Gandhi. 2011. "Economic Performance and Elite Defection from Hegemonic Parties." *British Journal of Political Science* 41 (1): 83–110.

Reuters Staff. 2013. *China's Xi Urges Swatting of Lowly "Flies" in Fight on Everyday Graft*. https://www.reuters.com/article/us-china-corruption-xi/chinas-xi-urges-swatting-of-lowly-flies-in-fight-on-everyday-graft-idUSBRE90L0AA20130122

Reuters Staff. 2017. "China's Xi: We Can't Be 'Blindly Optimistic' on Corruption inside the Communist Party." *Newsweek*, July. https://www.newsweek.com/communist-party-blindly-optimistic-about-corruption-643166

Ries, Tonia E., David M. Bersoff, Sarah Adkins, Cody Armstrong, and Jamis Bruening. 2018. *2018 Edelman Trust Barometer: Global Report*. Edelman. https://www.edelman.com/sites/g/files/aatuss191/files/2018-10/2018_Edelman_Trust_Barometer_Global_Report_FEB.pdf

Rios, Jesus and Julie Ray. 2015. "Brazilian's Trust in Country's Leadership at Record Low." *Gallup*. http://news.gallup.com/poll/190481/brazilians-trust-country-leadership-record-low.aspx.

Rix, K. 2008. "'The Elimination of Corrupt Practices in British Elections'? Reassessing the Impact of the 1883 Corrupt Practices Act." *The English Historical Review* 123 (500): 65–97. https://doi.org/10.1093/ehr/cen005.

Rose, Richard, William Mishler, and Christian Haerpfer. 1998. *Democracy and Its Alternatives: Understanding Post-Communist Societies*. Johns Hopkins University Press.

Rose, Richard, William Mishler, and Neil Munro. 2011. *Popular Support for an Undemocratic Regime: The Changing Views of Russians*. Cambridge University Press.

Ross, Michael L. 2001. "Does Oil Hinder Democracy?" *World Politics* 53 (3): 325–61.

Rothstein, Bo. 2009. "Creating Political Legitimacy." *American Behavioral Scientist* 53 (3): 311–30. https://doi.org/10.1177/0002764209338795.

Rothstein, Bo. 2011. *The Quality of Government: Corruption, Social Trust, and Inequality in International Perspective*. University of Chicago Press.

Rothstein, Bo and Jan Teorell. 2008. "What Is Quality of Government? A Theory of Impartial Government Institutions." *Governance* 21 (2): 165–90. https://doi.org/10.1111/j.1468-0491.2008.00391.x.

Rothstein, Bo and Aiysha Varraich. 2017. *Making Sense of Corruption*. Cambridge University Press.

Rozelle, Scott. 1996. "Stagnation without Equity: Patterns of Growth and Inequality in China's Rural Economy." *The China Journal* 35 (January): 63–92. https://doi.org/10.2307/2950276.

Rudolph, Josh. 2018a. *New Anti-Graft Ministry Heightens Rights Concerns*. https://chinadigitaltimes.net/2018/02/new-anti-graft-ministry-heightens-concerns-suspects-rights/

Rudolph, Josh. 2018b. *Premier's Call for Supervision of Government Censored*. https://chinadigitaltimes.net/2018/05/li-keqiangs-call-for-supervision-of-government-censored/

Rupp, Deborah E. and Chris M. Bell. 2010. "Extending the Deontic Model of Justice: Moral Self-Regulation in Third-Party Responses to Injustice." *Business Ethics Quarterly* 20 (1): 89–106. https://doi.org/10.5840/beq20102017.

Saich, Tony. 2009. *The Blind Man and the Elephant: Analysing the Local State in China*. Routledge.

Sampson, Steven. 2005. "Integrity Warriors: Global Morality and the Anti-Corruption Movement in the Balkans." In *Corruption: Anthropological Perspectives*, edited by Dieter Haller and Cris Shore, 103–30. Pluto Press.

Sampson, Steven. 2012. "Corruption and Anti-Corruption in Southeast Europe." In *Governments, NGOs, and Anti-Corruption: The New Integrity Warriors*, edited by Luís de Sousa, Peter Larmour, and Barry Hindess, 168–85. Routledge.

Samuels, David J. and Cesar Zucco. 2018. *Partisans, Antipartisans, and Nonpartisans: Voting Behavior in Brazil*. Cambridge University Press.

Santos, David and Reynaldo G. Rivera. 2015. "The Accessibility of Justice-Related Concepts Can Validate Intentions to Punish." *Social Influence* 10 (3): 180–92. https://doi.org/10.1080/15534510.2015.1031170.

Schaffner, Brian F. and Cameron Roche. 2017. "Misinformation and Motivated Reasoning: Responses to Economic News in a Politicized Environment."

Public Opinion Quarterly, 81(1): 86–110. https://doi.org/10.1093/poq/nfwo43.

Scheffler, Samuel. 1992. *Human Morality*. Oxford University Press on Demand.

Scheffler, Samuel. 2002. *Boundaries and Allegiances: Problems of Justice and Responsibility in Liberal Thought*. Oxford University Press on Demand.

Scher, Daniel and Christine MacAulay. 2010. "The Promise of Imihigo: Decentralized Service Delivery in Rwanda, 2006–2010." *Innovations for Successful Societies*. Princeton University. https://successfulsocieties.princeton.edu/publications/promise-imihigo-decentralized-service-delivery-rwanda-2006-2010

Scher, Daniel and Christine MacAulay. 2014. "How Tradition Remade Rwanda." *Foreign Policy*, January. https://foreignpolicy.com/2014/01/28/how-tradition-remade-rwanda/

Schimmel, Noam. 2012. "The Moral Case for Restorative Justice as a Corollary of the Responsibility to Protect: A Rwandan Case Study of the Insufficiency of Impact of Retributive Justice on the Rights and Well-Being of Genocide Survivors." *Journal of Human Rights* 11 (2): 161–88. https://doi.org/10.1080/14754835.2012.674454.

Schmidt, Diana. 2007. "Anti-Corruption: What Do We Know? Research on Preventing Corruption in the Post-Communist World." *Political Studies Review* 5 (2): 202–32. https://doi.org/10.1111/j.1478-9299.2007.00129.x.

Schnake, Mel. 1991. "Organizational Citizenship: A Review, Proposed Model, and Research Agenda." *Human Relations* 44 (7): 735–59.

Scott, James C. 1969. "The Analysis of Corruption in Developing Nations." *Comparative Studies in Society and History* 11 (3): 315. https://doi.org/10.1017/S0010417500005363.

Scott, James C. 1977. *The Moral Economy of the Peasant: Rebellion and Subsistence in Southeast Asia*. Yale University Press.

Seligson, Mitchell A. 2002. "The Impact of Corruption on Regime Legitimacy: A Comparative Study of Four Latin American Countries." *The Journal of Politics* 64 (2): 408–33. https://doi.org/10.1111/1468-2508.00132.

Sequeira, Ana Rita, Mark P. McHenry, Angus Morrison-Saunders, Hudson Mtegha, and David Doepel. 2016. "Is the Extractive Industry Transparency Initiative (EITI) Sufficient to Generate Transparency in Environmental Impact and Legacy Risks? The Zambian Minerals Sector." *Journal of Cleaner Production* 129 (August): 427–36. https://doi.org/10.1016/j.jclepro.2016.04.036.

Shani, Danielle. 2009. *On the Origins of Political Interest*. https://search.proquest.com/openview/b2b0b027fcaaac5ba96ff83125c2d45d/1.pdf?pq-origsite=gscholar&cbl=18750&diss=y.

Shehu, Garba. 2018. *Nigeria: Executive Order 6 - Buhari Acquires a Big Stick Against Corruption*. https://allafrica.com/stories/201807060033.html.

Shi, Tianjian. 2001. "Cultural Values and Political Trust: A Comparison of the People's Republic of China and Taiwan." *Comparative Politics* 33 (4): 401. https://doi.org/10.2307/422441.

Shih, Chih-Yu. 1994. "The Decline of a Moral Regime." *Comparative Political Studies* 27 (2): 272–301. https://doi.org/10.1177/0010414094027002005.

Shin, Doh Chull. 2012. *Confucianism and Democratization in East Asia.* Cambridge University Press.

Shultz, Thomas R., Christine Jaggi, and Michael Schleifer. 1987. "Assigning Vicarious Responsibility." *European Journal of Social Psychology* 17 (3): 377–80. https://doi.org/10.1002/ejsp.2420170314.

Shushi, Rao. 1950. *Summary of Experiences with Classic Land Reform Experiments in East China.*

Simões, Mariana. 2018. *Brazil's Polarizing New President, Jair Bolsonaro, in His Own Words.* www.nytimes.com/2018/10/28/world/americas/brazil-president-jair-bolsonaro-quotes.html.

Simpser, Alberto. 2013. *Why Governments and Parties Manipulate Elections.* Cambridge University Press. http://ebooks.cambridge.org/ref/id/CBO9781139343824.

Sjoberg, Fredrik M., Jonathan Mellon, Tiago Peixoto, Johannes Hemker, and Lily L. Tsai. 2019. "Voice and Punishment: A Global Survey Experiment on Tax Morale." *Policy Research Working Paper No. 8855.* World Bank. https://openknowledge.worldbank.org/handle/10986/31713. License: CC BY 3.0 IGO.

Smilansky, Saul. 2006. "The Paradox of Moral Complaint." *Utilitas* 18 (3): 284–90. https://doi.org/10.1017/S0953820806002044.

Smilov, Daniel. 2012. "Anti-Corruption Bodies as Discourse-Controlling Instruments: Experiences from South-East Europe." In *Governments, NGOs and Anti-Corruption,* edited by Luís de Sousa, Peter Larmour, and Barry Hindess, 85–101. Routledge.

Smith, C. Ann, Dennis W. Organ, and Janet P. Near. 1983. "Organizational Citizenship Behavior: Its Nature and Antecedents." *Journal of Applied Psychology* 68 (4): 653–63. https://doi.org/10.1037/0021-9010.68.4.653.

Smith, Craig E. and Felix Warneken. 2016. "Children's Reasoning about Distributive and Retributive Justice across Development." *Developmental Psychology* 52 (4): 613–28. https://doi.org/10.1037/a0040069.

Smith, Heather J. and Tom R. Tyler. 1996. "Justice and Power: When Will Justice Concerns Encourage the Advantaged to Support Policies Which Redistribute Economic Resources and the Disadvantaged to Willingly Obey the Law?" *European Journal of Social Psychology* 26 (2): 171–200. 3.0.CO;2-8",1,0,0 >https://doi.org/10.1002/(SICI)1099-0992(199603)26:2<171::AID-EJS P742>3.0.CO;2-8.

Smith, Heather J. and Tom R. Tyler. 1997. "Choosing the Right Pond: The Impact of Group Membership on Self-Esteem and Group-Oriented Behavior." *Journal of Experimental Social Psychology* 33 (2): 146–70. https://doi.org/10.1006/jesp.1996.1318.

Soifer, Hillel David. 2006. *Authority over Distance: Explaining Variation in State Infrastructural Power in Latin America.* https://www.worldcat.org/title/authority-over-distance-explaining-variation-in-state-infrastructural-power-in-latin-america/oclc/231799723

Soifer, Hillel and Matthias vom Hau. 2008. "Unpacking the Strength of the State: The Utility of State Infrastructural Power." *Studies in Comparative International Development* 43 (3–4): 219–30. https://doi.org/10.1007/s12116-008-9030-z.

Spegele, Brian. 2014. *China's Investigation of Ex-President's Aide Marks New Phase in War on Corruption.* https://www.wsj.com/articles/chinas-investiga tion-of-ex-presidents-aide-marks-new-phase-in-war-on-corruption-1419320403

Stern, Rachel E. and Jonathan Hassid. 2012. "Amplifying Silence." *Comparative Political Studies* 45 (10): 1230–54. https://doi.org/10.1177/0010414011434295.

Stinchcombe, Arthur L., Rebecca Adams, Carol A. Heimer, Kim Lane Scheppele, Tom W. Smith, and D. Garth Taylor. 1980. *Crime and Punishment: Changing Attitudes in America.* Jossey-Bass.

Stine, Kelsi. 2011. "A State of Inequality: Confronting Elite Capture in Post-Conflict Guatemala." PhD Thesis, Tufts University.

Stokes, Susan Carol. 2001. *Public Support for Market Reforms in New Democracies.* Cambridge University Press.

Strauss, Julia. 2006. "Morality, Coercion and State Building by Campaign in the Early PRC: Regime Consolidation and After, 1949–1956." *The China Quarterly* (188): 891–912. https://doi.org/10.1017/S0305741006000488.

Strauss, Julia C. 2002. "Paternalist Terror: The Campaign to Suppress Counterrevolutionaries and Regime Consolidation in the People's Republic of China, 1950–1953." *Comparative Studies in Society and History* 44 (1): 80–105.

Stroud, Natalie Jomini. 2011. *Niche News: The Politics of News Choice.* Oxford University Press on Demand.

Sunstein, Cass R., Sebastian Bobadilla-Suarez, Stephanie C. Lazzaro, and Tali Sharot. 2016. "How People Update Beliefs about Climate Change: Good News and Bad News." *Cornell Law Review* 102: 1431.

Svolik, Milan W. 2012. *The Politics of Authoritarian Rule.* Cambridge University Press.

Tang, Wenfang. 2005. *Public Opinion and Political Change in China.* Stanford University Press.

Tang, Wenfang. 2016. *Populist Authoritarianism: Chinese Political Culture and Regime Sustainability.* Oxford University Press.

Tang, Wenfang. 2018. "The 'Surprise' of Authoritarian Resilience in China." *American Affairs* 2 (1): 101–17.

Tang, Wenfang and Yang Zhang. 2016. "Political Trust: An Experimental Study." In *Populist Authoritarianism: Chinese Political Culture and Regime Stability,* edited by Wenfang Tang, 134–51. Oxford University Press.

Taub, Amanda. 2016. *How Countries Like the Philippines Fall Into Vigilante Violence.* https://www.nytimes.com/2016/09/12/world/asia/the-philippines-rodrigo-duterte-vigilante-violence.html

Tay, Alice. 1968. "Law in Communist China: Part One." *Sydney Law Review* 6 (2): 153–172.

Taylor, Donald M. and Fathali M. Moghaddam. 1994. *Theories of Intergroup Relations: International Social Psychological Perspectives.* Greenwood Publishing Group.

Teiwes, Frederick C. 1979. *Politics and Purges in China: Rectification and the Decline of Party Norms, 1950–1965.* 537. ME Sharpe.

Thaxton, Ralph. 2016. *Force and Contention in Contemporary China: Memory and Resistance in the Long Shadow of the Catastrophic Past.* Cambridge University Press.

Thompson, Edward P. 1974. "Patrician Society, Plebeian Culture." *Journal of Social History* 7 (4): 382–405.

Thompson, Roger A. 1985. *Photomultiplier Tube Assembly.* Google Patents. https://patents.google.com/patent/US4501366A/en

Thornton, Patricia M. 2007. *Disciplining the State: Virtue, Violence, and State-Making in Modern China.* Vol. 283. Harvard University Council on East Asian.

Tiedens, Larissa Z. 2001. "Anger and Advancement versus Sadness and Subjugation: The Effect of Negative Emotion Expressions on Social Status Conferral." *Journal of Personality and Social Psychology* 80 (1): 86–94. https://doi.org/10.1037//0022-3514.80.1.86.

Tilly, Charles. 2017. "From Mobilization to Revolution." In *Collective Violence, Contentious Politics, and Social Change: A Charles Tilly Reader*, edited by Ernesto Castañeda and Cathy Lisa Schneider, 71–91. Routledge.

Tisne, Martin and Daniel Smilov. 2004. *From the Ground Up. Assessing the Record of Anticorruption Assistance in Southeastern Europe.* Central European University Press.

Transparency International. 2016. "Corruption Perceptions Index 2016." www.transparency.org/news/feature/corruption_perceptions_index_2016.

Transparency International-Rwanda (TI-RW). 2015. *Rwanda Bribery Index 2015.* TI-RW and Norwegian People's Aid.

Treviño, Linda Klebe. 1992. "The Social Effects of Punishment in Organizations: A Justice Perspective." *Academy of Management Review* 17 (4): 647–676. https://doi.org/10.5465/amr.1992.4279054.

Treviño, Linda Klebe and Gail A. Ball. 1992. "The Social Implications of Punishing Unethical Behavior: Observers' Cognitive and Affective Reactions." *Journal of Management* 18 (4): 751–68. https://doi.org/10.1177/014920639201800409.

Treviño, Linda Klebe, Michael Brown, and Laura Pincus Hartman. 2003. "A Qualitative Investigation of Perceived Executive Ethical Leadership: Perceptions from Inside and Outside the Executive Suite." *Human Relations* 56 (1): 5–37. https://doi.org/10.1177/0018726703056001448.

Treviño, Linda Klebe, Laura Pincus Hartman, and Michael Brown. 2000. "Moral Person and Moral Manager: How Executives Develop a Reputation for Ethical Leadership." *California Management Review* 42 (4): 128–42. https://doi.org/10.2307/41166057.

Truex, Rory and Daniel Tavana. 2019. "Implicit Attitudes toward an Authoritarian Regime." *The Journal of Politics* 81 (3): 1014–27. http://cpd.berkeley.edu/wp-content/uploads/2018/04/CPC_Truex.pdf.

Tsai, Lily L. 2007. *Accountability without Democracy: Solidary Groups and Public Goods Provision in Rural China.* Cambridge University Press.

Tsai, Lily L. 2015. "Constructive Noncompliance." *Comparative Politics* 47 (3): 253–79. https://doi.org/10.5129/001041515814709329.

Tsai, Lily L. 2017. "Bringing in China." *Comparative Political Studies* 50 (3): 295–328. https://doi.org/10.1177/0010414016672236.

Tsai, Lily L., Varja Lipovsek, Benjamin S. Morse, and Guillermo Toral. 2018. *Effect of International Standards on Accountability Behaviors*. Washington, DC: Transparency and Accountability Initiative. https://www.transparency-initiative.org/wp-content/uploads/2018/12/effect-of-international-stand ards-on-accountability-behaviors-brief.pdf

Tsai, Lily L., Benjamin S. Morse, and Robert A. Blair. 2020. "Building Credibility and Cooperation in Low-Trust Settings: Persuasion and Source Accountability in Liberia during the 2014–2015 Ebola Crisis." *Comparative Political Studies* 53(10–11): 1582–1618.

Tsai, Lily L., Minh D. Trinh, and Shiyao Liu. "What Makes Anticorruption Punishment Popular? Individual-Level Evidence from China." *The Journal of Politics*, forthcoming.

Turner, John C. 1987. "The Analysis of Social Influence." In *Rediscovering the Social Group: A Self-Categorization Theory*, edited by John C. Turner, Michael A. Hogg, Penelope J. Oakes, Stephen D. Reicher, and Margaret S. Wetherell, 68–88. Blackwell.

Tyler, Tom R. Peter Degoey, and Heather Smith. 1996. "Understanding Why the Justice of Group Procedures Matters: A Test of the Psychological Dynamics of the Group-Value Model." *Journal of Personality and Social Psychology* 70 (5): 913–30. https://doi.org/10.1037/0022-3514.70.5.913.

Tyler, Tom R. 1997a. "Citizen Discontent with Legal Procedures: A Social Science Perspective on Civil Procedure Reform." *The American Journal of Comparative Law* 45 (4): 871. https://doi.org/10.2307/841024.

Tyler, Tom R. 1997b. "The Psychology of Legitimacy: A Relational Perspective on Voluntary Deference to Authorities." *Personality and Social Psychology Review* 1 (4): 323–45. https://doi.org/10.1207/s15327957pspr0104_4.

Tyler, Tom R. 1998. "Trust and Democratic Governance." In *Trust and Governance*, edited by Valerie Braithwaite and Margaret Levi, vol. 1, 269–294. Russell Sage Foundation.

Tyler, Tom R. 2000. "Social Justice: Outcome and Procedure." *International Journal of Psychology* 35 (2): 117–25. https://doi.org/10.1080/002075900399411.

Tyler, Tom R. 2003. "Procedural Justice, Legitimacy, and the Effective Rule of Law." *Crime and Justice* 30 (January): 283–357. https://doi.org/10.1086/652233.

Tyler, Tom R. 2006. *Why People Obey the Law*. Princeton University Press. htt ps://search.ebscohost.com/login.aspx?direct=true&db=cat00916a&AN=mi t.001396327&site=eds-live&scope=site.

Tyler, Tom R. and Steven L. Blader. 2000. *Cooperation in Groups: Procedural Justice, Social Identity, and Behavioral Engagement*. Psychology Press.

Tyler, Tom R., Robert J. Boeckmann, Heather J. Smith, and Yuen J. Huo. 1997. *Social Justice in a Diverse Society*. 1st ed. Routledge.

Tyler, Tom R. and Peter Degoey. 1995. "Collective Restraint in Social Dilemmas: Procedural Justice and Social Identification Effects on Support for Authorities." *Journal of Personality and Social Psychology* 69 (3): 482–97. https://doi.org/10.1037/0022-3514.69.3.482.

Tyler, Tom R. and Peter Degoey. 1996. "Trust in Organizational Authorities: The Influence of Motive Attributions on Willingness to Accept Decisions." In

Trust in Organizations: Frontiers of Theory and Research, edited by Roderick M. Kramer and Tom R. Tyler, 16–38. Sage.

Tyler, Tom R. and E. Allan Lind. 1992. "A Relational Model of Authority in Groups." *Advances in Experimental Social Psychology*, 25:115–91. http://li nkinghub.elsevier.com/retrieve/pii/S006526010860283X.

Tyler, Tom R. and Kathleen M. McGraw. 1986. "Ideology and the Interpretation of Personal Experience: Procedural Justice and Political Quiescence." *Journal of Social Issues* 42 (2): 115–28. https://doi.org/10.1111/j.1540-4560.1986 .tb00228.x.

Tyler, Tom R., Kenneth A. Rasinski, and Kathleen M. McGraw. 1985. "The Influence of Perceived Injustice on the Endorsement of Political Leaders." *Journal of Applied Social Psychology* 15 (8): 700–25. https://doi.org/10.111 1/j.1559-1816.1985.tb02269.x.

Tyler, Tom R. and Renee Weber. 1982. "Support for the Death Penalty; Instrumental Response to Crime, or Symbolic Attitude?" *Law & Society Review* 17 (1): 21. https://doi.org/10.2307/3053531.

Utne, Mary Kristine and Robert F. Kidd. 1980. "Equity and Attribution." In *Justice and Social Interaction*, edited by Gerold Mikula, 63–93. Springer-Verlag.

VanLandingham, Marta. 2002. *Transforming the State: King, Court and Political Culture in the Realms of Aragon (1213–1387)*. Vol. 43. Groupe de Boeck.

Vidmar, Neil. 2000. *An Assessment of Public Opinion in Frontenac County Ontario Regarding R. v. Louise Reynolds*. Superior Court of Ontario.

Vidmar, Neil. 2002. "Retributive Justice: Its Social Context." In *The Justice Motive in Everyday Life*, edited by Michael Ross and Dale T. Miller, 291–313. Cambridge University Press.

Vidmar, Neil and Dale T. Miller. 1980. "Socialpsychological Processes Underlying Attitudes toward Legal Punishment." *Law & Society Review*, 14 (3): 565–602. https://search.proquest.com/openview/4635b1e464 b0887oc5d022e30a58ba22/1?pq-origsite=gscholar&cbl=1818706.

Vigoda-Gadot, E. 2006. "Citizens' Perceptions of Politics and Ethics in Public Administration: A Five-Year National Study of Their Relationship to Satisfaction with Services, Trust in Governance, and Voice Orientations." *Journal of Public Administration Research and Theory* 17 (2): 291. https:// doi.org/10.1093/jopart/muj018.

Volkov, Vadim. 2016. *Violent Entrepreneurs: The Use of Force in the Making of Russian Capitalism*. Cornell University Press.

Wade, Samuel. 2013. *New Trial for New Citizen Transparency Activists*. https:// chinadigitaltimes.net/2013/12/new-trial-new-citizen-transparency-activists/

Wade, Samuel. 2018. *Party Tightens Rule Over Law With Supervisory Reforms*. https://chinadigitaltimes.net/2018/01/party-tightens-rule-law-supervisory-reforms/

Wager, Stefan and Susan Athey. 2018. "Estimation and Inference of Heterogeneous Treatment Effects Using Random Forests." *Journal of the American Statistical Association* 113 (523), June, 1228–42. https://doi.org/ 10.1080/01621459.2017.1319839.

Wagner, Alexander F., Friedrich Schneider, and Martin Halla. 2009. "The Quality of Institutions and Satisfaction with Democracy in Western

Europe – A Panel Analysis." *European Journal of Political Economy* 25 (1): 30–41. https://doi.org/10.1016/j.ejpoleco.2008.08.001.

Wang, Cynthia S., Niro Sivanathan, Jayanth Narayanan, Deshani B. Ganegoda, Monika Bauer, Galen V. Bodenhausen, and Keith Murnighan. 2011. "Retribution and Emotional Regulation: The Effects of Time Delay in Angry Economic Interactions." *Organizational Behavior and Human Decision Processes* 116 (1): 46–54. https://doi.org/10.1016/j.obhdp.2011.05.007.

Wang, Zhengxu. 2006. "Explaining Regime Strength in China." *China: An International Journal* 4 (2): 217–37. https://doi.org/10.1353/chn.2006.0018.

Weatherford, M. Stephen. 1987. "How Does Government Performance Influence Political Support?" *Political Behavior* 9 (1): 5–28. https://doi.org/10.1007/BF00987276.

Weber, Maximilian. 1947. "Theory of Social and Economic Organization." In *The Nature of Charismatic Authority and Its Routinization*, Translated by A. R. Anderson and Talcott Parsons. Free Press.

Wedeman, Andrew. 2005. "Anticorruption Campaigns and the Intensification of Corruption in China." *Journal of Contemporary China* 14 (42): 93–116. https://doi.org/10.1080/1067056042000300808.

Weisenthal, Joe. 2013. *Brazilian President's Popularity Takes Breathtaking Nosedive – And That Should Worry Investors.* www.businessinsider.com/dilma-rousseff-ratings-plunge-2013-7.

Wenhua, Mo. 1991. "Jiefang Zhanzheng Shiqi Liaodong Junqu de Zhengzhi Gongzuo (Political Work in the Liaodong Military Zone during the War of Liberation)." *Zhonggong Dangshi Ziliao (Chinese Communist Party History Materials)*, no. 39: 194.

Wenzel, Michael and Tyler G. Okimoto. 2010. "How Acts of Forgiveness Restore a Sense of Justice: Addressing Status/Power and Value Concerns Raised by Transgressions." *European Journal of Social Psychology* 40 (3), 401–17. https://doi.org/10.1002/ejsp.629.

What Is the Citizen's Initiative Ley3De3? 2016. http://ley3de3.mx/es/what-is-the-citizens-initiative-ley3de3-3-out-of-3-2/.

Whyte, Martin. 2010. *Myth of the Social Volcano: Perceptions of Inequality and Distributive Injustice in Contemporary China.* Stanford University Press.

Williams, Peter. 1983. "Concept of an Independent Organisation to Tackle Corruption." In International Conference on Corruption and Economic Crime against Government. Washington, DC.

Wojciszke, Bogdan and Bożena Klusek. 1996. "Moral and Competence-Related Traits in Political Perception." *Polish Psychological Bulletin* 27 (4): 319–24. https://www.researchgate.net/publication/232539438_Moral_and_competence-related_traits_in_political_perception

World Bank Group. 2016. *Making Politics Work for Development: Harnessing Transparency and Citizen Engagement.* Washington, DC: The World Bank. https://doi.org/10.1596/978-1-4648-0771-8.

World Economic Forum. 2017. "Partnering against Corruption Initiative – Infrastructure and Urban Development: Building Foundations for Trust and Integrity." *World Economic Forum in Collaboration with Deloitte.* www3.weforum.org/docs/WEF_PACI_IU_Report_2017.pdf.

Wright, Louis B. 1944. *Religion and Empire: The Alliance between Piety and Commerce in English Expansion, 1558–1625.* University of North Carolina Press. https://uncpress.org/book/9781469612287/religion-and-empire/

Wu, Guo. 2014. "Speaking Bitterness: Political Education in Land Reform and Military Training under the CCP, 1947–1951." *The Chinese Historical Review* 21 (1): 3–23. https://doi.org/10.1179/1547402X14Z.00000000026.

Wu, Yiping and Jiangnan Zhu. 2011. "Corruption, Anti-Corruption, and Inter-County Income Disparity in China." *The Social Science Journal* 48 (3): 435–48. https://doi.org/10.1016/j.soscij.2011.05.001.

Xi, Tianyang, Yang Yao, and Qian Zhang. 2018. "Dilemmas of Autocratic Governance: Theory and Evidence from the Anti-Corruption Campaign in China." https://www.aeaweb.org/conference/2019/preliminary/668?q=eNqrVipOLS7OzM8LqSxIVbKQhnGVrAxrawGlCArI

Xinhua. 2014. *China Issues Real Estate Registration Rules.* https://www.globaltimes.cn/content/898050.shtml

Yang, Hongxing and Dingxin Zhao. 2015. "Performance Legitimacy, State Autonomy and China's Economic Miracle." *Journal of Contemporary China* 24 (91): 64–82. https://doi.org/10.1080/10670564.2014.918403.

Yardley, Jim. 2008. *Beijing Olympics Building Chief May Be Executed for Corruption. The New York Times.* https://www.nytimes.com/2008/10/20/sports/olympics/20beijing.html

Yep, Ray. 2013. "The Crusade against Corruption in Hong Kong in the 1970s: Governor MacLehose as a Zealous Reformer or Reluctant Hero?" *China Information* 27 (2): 197–221. https://doi.org/10.1177/0920203X13482244.

Yuan Can, Bianji. 2016. *Xi Warns of Party "Cabals and Cliques."* http://en.people.cn/n3/2016/0504/c90785-9052699.html

Yukl, Gary. 1989. "Managerial Leadership: A Review of Theory and Research." *Journal of Management* 15 (2): 251–89. http://en.people.cn/n3/2016/0504/c90785-9052699.html

Zacka, Bernardo. 2017. *When the State Meets the Street: Public Service and Moral Agency.* Harvard University Press.

Zhao, Dingxin. 2009. "The Mandate of Heaven and Performance Legitimation in Historical and Contemporary China." *American Behavioral Scientist* 53 (3): 416–33. https://doi.org/10.1177/0002764209338800.

Zhu, Yuchao. 2011. "'Performance Legitimacy' and China's Political Adaptation Strategy." *Journal of Chinese Political Science* 16 (2): 123–40. https://doi.org/10.1007/s11366-011-9140-8.

Index

Made in United States
North Haven, CT
25 October 2021